Sugar-Free Cooking and Baking

by Liz Scott

ALPHA

A member of Penguin Group (USA) Inc.

ALPHA BOOKS

Published by Penguin Group (USA) Inc.

Penguin Group (USA) Inc., 375 Hudson Street, New York, New York 10014, USA • Penguin Group (Canada), 90 Eglinton Avenue East, Suite 700, Toronto, Ontario M4P 2Y3, Canada (a division of Pearson Penguin Canada Inc.) • Penguin Books Ltd., 80 Strand, London WC2R 0RL, England • Penguin Ireland, 25 St. Stephen's Green, Dublin 2, Ireland (a division of Penguin Books Ltd.) • Penguin Group (Australia), 250 Camberwell Road, Camberwell, Victoria 3124, Australia (a division of Pearson Australia Group Pty. Ltd.) • Penguin Books India Pvt. Ltd., 11 Community Centre, Panchsheel Park, New Delhi—110 017, India • Penguin Group (NZ), 67 Apollo Drive, Rosedale, North Shore, Auckland 1311, New Zealand (a division of Pearson New Zealand Ltd.) • Penguin Books (South Africa) (Pty.) Ltd., 24 Sturdee Avenue, Rosebank, Johannesburg 2196, South Africa • Penguin Books Ltd., Registered Offices: 80 Strand, London WC2R 0RL, England

International Standard Book Number: 978-1-61564-184-0
Library of Congress Catalog Card Number: 2011945184

14 13 12   8 7 6 5 4 3 2 1

Interpretation of the printing code: The rightmost number of the first series of numbers is the year of the book's printing; the rightmost number of the second series of numbers is the number of the book's printing. For example, a printing code of 12-1 shows that the first printing occurred in 2012.

Printed in the United States of America

Note: This publication contains the opinions and ideas of its author. It is intended to provide helpful and informative material on the subject matter covered. It is sold with the understanding that the author and publisher are not engaged in rendering professional services in the book. If the reader requires personal assistance or advice, a competent professional should be consulted.

The author and publisher specifically disclaim any responsibility for any liability, loss, or risk, personal or otherwise, which is incurred as a consequence, directly or indirectly, of the use and application of any of the contents of this book.

Most Alpha books are available at special quantity discounts for bulk purchases for sales promotions, premiums, fund-raising, or educational use. Special books, or book excerpts, can also be created to fit specific needs. For details, write: Special Markets, Alpha Books, 375 Hudson Street, New York, NY 10014.

Publisher: *Marie Butler-Knight*
Associate Publisher: *Mike Sanders*
Executive Managing Editor: *Billy Fields*
Executive Acquisitions Editor: *Lori Cates Hand*
Senior Development Editor: *Christy Wagner*
Senior Production Editor: *Kayla Dugger*

Copy Editor: *Jan Zoya*
Cover Designer: *Kurt Owens*
Book Designers: *William Thomas, Rebecca Batchelor*
Indexer: *Johnna VanHoose Dinse*
Layout: *Ayanna Lacey*
Proofreader: *John Etchison*

Contents

Appendixes

Introduction

Whether you've decided to go sugar free for specific health reasons such as diabetes, are looking to lose weight, or simply want a way to cut back on your sugar consumption, you've come to the right place. Whatever your goals may be, let this book be your guide to the ins and outs of cooking, baking, and eating sugar free.

It can be stressful enough to start on a new culinary journey, so I want you to feel as at ease as you can be. To that end, I try to answer all your most pressing questions in simple, understandable terms. That's my job. Your job is to enjoy the luscious sugar-free recipes that fill this book. From soup to nuts—chocolate-covered nuts, that is—I share over 200 delicious recipes you'll enjoy so much you'll never miss the added sugar!

How This Book Is Organized

I've organized this book in seven parts:

Part 1, The Sweet, Sugar-Free Life, answers your questions about saying good-bye to sugar, including how cutting out sugar can improve your health, your weight, and your mood, even if you're not diabetic or dieting. You also meet all the sugar substitutes out there and discover some helpful advice on setting up your sugar-free kitchen.

Part 2, Delightfully Sweet Beginnings, launches you straight into the first meal of the day with terrific ideas for hot and cold cereals, pancakes, muffins, and even some delightfully sweet sugar-free jams, jellies, and syrups.

Part 3, Light Fare and Go-Withs, shares recipes for soups, salads, snacks, and more worthy of your lunchbox or your mid-afternoon snack.

Part 4, Dinner Entrées and Side Dishes, is chock-full of sensational sugar-free main courses as well as some delicious sides to round out your evening meal.

Part 5, Bakery Favorites, dives into all those enticing goodies like cookies, brownies, cakes, and pies, and shows you how easy it is to create fabulous sugar-free versions without sacrificing a crumb of flavor.

Part 6, Old-Fashioned Desserts and Treats, takes on puddings, dessert toppings, and candies so notorious for being sugar laden and provides you with tastefully amazing solutions.

Part 7, Frozen Desserts, tackles icy and refreshing dishes like sorbets and ice creams and shows you how flavorful they can really be when created with sugar-free flair.

Extras

Throughout the book, you'll come across many sidebars that offer extra information. Watch for these:

DEFINITION

Here you'll find helpful definitions of some unusual terms and ingredients.

HONEY DON'T!

Be sure to heed these warnings and alerts concerning sugar-free cooking and baking.

SWEET SECRET

These sidebars contain a wealth of facts, figures, and amusing trivia to entertain and educate you.

TASTY TIP

Look to these sidebars for tips and hints to make your sugar-free cooking and baking easier.

Acknowledgments

No book ever sees the light of day without the hard work and loving care of many, many people.

I'd like to thank the staff at Alpha Books, in particular, Lori Hand and Christy Wagner, for their terrific support and patience. Marilyn Allen at the Allen O'Shea Literary Agency deserves applause for standing by me so staunchly.

I am blessed with a wonderful group of friends and family who have always been my biggest fans. Thanks to all of you. And of course, to Bella.

Special Thanks to the Technical Reviewer

The Complete Idiot's Guide to Sugar-Free Cooking and Baking was reviewed by an expert who double-checked the accuracy of what you'll learn here, to help us ensure that this book gives you everything you need to know about enjoying delicious foods that aren't loaded with extra sugar. Special thanks are extended to Lucy Beale.

Lucy Beale is a weight-loss and wellness coach and author of nine *Complete Idiot's Guides*, including *The Complete Idiot's Guide to Terrific Diabetic Meals*, *The Complete Idiot's Guide to Glycemic Index Weight Loss*, *The Complete Idiot's Guide to Glycemic Index Cookbook*, *The Complete Idiot's Guide to Glycemic Index Snacks*, and *The Complete Idiot's Guide to Low-Carb Meals*.

Trademarks

All terms mentioned in this book that are known to be or are suspected of being trademarks or service marks have been appropriately capitalized. Alpha Books and Penguin Group (USA) Inc. cannot attest to the accuracy of this information. Use of a term in this book should not be regarded as affecting the validity of any trademark or service mark.

The Sweet, Sugar-Free Life

Before starting to cook and bake sugar free, it pays to learn a little background information first, and in Part 1, we do just that. Even if you already know you need to reduce or eliminate sugar from your diet, you might find a few more interesting reasons why sugar can be detrimental to your health in the following chapters. You may be surprised to find that dieters and diabetics are not the only people who should consider sugar-free alternatives, and you learn exactly what those alternatives are, from artificial to natural.

You also get a solid primer on how to set up your sugar-free kitchen, with a list of all the essentials you'll want to obtain—and eliminate—from your pantry and fridge. I also show you how priming your palate for the change and eating sugar free doesn't mean neglecting your other nutritional needs.

Armed with these essentials, you'll be ready to dive into your sugar-free cooking with confidence.

Saying So Long to Sugar

In This Chapter

- The benefits of giving up sugar
- Discovering some sweet facts
- The pros and cons of sweeteners
- The best sweeteners for cooking and baking

I probably don't have to tell you that sugar isn't the best thing for you. From obesity to diabetes to feelings of fatigue after coming down from a "sugar high," it seems the more sugar we consume, the more unwell we become. Increased rates of heart disease and type 2 diabetes essentially can be blamed on the nutritionally void diet we have come to enjoy, which contains a large amount of refined sugar.

Refined sugar, like refined carbohydrates, is highly processed, and in the case of sugar, it's usually clarified, decolorized, and dried. And like all highly processed foods, refined sugars and carbs are simply not good for us.

In this chapter, we take a close look at why we crave sugar in the first place and examine all the different shapes and forms it can take in our food. I also cover a little more about sugar and your health as well as touch on the subject of glucose levels and what they mean in connection to sugar consumption.

Finally, we'll take a look at some sugar replacers and discuss the pros and cons of each. Not all sugar substitutes are created equal, so it pays to know which alternatives you'll want to rely on and which ones you may want to steer clear of.

Why Go Sugar Free?

If you have *diabetes* or are dieting, the reason for eighty-sixing the sugar is pretty self-explanatory. While diabetics are medically advised to reduce sugar intake—which I discuss in a little more detail coming up—dieters know that with all those empty sugar-laden calories, they'll never reach their goal weight unless they replace sugary snacks and treats with healthier alternatives. But what about the rest of us?

> **DEFINITION**
>
> **Diabetes** is a disease in which blood glucose (blood sugar) levels are above normal. Type 2 diabetes, also known as adult-onset or non-insulin-dependent diabetes mellitus, is the most common form of diabetes.

Too much sugar is not a good thing for anyone. If you're not already suffering as a direct result of excess sugar consumption, there's a good chance you eventually will if you maintain a high-sugar diet. From arthritis to attention deficit disorder (ADD) to Alzheimer's disease, people who eat a diet of highly processed foods, including refined sugar, are more likely than others to develop problems in the future. By reducing your sugar intake before the problems actually occur, you could be doing a world of good for your body and your future health.

Why We Crave Sugar

Sugar is the only one of the five taste sensations—the others being sour, bitter, salty, and umami—you're born with. That's right, you're born with a "sweet tooth."

> **SWEET SECRET**
>
> Eastern philosophies believe there are actually additional tastes, including pungent, an important sensation believed to help balance our taste for sugar. As Americans, we eat fewer pungent foods such as ginger and red pepper, which could in part account for our tremendous sugar cravings.

Researchers believe early humans were genetically selected for sugar consumption, because those who ate it, probably in the form of ripened fruit and perhaps honey, had more immediate energy than those who consumed only protein. Consequently, sugar eaters were more likely to outwit, outrun, and outlast their sluggish counterparts. Having a taste for sweet was definitely a plus for survival.

These days, we're not chasing bison too often for dinner, nor are we constantly on the go, expending great amounts of energy. So all that sugar we consume is stored as fat, setting us on a path toward becoming overweight, unhealthy, and, eventually, diseased.

Sugar in All Its Forms

Sugar isn't just the white grainy stuff you have in your sugar canister brought home from the supermarket. It can find its way into your life by a number of guises and names, so it pays to know what sugar's many names are.

For example, brown sugar doesn't look like traditional table sugar, and neither does organic sugar or sugar in the raw. But basically they're all refined and processed products and make no difference whatsoever to your body when you consume them.

All these types of sugar come from either sugarcane or sugar beets, and none is any healthier than the next. Sugar from these two sources is primarily made up of *sucrose*, which, when digested, breaks down into *glucose* and *fructose* and is rapidly digested by the body.

DEFINITION

Sucrose, glucose, and **fructose** are all sugar compounds digested by the body and provide energy for it to function properly. Overeating of sucrose-containing products (that contain both glucose and fructose) can force your pancreas to work harder and release more insulin to lower blood glucose levels. Fructose, the sugar compound found in fruit, does not stress insulin production in exactly the same way but can also cause unhealthy fluctuations, weight gain, and even fatty liver if eaten in excess.

Corn syrup and high-fructose corn syrup are actually derived from the starch of maize, which is primarily glucose to begin with. In fact, corn syrup is sometimes referred to as glucose syrup and was originally used as a sweetener before the prevalence of high-fructose corn syrup in the food industry.

High-fructose corn syrup has undergone an enzymatic process to raise its fructose level and make it sweeter than traditional corn syrup. Because of this process, and because fructose is metabolized by the liver, concerns about high-fructose corn syrup's health risks have risen, and questions about its ultimate effect on the liver, pancreas, insulin resistance in general, and digestive health overall prevail.

SWEET SECRET

Sugar tariffs and quotas imposed in 1977 in the United States significantly increased the cost of imported sugar, leading U.S. food and beverage producers to seek cheaper sources. High-fructose corn syrup became the economical choice.

The Diabetes and Glucose Connection

Diabetics of both types need not only monitor their sugar intake but must also be aware of their carbohydrate intake, of which sugar is one of the elements. Eating of excess carbohydrates, especially those that are highly processed and refined, can wreak havoc on glucose levels and exacerbate the disease. Unlike the other macronutrients—protein and fat—that don't influence blood sugar levels directly, carbohydrates can quickly disrupt healthy levels of blood sugar, particularly if they contain a good deal of sucrose.

Choosing to eat complex carbohydrates rather than simple carbohydrates can help stabilize blood glucose levels in diabetics (and nondiabetics) because the digestion process is slowed by the presence of *dietary fiber* that requires time and effort to break down by the body. The longer it takes to digest these types of complex carbohydrates, the better it is for your health and the better you will feel. You'll have a steady stream of energy and won't experience the dramatic highs and lows that can occur after eating large quantities of simple carbohydrates.

DEFINITION

Dietary fiber is the indigestible part of plant foods that moves through the digestive system. It can be soluble (dissolves in water) or insoluble (stays intact). Both types of fiber are essential for moving waste through the digestive tract and maintaining overall good health.

Sugar gets a particularly bad rep because it's usually part of a simple-carbohydrate food product that's metabolized quickly. Things like highly processed sugar breakfast cereals, cookies, cakes, and even white-flour breads are the usual culprits. However, when sugar is a small part of something less processed like a high-fiber cereal bar or 12-grain bread, its effect can be slowed. This is why complex carbohydrates are better all-around choices for a healthy diet.

The best and most simple advice on making carbohydrate selections is to pick something your body needs to process to gain its nutritional value and not something the manufacturing plant has already processed for you and stripped of its nutritional value. Think bran flakes over frosted flakes, or sugar-free oatmeal cookies over sugar cookies.

Once you start looking at your choices in this way, making the right ones will become a snap. The added bonus is that most complex carbohydrates naturally contain less sugar.

More on Sugar and Your Health

If you're still not convinced that eliminating sugar from your diet makes a difference to your health, here's a list of some surprising conditions that have been associated with high sugar consumption:

- A suppressed immune system
- Interference with absorption of essential minerals, including calcium
- Elevation of anxiety and hyperactivity in children and adults
- Elevation of bad cholesterol and triglycerides
- Loss of tissue elasticity and function
- Increased risk of certain cancers, including breast, prostrate, pancreas, lung, and gallbladder
- Weakened eyesight
- Increased risk of acid reflux disease, Crohn's disease, and other digestive disorders
- Tooth decay and periodontal disease
- Increased blood pressure
- Hemorrhoids and gallstones
- Premature aging

Eliminating sugar can help you stay healthy and avoid unnecessary future problems—many of which could be quite severe—while making you feel better, more energetic, and perhaps a lot more trim and fit (if weight loss is your goal).

Natural Sugar Alternatives

When you cut out the sugar from your cooking and baking, you need to replace it with something else. You can't just remove an ingredient and expect the same results from a recipe. In the following sections, I explain all your sugar-free options—some good, some not so good—so you can make your own choice based on taste, ease of use, and overall preference.

First, let's look at the natural substitutes (as opposed to artificial substitutes—more on those later), made with sugar alternatives actually found in nature and man-made to replicate the qualities of sugar.

HONEY DON'T!

Natural, by the way, doesn't always imply better, as a natural substitute can be subjected to unnatural processes, like high-fructose corn syrup, causing its intrinsic nature to come under question.

Stevia

Stevia is the newest darling among sugar substitutes. Made from a leaf that's extremely strong in its sweet taste (a little goes a long way), stevia can have a slight licorice aftertaste as well. Initially this was the universal case, but since stevia's popularity has grown as a safe sugar substitute, companies have attempted—and quite successfully at that—to eliminate both of these qualities.

Stevia is available in sweetener packets and large bags of cup-for-cup granulated stevia in the supermarket baking aisle. It's also available in liquid form, and some companies offer flavored stevia drops for use in making beverages and flavoring teas. It's also now popping up in sodas and other commercial beverages, including old standards like Coke and Pepsi.

If you haven't yet tried stevia, be sure to give it a fair shot. More than other types of sweeteners, stevia truly seems to be an acquired taste, regardless of the progress made in the manufacturing area. As a safe alternative, it's probably the best of the bunch, and user-friendly packaging has now made this 0 calorie sweetener a lot easier to use in cooking and baking.

Agave Nectar

Also known as agave syrup or just plain agave, agave has been used by health food and raw-food enthusiasts for a very long time. (Yes, there is a raw version, too!)

Usually available in light and amber varieties, you'll often find squeeze bottles of agave nectar in the baking section near other sugar substitutes. Some companies are also producing flavored agave nectar to compete with the stevia offerings, but these have not taken hold much. Agave, especially the amber version, already has a slight maple syrup flavor, which is often used in place of maple syrup and can add a nice layer of flavor to cooking and baking.

Agave is an ancient plant that's been used medicinally for centuries. It's also the same plant tequila is made from. The liquid from the core of the plant, sometimes referred to as honey water, is what's extracted and processed into the nectar. Many argue this is really no different from any other type of refined sugar and warn against its excessive use.

SWEET SECRET

Agave nectar has come under a bit of scrutiny lately because of its high fructose content and the intensive processing it undergoes, which is not unlike turning corn syrup into high-fructose corn syrup. But the jury is still out on this.

However, agave's saving grace—particularly important for diabetics and those watching blood glucose levels—is its low number on the glycemic index compared to other sugars. The lower the number, the less the immediate and direct impact on blood sugar, which is always a good thing. Per tablespoon, agave nectar has 60 calories per tablespoon, while sugar itself is only 40. But because agave is $1\frac{1}{2}$ times sweeter than sugar, much less is required.

No sugar substitute is perfect, and none should be used in excess, but agave definitely has a place for occasional cooking and baking, especially for diabetics and health food enthusiasts. And as an occasional substitute for maple syrup or honey, it's ideal.

Honey

As far as carbohydrates are concerned, honey isn't any better or worse for you than sugar, whether or not you have type 2 diabetes. Honey contains fructose, glucose, and water, plus other sugars. Also in the lineup are trace enzymes, minerals, amino acids, and a wide range of B vitamins. The amount of these micronutrients varies depending on where the honey comes from. In general, darker honeys contain more vitamins than lighter ones and also provide more trace minerals such as calcium, magnesium, and potassium.

If you consult the glycemic index, you'll see that honey and table sugar rank very closely together, with honey at 62 and sugar at 64. So as far as glycemic control is concerned, honey isn't a recommended substitute for plain old sugar. But because it can offer other nutrients, especially organic and raw locally produced honey, honey isn't a bad selection for adding to teas and yogurts or spreading on toast in small amounts. However, cooking with honey in large quantities is not an acceptable option over sugar. One tablespoon of honey contains about 64 calories.

Use honey sparingly to highlight a dish's flavor but not as a substitute for sugar. Light agave fills in much better when liquid syrupy sweeteners are required, and agave has a subtler taste that won't interfere with your recipe outcome.

Molasses and Maple Syrup

Molasses is the dark, syrupy liquid left behind when sugar cane is made into white sugar. It comes in three grades: the first and second grades are fairly sweet, while the third, blackstrap molasses, is the most intense.

Blackstrap isn't very sweet, but it does have the highest vitamin and mineral content of the three. In fact, blackstrap molasses is a good source of iron and is often added to smoothies, protein drinks, and other concoctions. But as a substitute for sugar in cooking and baking, molasses—with its strong distinct flavor, not to mention its high sugar content—is not a good option. Blackstrap contains 47 calories per tablespoon, a little less than its first- and second-grade cousins.

SWEET SECRET

Blackstrap molasses—unlike refined sugars—contains significant amounts of vitamin B$_6$, calcium, magnesium, potassium, and iron and has long been sold as a health supplement.

Maple syrup, produced by boiling down sap from specific maple trees to increase its concentration of flavor and consistency, is often touted as a healthy alternative to sugar. However, 1 tablespoon contains about 55 calories, and its effect on glycemic control is no better than sugar. In addition, this is specifically the case for pure maple syrup, which has no added corn syrup or glucose that would hike up these numbers even more. It's true that maple syrup contains a number of antioxidants, but you'd need to consume a large amount of it to reap any serious benefits. As a liquid substitute for sugar in cooking and baking, it has its place, but not on a regular basis.

Using syrups like maple and molasses is best done in small amounts when you really want the essence of flavor they offer in your recipe. Be mindful, however, that it won't give you a sugar-free result, and in most cases, they're quite the same as using refined processed sugar.

Sugar Alcohols

This misnomer (neither a sugar nor an alcohol) is used to describe popular sweeteners used primarily in the commercial food world such as xylitol, sorbitol, and erythritol. As exotic as they sound, they are indeed natural substances that occur in fruits and vegetables. Because they have very few calories and do not disrupt blood sugar as natural sugar products do (except for stevia), they are labeled "sugar-free" ingredients and are often found in sugar-free candies and other confections.

Working with them in the home kitchen is not unheard of, but for the most part, these substances are primarily utilized in the food industry, although xylitol is gaining in popularity with many home cooks. Difficult to use and often difficult to find, sugar alcohols are not a recommended sugar substitute for home cooking and baking. In addition, one of their annoying side effects, if eaten in excess, is gastrointestinal distress including bloating, constipation, and diarrhea.

Artificial Sugar Alternatives

Any food or ingredient with the term *artificial* in front of it should raise a concern, but unfortunately, we've been living with artificial sugar alternatives for so long, many of us accept their existence and continue to consume them in everything from soda to medicines for lack of any better choices.

Today, however, with a focus on natural ingredients and the growing popularity of stevia, many people are revisiting these supposedly tried-and-true artificial sweeteners with a more discerning eye. Let's take a look at them in a little depth, find out what they're really all about, and decide if they have a place in your sugar-free kitchen.

Sucralose

Sucralose is best known for its claim to be made from sugar. It can be found and used alone or in the sugar substitute Splenda, and it's 600 times sweeter than table sugar. In 1999, sucralose was given approval for use as a general-purpose sweetener and is now found in more than 4,500 products. Because sucralose performs so well in cooking and baking, it has become the most popular and highly consumed artificial sweetener on the market. It's available in concentrated packets or in cup-for-cup granulated form.

TASTY TIP

Sucralose is sold under the brand names Splenda, Sukrana, SucraPlus, Candys, Cukren, and Nevella.

The most misunderstood fact about sucralose is that it's nothing like sugar even though the marketing implies that it is. Sucralose was actually discovered while trying to create a new insecticide. It may have started out as sugar, but the final product is anything but sugar and far from natural. Still, it's the most ubiquitous sweetener available and has yet to be irrevocably determined to be dangerous to your health. The use of chlorine in its production is the most mentioned detriment, and some evidence has shown that sucralose passes through the body and into the ecosystem with as-yet-unknown repercussions.

Splenda itself also contains dextrose and maltodextrin, two carbohydrates added to increase bulk. These are also added to other cup-for-cup sweeteners such as stevia. They contribute a small amount of calories, but have yet to be studied, along with sucralose, on a long-term basis to determine what potential effects they could have on human health. Anecdotally, some people complain of anxiety, headaches, and digestive discomfort.

Most people enjoy the taste of sucralose and say it's closest to the flavor of sugar compared to the other alternatives. Although 1 cup still contains about 96 calories, unless you're eating an entire batch of cookies made from that amount, you'll be able to reduce the amount of sugar and calories you're consuming by baking with it.

Sucralose can be used in cooking and baking to create many authentic-tasting sugar-free treats. If you're going to indulge, nibbling on something made with a bit of sucralose isn't a bad choice.

Aspartame

Aspartame, also known as NutraSweet, Equal, and Sugar Twin, was discovered in 1965 by a scientist trying to make new ulcer drugs, and in 1981, the Food and Drug Administration (FDA) approved it for dry use in tabletop sweeteners, chewing gum, cold breakfast cereals, gelatins, and puddings. In 1983, it began to be included in carbonated beverages. In 1996, the FDA approved its use as a "general purpose sweetener." Aspartame does provide calories, but because it's 160 to 220 times sweeter than sucrose, very small amounts are needed, so the caloric intake is pretty negligible.

Although often targeted as having links with depression, dementia, and even hair loss, no definitive studies have shown aspartame to be detrimental to health except for those people who suffer from *phenylketonuria*. Approved for use in more than 100 countries, aspartame still remains controversial and is quickly losing its popularity in the individual-use market but remains a common sweetener in the food industry.

DEFINITION

Phenylketonuria (commonly known as PKU) is an inherited disorder that increases the levels of a substance called phenylalanine in the blood, a building block of proteins. If PKU is not treated, phenylalanine can build to harmful levels in the body, causing intellectual disability and other serious health problems.

Given its continuing bad rep, and its poor performance in baking, using aspartame as a sugar-free substitute probably isn't ideal. However, until further definitive information emerges, it will be available for use.

Saccharin

Saccharin has been around for more than 100 years and claims to be the "best researched sweetener." Also known as Sweet Twin, Sweet'N Low, and Necta Sweet, saccharin doesn't contain any calories, doesn't raise blood sugar levels, and its sweetness is 200 to 700 times sweeter than table sugar, even if it has a bitter aftertaste.

In 1977, research showed bladder tumors in male rats with high ingestion of saccharin. The FDA proposed a ban on saccharin based on the Delaney Clause of the Federal Food, Drug, and Cosmetic Act enacted in 1958. This clause prohibits the addition to the human food supply of any chemical that had caused cancer in humans or animals. However, Congress intervened after public opposition to the ban because this was the only artificial sweetener available at that time. Congress allowed saccharin to remain in the food supply as long as the label carried this warning: "Use of this product may be hazardous to your health. This product contains saccharin, which has been determined to cause cancer in laboratory animals."

Since then, more than 30 human studies have been completed and found that the results found in rats did not translate to humans, making saccharin safe for human consumption. In 2000, the National Toxicology Program (NTP) of the National Institutes of Health concluded that saccharin should be removed from the list of potential carcinogens. The warning has now been removed from saccharin-containing products.

Out of the five FDA-approved artificial sweeteners, saccharin is often chosen to be the safest, and recently it has enjoyed resurgence among sweetener users, while some nutritionists recommend it over other sweeteners.

Old beliefs die hard, however, and many people prefer not to consume saccharin at all. There also have been suggestions of allergic responses to it because of its designation as a sulfanomide, a compound found in sulfa-based drugs. Reactions can include headaches, breathing difficulties, skin eruptions, and diarrhea. It's also believed that the saccharin found in some infant formulas can cause irritability and muscle dysfunction. For these reasons, many people still believe the use of saccharin should be limited in infants, children, and pregnant women. Without research to support these claims, the FDA has not imposed any limitations.

If you remember the days when saccharin was your only option, you may not be averse to picking it up again as an occasional sweetener in coffee and other drinks. But for the most part, saccharin won't help much in baking unless you're keen on calculating the conversion from the amount of sugar to the concentrated packets. For ease of preparation, cup-for-cup sugar substitutes offer the best alternative.

The Least You Need to Know

- Eliminating sugar is a healthy idea, not just for diabetics and dieters, but for anyone who wants to maintain excellent health and an acceptable weight.
- The taste for sugar is something we're born with, along with the taste for sour, bitter, salt, and sometimes pungent, so craving something sweet isn't unnatural.
- Sugar comes in many different processed refined forms, but all have more or less the same effect on the body and blood glucose control.
- Natural sugar alternatives include stevia, agave, honey, molasses, maple syrup, and sugar alcohols, some of which can be utilized in sugar-free cooking and baking with great success.
- Artificially made sugar alternatives still remain popular and, according to preference, could also be used in the sugar-free kitchen.

The Sugar-Free Kitchen

In This Chapter

- Getting your kitchen in order
- Stocking useful ingredients
- Identifying hidden sugar
- Adapting your taste buds

As with any type of specialty diet, certain ingredients need to be included in—and eliminated from—your sugar-free kitchen to give you the best start possible on your new quest to a sugar-free diet.

Sugar-free cooking and baking is really no different from gluten- or dairy-free cooking, but in this case, it's probably more of a temptation issue than a health or safety issue. Having sugar-laden products and ingredients easily accessible in your kitchen can cause you to fall prey to temptation and consume sugar-laden foods or drinks taunting you from the fridge or pantry.

It really pays to clean shop and remove those sugary triggers—*now*—and replace them with sugar-free ingredients. Plus, when you have what you need at your fingertips, creating delicious sugar-free dishes will be a snap. In this chapter, we take a look at the essentials you need to follow a sugar-free plan, as well as those you should say good-bye to. We also look at how to decipher food labels to find hidden sugar and learn some of the other names sugar goes by.

I also talk a little about how to help your palate adapt to these somewhat different sugary tastes that at first might seem unusual, especially if you have little experience eating and cooking with sugar substitutes. But not to worry—your taste buds easily adapt to what you choose to consume, and you may be surprised how quickly you come to enjoy the absence of heavy, sugar-laden ingredients and foods. Finally, we also look at the nutritional side of the sugar-free life with some basic tips and advice on ensuring your body gets all the nourishment you need.

Stocking Up on Sugar-Free Essentials

If you're going to replace the sugar in your diet, you need to determine which sugar alternatives you'd like to use instead. In Chapter 1, you learned about the different substitutes available, and you may already have an idea of which ones you prefer.

If you're completely new to the idea of cooking and baking with sugar substitutes, you might want to try out several different ones before you decide which you'll be using on a regular basis. Everyone's taste is slightly different, so what might seem a bit bitter to someone else might be perfect for your palate.

Whichever brands or types of sugar alternatives you choose, whether natural or artificial, be sure to have the following on hand to make the recipes in this book. You'll also want to stock up on some of the other helpful ingredients listed here, too.

For the Pantry

Packets of concentrated sweetener   This is the sweetener you see most often on the shelf in boxes of 50, 100, or more. This concentrated version is used primarily for sweetening coffee, tea, and other beverages. Some recipes lend themselves to using this version rather than a granulated version for cooking-volume concerns, too.

Granulated cup for cup   Ever since Splenda came out with their measure-for-measure cooking and baking substitute, many other brands of sucralose, as well as stevia and even aspartame, have produced similar products. Depending on your preference, you might want to have just one of these on hand. However, you can always try others and see if they're better suited to your palate.

Splenda also makes a brown sugar blend (which is part brown sugar) as well as a baking blend (which is part real sugar). These products aren't completely sugar free, but you might want to keep them on hand anyway.

Plain or flavored liquid sweetener   Many brands are now coming out with liquid versions of their concentrated sugar substitutions, and some are even flavored with artificial fruit taste or vanilla. The recipes in this book don't call for these sweeteners, but you could certainly try them as an option for flavoring hot and cold drinks on your own.

TASTY TIP

Some commercial brands of liquid stevia now have flavor drops that contain popular concentrated flavors such as chocolate, strawberry, and root beer. These are great to use in flavoring beverages and for cooking and baking. Look for them online and in health food stores.

Light and amber agave nectar   Many delicious baked recipes make use of both these sweeteners, which add a lovely faint honey (light) or maple (amber) flavor to the result. These sweeteners don't require refrigeration and have a relatively long shelf life, so it's definitely worth having one of each at the ready when the baking urge hits.

No-sugar-added canned fruit   These can come in extremely handy when fresh fruit isn't available or when canned versions are the preferred ingredient. Stocking only sugar-free or reduced-sugar products like these helps keep you from being tempted to grab the fruit packed in heavy syrup.

No-sugar-added sauces and condiments   These days it's quite easy to find reduced-sugar versions of everything from marinara sauce to ketchup to bottled Chinese sauces. When you run across such products, grab a bottle or two to stock your pantry. You'll be glad you did. Once opened, refrigerate them for safety and use by the expiration date.

Unsweetened cocoa powder   This product, along with unsweetened baking chocolate and sugar-free chocolate for drizzling and melting, will probably get a lot of use if you're a big chocolate fan. Don't skimp on lesser quality. Let the luxurious flavor of stellar chocolate highlight your sugar-free desserts.

HONEY DON'T!

Don't confuse the term *sugar free* with *unsweetened* when looking at chocolate labels. Remember, an unsweetened chocolate or cocoa powder has no sugar flavor at all, not even an artificial one.

For the Refrigerator

Maple syrup   For flavor emphasis, you occasionally might want to add maple syrup to specific recipes. Choose a good-quality pure maple syrup, and keep it refrigerated for freshness.

Sugar-free jams   In some instances, you'll want to add a touch of sweetness to a recipe, particularly with something like a jam or jelly that contains pectin and can help thicken the result. Also in this group is 100 percent fruit preserves. Keep several flavors on hand (and of course make your own as well) to quickly add to a dish when required.

Sugar-free fruit juices   In addition to being refreshing beverages, these juices can be useful in the sugar-free kitchen when making sauces, soups, and all kinds of desserts, especially frozen ones. Stock up on whatever flavors you enjoy. For kids, grape is always popular, while for adults, pomegranate or cranberry might do the trick.

Unsweetened milks, yogurts, and nondairy products   If you're a fan of soy, coconut, almond, or other nondairy milks as well as flavored milks, be sure to purchase the unsweetened varieties. Store them in the refrigerator according to the manufacturer's instructions. Sugar-free coffee creamers are handy as well.

For the Freezer

No-sugar-added frozen fruit   Many bags and boxes of frozen fruit, including berries of all types, come in a light or heavy sugar-laden syrup or sauce. Steer clear of these, and keep only sugar-free versions on hand for baking and dessert-making.

Sugar-free ice creams and whipped toppings   Because you can't always make your own ice cream or dessert topping, keep these in your freezer for last-minute dolloping on your sugar-free cobblers or pies. Don't ruin all your fabulous sugar-free effort by reaching for the high-sugar tub of vanilla ice cream simply because that's all you can find in your freezer.

A Sugar by Any Other Name ...

As you probably already know, sugar can appear under many guises on ingredient lists and still be sugar. You might know that corn syrup or high-fructose corn syrup is obvious code for "sugar," but what about the other, more elusive names? Here are other terms that mean sugar:

Confectioners' sugar	Maltose
Dextrose	Raw sugar
Galactose	Sucrose
Glucose	Turbinado sugar
Invert sugar	

As you start reading labels, you'll find that sugar seems to be in everything—even toothpaste! You can't always avoid it everywhere, but you can be conscious of the sugar already contained in an ingredient you'll be cooking or baking with so you can keep track of how much you may actually be getting in the end result. What you find may surprise you.

Reading Labels

Let's face it. Packaging on processed goods is meant to grab your attention. If something announced it was a great source of refined sugar, would you buy it? Probably not. Instead, manufacturers highlight some other quality of their product that makes it more appealing to the average consumer. Something like "low in fat" or "a low-calorie food" is an option, but of course that doesn't preclude the food is loaded with sugar.

Let's look at an example: ruby red grapefruit is a fabulous and healthy fruit, but ruby red grapefruit juice drink can teem with sugar. In fact, a 10-ounce glass of grapefruit juice drink contains at least 10 teaspoons of sugar.

Here's where a bit of label reading reveals the facts in far better detail. First, check the ingredient list. Remember that ingredients are listed according to the amount they're present in the product. So the first ingredient is always the one highest in quantity, and the last is always the lowest. In the case of grapefruit juice drink, you might see grape juice concentrate at the top, followed by grapefruit juice, which means you're getting more concentrated flavor than actual grapefruit juice. Yet the bottle says 100 percent juice. That's not exactly a fib, but it's not what you were expecting, is it? Consequently, it probably has much more sugar content than plain old grapefruit juice, as fruit concentrates are known to have.

Next, take a look at the nutritional percentages, in particular the number of carbohydrate and sugar grams per serving. In the case of grapefruit juice, anything over about 17 grams sugar is a red flag you're getting more sugar than you may want to drink.

SWEET SECRET

Fresh-squeezed grapefruit juice—or even better, the whole fruit—contains just 17 grams of sugar. It also offers healthy dietary fiber and a number of antioxidants, including cancer-fighting lycopene and cholesterol-lowering pectin.

Training Your Taste Buds

Before you delve into the sweet world of sugar-free cooking and baking, let me say a few last words about taste. As mentioned earlier, if you're relatively unaccustomed to eating sugar-free products or using sugar substitutes in any capacity, you'll likely want to ease into the switch as your palate and taste buds adapt.

This type of taste adaptation is not limited to going sugar free. Perhaps you've reduced or eliminated salt from your diet, or were required to eat only nonfat meals or meals without any dairy. The change may have shocked your palate initially, but the human body is amazingly resilient and can adapt to just about any change you decide to throw at it (within reason).

After reducing salt and getting used to eating salt free, many people can't tolerate even small amounts of salt. Ideally, this will happen to you as well as you cut out the sugar. After eating primarily reduced-sugar and sugar-free items for a while, sugary treats will seem unpleasantly sweet and maybe even sickeningly sweet.

Once away from sugar, your body learns to do without it, and that, in essence, is really the goal: not to simply replace sugar with sugar substitutes, but to learn that sugar, in any form, in small amounts and only on occasion, can be part of a healthy diet.

Mind Your Nutrition

Finally, always be sure you're eating a well-balanced diet throughout the day. Sure, at first you'll be tempted to try out all those delicious cookies, puddings, and snacks—completely smitten by their uncanny sugary taste. Go ahead and indulge for a while. You deserve it.

Just remember to eat properly—get in those veggies, fruits, lean proteins, and fiber-rich carbs, too. Then sit back and treat yourself to a bite of heavenly sugar-free bliss.

The Least You Need to Know

- Keeping a good supply of sugar substitutes in different forms makes sugar-free cooking and baking easy as pie.
- Stocking your pantry, fridge, and freezer with sugar-free ingredients prevents you from reaching for sugar-laden substitutes.

- Learning to read labels and recognizing hidden sugar in purchased products are two important elements of sugar-free cooking.

- Give your taste buds and palate time to adapt to sugar-free tastes and flavors.

- Ensuring your nutritional needs are met with a healthy diet is important for all sugar-free eaters.

Delightfully Sweet Beginnings

Breakfast is the most important meal of the day. So it's that much more important not to begin on the wrong foot and grab sugar-laden breakfast selections simply because they're quick and convenient. Fortunately, with sugar-free cooking, that won't be the case, as you'll see when you begin enjoying the recipes in Part 2.

From hot and cold cereals to favorites like pancakes, waffles, and muffins, the following chapters offer a terrific choice of sugar-free options everyone will love.

In addition, I share a collection of delicious jams and syrups to top all your fabulous breakfast selections so your sugar-free morning table is complete.

Hot and Cold Cereals

In This Chapter

- Creating healthier breakfast cereals
- Swapping out sugar for real flavor
- Easy recipes for quick morning prep
- Sweet satisfaction without sugar

When you're looking for ways to cut sugar from your diet, one of the first places to look is in that traditionally "healthy" morning bowl of cereal.

Believe it or not, the majority of processed breakfast cereals—from delightfully crunchy and nutty cold versions to the creamy, fruity, and oh-so-good-for-you bowls of oatmeal and grains—are teeming with added sugar. Take a quick glance at the nutritional label to see just how much sugar they contain. What's a breakfast cereal lover to do?

The Great Sugar Trade

Learning to swap out sugar for real flavor in your breakfast bowl is as easy as (sugar-free) pie when you have the perfect ingredients at your fingertips. Naturally sweet fresh and dried fruits, flavorful nuts and grains, enticing spices, as well as the thoughtful use of sugar alternatives like agave or stevia provide the subtle boost of sweetness you crave.

Sweet Inspiration

From luscious apple pie–flavored oatmeal to quick strawberry muesli, you'll be amazed at how tantalizingly "sweet" your sugar-free breakfast can be. Use the recipes in this chapter to inspire your cereal creativity even further, and discover that when it comes to your breakfast bowl, sugar free can be the sweetest thing under the morning sun.

Oatmeal in an Instant

You can customize this quick scoop-and-cook sugar-free oatmeal to your liking with the sweetness of dried fruit and the crunchiness of nuts.

Yield:	Prep time:	Cook time:	Serving size:
5 cups	3 minutes	1 minute	½ cup

5 cups plain instant oatmeal

3 TB. granulated sugar substitute

3 TB. dry milk powder

2 tsp. ground cinnamon

1 cup dried raisins, cranberries, or cherries

½ cup chopped pecans, walnuts, or hazelnuts

Dash salt

1. In a large bowl, whisk together instant oatmeal, granulated sugar substitute, dry milk powder, and cinnamon.

2. Stir in dried raisins, pecans, and salt, and transfer to an airtight container.

3. To prepare, scoop ½ cup oatmeal mixture into a serving bowl and add ¼ to ⅓ cup boiling water. Stir until thickened, and serve.

TASTY TIP

Dry milk powder provides creaminess in this recipe and additional nutrition in other cereal and baked good recipes.

Nutz Over Banana Oatmeal

You'll go bananas for this nutty combination that's full of crunch and flavor with just the right amount of sweetness and spice.

Yield:	Prep time:	Cook time:	Serving size:
1 cup	8 minutes	8 minutes	1 cup

½ cup water

½ cup milk

½ cup old-fashioned oats

¼ tsp. vanilla extract

1½ tsp. granulated sugar substitute

Dash salt

½ medium banana, peeled and diced

Dash ground nutmeg

2 TB. chopped mixed nuts, such as pecans, walnuts, and almonds

1. In a small saucepan over medium heat, bring water and milk to a boil. Stir in old-fashioned oats, vanilla extract, 1 teaspoon granulated sugar substitute, and salt, and cook over low heat, stirring occasionally, for 5 minutes or until soft and creamy.

2. Remove from heat, and stir in banana. Set aside for 1 minute.

3. In a small bowl, combine remaining ½ teaspoon granulated sugar substitute, nutmeg, and mixed nuts.

4. Transfer oatmeal to a serving bowl, top with nut mixture, and serve.

TASTY TIP

Old-fashioned oats are rolled oats that are less processed than quick-cooking oats but more processed than the much-longer-cooking steel-cut oats. Still a good source of fiber and requiring only 5 minutes of cooking time, they're an excellent compromise for making healthy oatmeal on busy mornings.

Agave Apple Pie Oatmeal

Subtly sweet, light agave nectar highlights the natural sweetness of apples and the familiar allure of *apple pie spice* in this comfortingly warm start to the day.

Yield:	Prep time:	Cook time:	Serving size:
1 cup	10 minutes	7 minutes	1 cup

²/₃ cup water

¹/₃ cup no-sugar-added apple juice

¹/₂ cup old-fashioned oats

Dash salt

Dash ground cinnamon

¹/₂ medium apple, peeled, cored, and grated

¹/₈ tsp. apple pie spice

2 tsp. light agave nectar

1 TB. milk or light cream

1. In a small saucepan over medium heat, bring water and no-sugar-added apple juice to a boil. Stir in old-fashioned oats, salt, and cinnamon. Reduce heat to low, and cook, stirring occasionally, for 5 minutes or until soft and creamy.

2. In a small serving bowl, stir together apple, apple pie spice, and agave nectar just to combine.

3. Spoon cooked oatmeal over apple mixture, and gently stir. Drizzle milk around the edges, and serve.

DEFINITION

Apple pie spice is a ground blend of cinnamon, nutmeg, and allspice. Find it in the baking and spice aisle of your supermarket.

Creamy "Maple" Cream of Wheat

Amber agave nectar, with its remarkable maple-sweet flavor, deliciously fills in for sugar-rich maple syrup, while plump, juicy raisins add their own fruity sweetness in this yummy dish.

Yield:	Prep time:	Cook time:	Serving size:
2 cups	5 minutes	5 minutes	1 cup

2 cups milk

2 TB. amber agave nectar

2 TB. seedless raisins

Dash salt

$\frac{1}{3}$ cup cream of wheat

2 tsp. unsalted butter

1. In a medium saucepan over medium-high heat, bring milk, amber agave nectar, raisins, and salt to a boil, stirring occasionally.

2. Slowly pour in cream of wheat, stirring constantly until mixture returns to a boil. Remove from heat, cover, and set aside for 1 minute.

3. Stir, and divide cream of wheat between 2 serving bowls. Top each with 1 teaspoon unsalted butter, and serve.

SWEET SECRET

The crème de la crème of raisins is the Chilean flame raisin, which is larger, plumper, and sweeter than any of its common cousins. Dried from jumbo flame table grapes, they can't be beat for a mouthful of natural sweetness.

Orange Cranberry Oat Bran

Sweetening your morning with OJ rather than sugar makes for a tangy and terrific-tasting bowl of healthy oat bran, while tart cranberries add even more fruity flavor.

Yield:	Prep time:	Cook time:	Serving size:
1 cup	5 minutes	10 minutes	½ cup

½ cup no-sugar-added orange juice

½ cup water

⅓ cup oat bran

1 TB. dried no-sugar-added cranberries

Dash ground cinnamon

Dash salt

1 TB. milk (optional)

1. In a small saucepan over medium heat, bring no-sugar-added orange juice, water, oat bran, no-sugar-added cranberries, cinnamon, and salt to a boil. Reduce heat to low, and cook, stirring often, for 1 minute.

2. Remove from heat, and set aside for 3 to 5 minutes or until thickened.

3. Stir, and divide between 2 serving bowls. Drizzle milk (if using) over the top, and serve.

HONEY DON'T!

Avoid fruit juices that have added sugar when purchasing juice for drinking or cooking. Seek out buzzwords such as *fresh squeezed, all natural,* and *not from concentrate.* Better yet, squeeze your own orange juice from fresh oranges whenever possible. Try to retain the pulp for added flavor and fiber.

Brown Sugary Ginger Pecan Granola

Brown sugar substitute adds a deep, molasses-like flavor to this crunchy, nutty, and "sugary" granola.

Yield:	Prep time:	Cook time:	Serving size:
4 cups	10 minutes	30 to 35 minutes	⅔ cup

3 cups old-fashioned oats

1 tsp. ground cinnamon

1 tsp. ground ginger

½ tsp. baking powder

¼ tsp. salt

½ cup granulated brown sugar substitute

½ tsp. vanilla extract

¼ cup canola oil

2 large egg whites, slightly beaten

¼ cup unsweetened shredded coconut

¼ cup chopped pecans

1. Preheat the oven to 350°F. Line a jelly roll or rimmed baking pan with parchment paper.

2. In a large bowl, combine old-fashioned oats, cinnamon, ginger, baking powder, salt, and granulated brown sugar substitute.

3. In a small bowl, combine vanilla extract, canola oil, and egg whites.

4. Pour wet mixture over oat mixture, and stir well to coat. Spread evenly on the prepared jelly roll pan, and bake for 30 to 35 minutes or until oats are well browned.

5. Allow to cool, transfer to an airtight container, and stir in coconut and pecans. Store in a cool, dry place for up to 1 month.

TASTY TIP

"Sweeten" plain unflavored yogurt with diced fruit and a sprinkling of granola for a scrumptious dessert or snack.

Chunky Chocolate Granola

You'll love this sweet and chocolaty granola, flavored with chocolate-covered nuts and a hint of pure vanilla, drowned in cold milk or even as a snack.

Yield:	Prep time:	Cook time:	Serving size:
5 cups	5 minutes	30 minutes	½ cup

4½ cups old-fashioned oats

½ cup light agave nectar

3 TB. unsweetened cocoa powder

1½ tsp. vanilla extract

½ tsp. salt

⅔ cup sugar-free chocolate-covered nuts

1. Preheat the oven to 300°F. Line a jelly roll pan or rimmed baking sheet with parchment paper.

2. In a large bowl, combine old-fashioned oats, light agave nectar, cocoa powder, vanilla extract, and salt.

3. Transfer to the prepared pan, and spread into an even layer. Bake for 30 minutes, stirring every 5 to 10 minutes to cook evenly, or until toasted and lightly browned.

4. Allow mixture to cool completely before adding sugar-free chocolate-covered nuts. Keep in an airtight container for up to 3 weeks.

HONEY DON'T!

Always be careful when adding chocolate chips or chocolate-coated ingredients to a recipe. If the dish is the least bit warm, your chocolate additions will quickly melt.

Quick-and-Easy Strawberry Muesli

No overnight soaking is required for this fresh version of a delicious fruit-and-cereal classic featuring sweet, juicy strawberries and crunchy, honey-flavored cereal flakes.

Yield:	Prep time:	Serving size:
2 cups	15 minutes	1 cup

1 cup sliced strawberries

1 TB. chopped dried strawberries

1 (1-g) pkt. concentrated sugar substitute

1 cup organic, no-sugar-added corn flakes

2 tsp. honey

1/2 cup sugar-free smooth strawberry yogurt

1/2 cup milk

1 TB. unsalted sunflower seeds

1. In a small bowl, combine fresh strawberries and dried strawberries. Sprinkle concentrated sugar substitute over top, and toss gently to coat. Set aside for 10 minutes.

2. Divide organic, no-sugar-added corn flakes between 2 serving bowls. Drizzle 1 teaspoon honey over each, and toss gently.

3. In a separate small bowl, whisk together sugar-free strawberry yogurt and milk until smooth and thin. Pour 1/2 of mixture in each bowl of corn flakes.

4. Stir strawberry mixture, and mound on top of cereal, dividing between the 2 bowls. Sprinkle sunflower seeds over each, and serve immediately.

SWEET SECRET

Developed by a Swiss physician for his patients in 1900, muesli has become a popular breakfast cereal around the world. Traditionally muesli is made with rolled oats and requires a lengthy overnight soaking in milk to soften. A variety of cereals, fruits, and nuts are often added today in place of the original mainstays of oats and grated apples, and many versions do not require an overnight soak.

Pancakes, Waffles, and Griddle Favorites

In This Chapter

- Saying good-bye to sugar-laden shortcuts
- Turning traditional treats sugar free
- Savoring authentic ingredients and flavors
- Flipping over healthier versions

When it comes to convenience, there's definitely no shortage of breakfast foods in your supermarket's frozen section. From buttermilk pancakes to whole-grain waffles and cinnamon French toast, they're all there, just waiting to be toasted or zapped in your microwave—and loaded with plenty of sugar! Take a quick look at the labels, and you'll see the unfortunate sugar-laden truth.

And that's not all. Boxed mixes and even Mom's old standard recipes have sugar lurking in the ingredient list somewhere. There seems to be no getting away from our modern American propensity to add a pinch (and usually more!) of sugar to just about every breakfast item on the menu.

If you're aiming to go sugar free and still hoping to enjoy all your traditional breakfast favorites, frustration and disappointment have no doubt been your companions—until now!

Pinch-Hitting for Sugar

In this chapter, I share incredibly tasty revamped sugar-free versions of familiar breakfast fare as well as some surprising and unique menu selections like waffles flavored with pumpkin spice that will surely become a part of your sugar-free breakfast tradition on first bite.

No longer will you be missing out on digging into a satisfying stack of flapjacks or French toast hot off the griddle. With these sugar-free recipes in your breakfast repertoire, even the most skeptical breakfast fans will walk away from the table happy.

Finding Flavor *au Naturelle*

And don't worry that you'll be sacrificing any flavor when kicking out the sugar—quite the opposite. By replacing the usual dominating taste of sugar, you allow all the delicious natural ingredients to provide genuine taste and excitement.

For an even bigger boost of sugar-free flavor, consider serving the recipes in this chapter with any of the breakfast jams, jellies, and syrups in Chapter 6.

Best-Ever Buttermilk Pancakes

Rich and creamy buttermilk provides the marvelous, country-style flavor in this traditional favorite pancake.

Yield:	Prep time:	Cook time:	Serving size:
8 pancakes	20 minutes	15 minutes	2 pancakes

1½ cups all-purpose flour

2 (1-g) pkt. concentrated sugar substitute

1 tsp. baking powder

½ tsp. baking soda

¼ tsp. salt

1 cup buttermilk

2 large eggs

2 TB. unsalted butter, melted

1. In a medium bowl, whisk together all-purpose flour, concentrated sugar substitute, baking powder, baking soda, and salt.

2. In a small bowl, whisk together buttermilk, eggs, and melted unsalted butter.

3. Add buttermilk mixture to flour mixture, and stir with a fork until well combined. Let rest 10 minutes.

4. Heat a large griddle or pan over medium heat, and lightly coat with oil. Pour batter onto the griddle by ¼ cupfuls, and cook for about 2 minutes per side or until lightly golden. Serve hot with sugar-free syrup or jam.

TASTY TIP

Whip up an extra batch of these sugar-free pancakes, and freeze or refrigerate them for a convenient and ready-made breakfast later in the week.

Honey Banana Pancakes

A touch of healthy honey and super-sweet ripe bananas are all the sweetness required for these delectable dessertlike pancakes that will keep 'em coming back for more.

Yield:	Prep time:	Cook time:	Serving size:
12 pancakes	10 minutes	15 minutes	2 pancakes

1 cup all-purpose flour

2 tsp. baking powder

⅛ tsp. salt

1 large egg, beaten

1 cup milk

2 TB. canola oil

2 tsp. honey

2 medium ripe bananas, peeled and mashed

1. In a medium bowl, whisk together all-purpose flour, baking powder, and salt.

2. In another medium bowl, whisk together egg, milk, canola oil, honey, and bananas.

3. Stir flour mixture into banana mixture. Do not overmix; batter should be slightly lumpy.

4. Heat a large nonstick griddle or pan over medium heat, and coat lightly with oil. Spoon batter onto the griddle by ¼ cupfuls, and cook for 1 or 2 minutes per side or until golden. Serve hot.

SWEET SECRET

During their ripening, bananas produce amylase, an enzyme that breaks down starch into sugar. This is why ripe bananas are less starchy in texture than their green counterparts and smell and taste much sweeter, too—the perfect condition for baking and cooking.

Corny Blueberry Flapjacks

The natural sweetness of cornmeal adds another layer of flavor to these popular breakfast treats highlighted by bursting juicy and fruity blueberries.

Yield:	Prep time:	Cook time:	Serving size:
6 pancakes	20 minutes	15 minutes	2 pancakes

½ cup yellow cornmeal

½ cup all-purpose flour

1 (1-g) pkt. concentrated sugar substitute

2 tsp. baking powder

⅛ tsp. salt

1¼ cups milk

2 large eggs

1 TB. unsalted butter, melted

1 cup fresh or frozen no-sugar-added blueberries

1. In a medium bowl, whisk together yellow cornmeal, all-purpose flour, concentrated sugar substitute, baking powder, and salt.

2. In a small bowl, whisk together milk, eggs, and unsalted butter.

3. Add milk mixture to flour mixture, and stir with a fork until well combined. Let rest for 10 minutes.

4. Gently stir in no-sugar-added blueberries.

5. Heat a large nonstick griddle or pan over medium heat, and coat lightly with oil. Spoon batter onto the griddle to make 6 pancakes, distributing blueberries with a spoon as necessary. Cook for 1 or 2 minutes per side or until golden. Serve hot.

HONEY DON'T!

Always check frozen fruit package labels for the addition of sugar or syrup, and avoid purchasing those that have been processed or cooked with high-fructose corn syrup.

Whip-'Em-Up Waffles

Making waffles is a snap with this simple recipe. The finished waffles are crispy on the outside and delectably moist and flavorful on the inside.

Yield:	Prep time:	Cook time:	Serving size:
6 to 8 waffles	10 minutes	15 minutes	1 or 2 waffles

$1\frac{1}{2}$ cups all-purpose flour

1 (1-g) pkt. concentrated sugar substitute

2 tsp. baking powder

1 tsp. baking soda

$\frac{1}{4}$ tsp. salt

$1\frac{1}{4}$ cups buttermilk

3 large eggs

$\frac{1}{4}$ cup vegetable oil

1. In a medium bowl, whisk together all-purpose flour, concentrated sugar substitute, baking powder, baking soda, and salt.

2. In a small bowl, whisk together buttermilk, eggs, and vegetable oil. Add to flour mixture, and stir with a fork until well combined. Let rest for 10 minutes.

3. Heat a waffle iron according to the manufacturer's instructions, and lightly coat with cooking spray. Pour batter into the waffle iron in batches, and cook for about 5 minutes or until crisp and golden.

4. Serve hot with your favorite topping.

TASTY TIP

Use leftover waffles to make a delightful frozen dessert sandwich by filling with sugar-free ice cream or frozen yogurt.

Wholesome Whole-Grain Waffles

Light agave nectar steps in for a touch of sweetness in these healthy whole-wheat yet light waffles flavored with a hint of cinnamon and vanilla.

Yield:	Prep time:	Cook time:	Serving size:
10 waffles	10 minutes	20 minutes	2 waffles

2 cups *whole-wheat pastry flour*

1 TB. baking powder

½ tsp. salt

½ tsp. baking soda

¼ tsp. ground cinnamon

2 cups milk

2 large eggs, beaten

¼ cup canola oil

2 TB. light agave nectar

1 tsp. vanilla extract

1. In a medium bowl, whisk together whole-wheat pastry flour, baking powder, salt, baking soda, and cinnamon.

2. In another medium bowl, whisk together milk, eggs, canola oil, light agave nectar, and vanilla extract.

3. Add flour mixture to milk mixture, and stir until just combined. Do not over-mix; batter should be lumpy.

4. Heat a waffle iron according to the manufacturer's instructions, and coat lightly with cooking spray or oil. Pour batter into the waffle iron in batches, and cook for about 3 minutes or until golden and crisp. Serve hot.

DEFINITION

Whole-wheat pastry flour, like whole-wheat flour, contains the whole grain. It has less gluten and has also been ground finer and softer to lessen its weight when used for pastry and delicate baking.

Pumpkin Spice Waffles

Fragrant with familiar fall spices, you'll want to enjoy these sweet and toasty waffles all year long to savor their delicate buttery pumpkin flavor.

Yield:	Prep time:	Cook time:	Serving size:
12 waffles	15 minutes	15 minutes	2 waffles

1 cup all-purpose flour

1 tsp. baking powder

½ tsp. ground ginger

½ tsp. ground cinnamon

½ tsp. baking soda

⅛ tsp. salt

Dash ground nutmeg

1 cup buttermilk

¼ cup canned unsweetened pumpkin purée

1 large egg

1 TB. canola oil

2 TB. granulated brown sugar substitute

1. In a medium bowl, whisk together all-purpose flour, baking powder, ginger, cinnamon, baking soda, salt, and nutmeg.

2. In a separate medium bowl, whisk together buttermilk, unsweetened pumpkin purée, egg, canola oil, and granulated brown sugar substitute.

3. Add flour mixture to pumpkin mixture, and stir until just combined. Do not overmix; batter should be lumpy.

4. Heat a waffle iron according to the manufacturer's instructions and coat lightly with cooking spray or oil. Pour batter into the waffle iron in batches, and cook for about 4 minutes or until golden and crisp. Serve hot.

HONEY DON'T!

When purchasing plain canned pumpkin purée, be careful not to pick up canned pumpkin pie filling instead. The latter is already sweetened with sugar and flavored with spices.

Perfect Cinnamon French Toast

Who can resist the crispy-edged, moist sweet center of perfect French toast—especially when each bite contains the intoxicating flavor of cinnamon? No need to any longer with this go-to recipe for sugar-free diners.

Yield:	Prep time:	Cook time:	Serving size:
6 slices	10 minutes	18 minutes	2 slices

4 large eggs

¼ cup milk

1 (1-g) pkt. concentrated sugar substitute

1 tsp. ground cinnamon

1 tsp. vanilla extract

6 slices white sandwich bread

1. In a large, shallow bowl, whisk together eggs, milk, concentrated sugar substitute, cinnamon, and vanilla extract.

2. Heat a large griddle or pan over medium heat, and coat lightly with oil.

3. Dip each bread slice into egg mixture to saturate, and transfer to the griddle. Cook for about 2 minutes per side or until golden and crispy on edges and puffed in middle. Serve hot.

TASTY TIP

French toast goes perfectly with fresh fruit as well as sugar-free syrup. Top yours with berries or sliced peaches with a light sprinkling of granulated sugar substitute if desired.

Berry Good Baked French Toast

Great for make-ahead breakfasts, this delicious French toast features the flavor of fresh fruit, from oranges to sweet succulent berries.

Yield:	Prep time:	Cook time:	Serving size:
8 slices	70 minutes	15 minutes	2 slices

4 large eggs

½ cup orange juice

½ cup milk

½ tsp. vanilla extract

3 (1-g) pkt. concentrated sugar substitute

8 (1-in.-thick) slices French bread loaf or *baguette*

1 cup mixed fresh berries

1. In a medium bowl, whisk together eggs, orange juice, milk, vanilla extract, and 2 packets concentrated sugar substitute.

2. Place French bread, cut sides down, in a 13×9-inch baking dish. Pour egg mixture over bread, turn slices to absorb liquid, cover with aluminum foil, and refrigerate for 1 hour or overnight.

3. Preheat the oven to 400°F. Lightly coat a large baking sheet with cooking spray or butter.

4. Place bread slices on the prepared baking sheet 1 inch apart, and bake for about 15 minutes or until golden brown, turning over slices halfway through to cook evenly.

5. Meanwhile, combine remaining 1 packet sugar substitute and mixed fresh berries.

6. Serve French toast slices hot, topped with a spoonful of berries.

DEFINITION

A **baguette** is a long, thin loaf of French bread, characterized by a crispy crust and a chewy interior. Day-old baguettes make excellent French toast and also can be used in soups and stews as thickeners.

Berry Patch Sweet Soufflé Omelet

Succulent and juicy berries highlight this dessertlike breakfast treat that can be made with any naturally sweet seasonal fruit and flavored with a variety of extracts.

Yield:	Prep time:	Cook time:	Serving size:
1 omelet	20 minutes	5 minutes	½ omelet

1½ cups fresh mixed berries, such as raspberries, blueberries, and sliced strawberries

1 TB. plus 2 tsp. granulated sugar substitute

3 large eggs, separated

½ tsp. vanilla extract

Dash salt

2 TB. unsalted butter

1. In a small bowl, combine mixed berries and 1 tablespoon granulated sugar substitute. Stir gently, and set aside for 10 minutes.

2. In a medium bowl, whisk together egg yolks, remaining 2 teaspoons granulated sugar substitute, and vanilla extract until pale yellow.

3. In another medium bowl, beat egg whites with salt until soft peaks form. Fold beaten egg whites into yolks.

4. In a large, nonstick skillet over medium heat, melt unsalted butter. Pour in eggs, spread evenly in the pan, cover, reduce heat to low, and cook for 5 or 6 minutes or until lightly golden on the bottom and set on top.

5. Using a slotted spoon, transfer berries to center of omelet, and spread slightly. Reserve berry juices. Use a spatula to fold omelet in half, and cook for 1 more minute.

6. Transfer omelet to a heated platter, pour reserved berry juice over top, and serve warm.

Variation: For a **Peachy Almond Sweet Soufflé Omelet,** substitute fresh sliced peaches for the mixed berries and almond extract for the vanilla extract. Sprinkle the top with 1 tablespoon sliced almonds before serving.

TASTY TIP

To separate eggs, crack them over a bowl and allow the whites to run down while keeping the yolk intact. To fold beaten egg whites into a mixture, use a rubber spatula and cut down vertically through both mixtures, "folding" up and over. Shift the bowl a quarter turn, and repeat until combined.

Quick Breads, Muffins, and Scones

In This Chapter

- Baking better breads and breakfast treats
- Finding flavor in fruit and spices
- Guilt-free bakery favorites
- Terrific taste temptations

Sweet quick breads and muffins are always on the menu when morning rolls around, but these delicious treats can often contain much unwanted sugar and carbs. More cakelike than wholesome breakfast fare, many purchased goodies can do more harm than you think if you're monitoring your sugar and calorie intake. Does it mean they are permanently off *your* menu?

I'm happy to answer that with "No!" Not when you've got the recipes in this chapter to help you along. Baking more healthful and less-sugar-laden breads, muffins, and scones is a snap when you follow these recipes.

From great-tasting orange cranberry bread to agave-sweetened whole-grain scones, you'll be jumping for joy each morning when you sit down to breakfast with these amazing selections on your plate.

A Treat for Your Taste Buds

Ingredients like grated orange peel or a variety of spices can really add tang to the flavor of your baked goods. And your taste buds will definitely thank you after you've tried the treats coming up in this chapter.

Fresh pineapple, sweet ripe bananas, and yes—even chocolate—unite to create a feast of flavor. With the strategic use of terrific sugar substitutes when needed, you won't even notice that sugar has taken a walk.

Old Faves with Guiltless Flare

And don't worry. All your favorites are here with a new and healthful twist. I've revamped blueberry muffins, zucchini bread, and traditional scones to our sugar-free specifications, and they sure do taste terrific.

So let's get to baking sugar-free breakfasts—and enjoying the sweet results!

Zesty Orange Cranberry Bread

You'll love the intense citrus flavor orange zest brings and the flavorful balance of sweet, yet tart dried cranberries when you bite into this morning tea bread that's especially tasty when toasted and topped with butter.

Yield:	Prep time:	Cook time:	Serving size:
1 (9×5-inch) loaf	20 minutes	30 to 40 minutes	1 (1-inch) slice

2 cups all-purpose flour	$^2/_3$ cup milk
1 tsp. baking powder	1 tsp. vanilla extract
$^1/_2$ tsp. baking soda	2 TB. fresh orange juice
Dash salt	1 TB. grated orange zest
2 large eggs	$^2/_3$ cup dried no-sugar-added cranberries
$^2/_3$ cup granulated sugar substitute	
6 TB. unsalted butter, melted	

1. Preheat the oven to 350°F. Lightly coat a 9×5-inch loaf pan with cooking spray.

2. In a medium bowl, whisk together all-purpose flour, baking powder, baking soda, and salt.

3. In a large bowl, and using an electric mixer on high speed, beat together eggs and granulated sugar substitute for 3 minutes or until yellow and smooth.

4. Add unsalted butter, and beat on medium speed for 1 minute.

5. Add milk, vanilla extract, orange juice, and orange zest, and beat on medium speed for 2 minutes. Stir in no-sugar-added cranberries.

6. Pour batter into the prepared pan, and bake for 30 to 40 minutes or until lightly golden and a toothpick inserted in the center comes out clean.

7. Cool on a wire rack for 10 minutes before loosening the edges and removing bread from the pan. Slice with a serrated knife, and serve.

> **TASTY TIP**
>
> Grating and zesting fruit rind and cheeses couldn't be quicker or easier using a Microplane. This handy kitchen tool comes in various shapes and sizes and can be found in most stores that carry kitchen supplies.

Nutty Spiced-Up Zucchini Bread

Definitely not your mother's zucchini bread, in this not-too-sweet version, the intense flavors of intoxicating spices rule while buttery pecans add crunch.

Yield:	Prep time:	Cook time:	Serving size:
1 (9×5-inch) loaf	15 minutes	35 to 45 minutes	1 (1-inch) slice

1½ cups all-purpose flour	1 large egg
1 tsp. ground cinnamon	½ cup granulated sugar substitute
½ tsp. ground cloves	¼ cup buttermilk
¼ tsp. ground nutmeg	2 TB. unsalted butter, melted
¼ tsp. ground ginger	½ tsp. vanilla extract
½ tsp. baking powder	1¼ cups shredded unpeeled zucchini
¼ tsp. baking soda	⅔ cup roughly chopped pecans
¼ tsp. salt	

1. Preheat the oven to 350°F. Lightly coat a 9×5-inch loaf pan with cooking spray.

2. In a medium bowl, whisk together all-purpose flour, cinnamon, cloves, nutmeg, ginger, baking powder, baking soda, and salt.

3. In a large bowl, and using an electric mixer on high speed, beat together egg and granulated sugar substitute for 2 minutes or until yellow and smooth.

4. Add buttermilk, melted unsalted butter, and vanilla extract, and beat on medium speed for 1 minute.

5. Add ½ of flour mixture to wet mixture, and beat on medium speed until just combined. Repeat with remaining flour mixture. Stir in zucchini and pecans, and scrape batter into the prepared loaf pan, smoothing the top.

6. Bake for 35 to 45 minutes or until golden and a toothpick inserted in the center comes out clean.

7. Cool on a wire rack for 10 minutes before loosening the edges and removing bread from the pan. Slice with a serrated knife, and serve.

TASTY TIP

You can shred zucchini in your food processor using the shredder disc or the steel blade. If you don't have a food processor, you can grate zucchini on the large-hole side of a cheese grater.

Double-Citrus Poppy Seed Bread

Deliciously tangy with the flavors of both lemon and orange, this bread is delightful toasted and topped with a smear of whipped butter.

Yield:	Prep time:	Cook time:	Serving size:
12 slices	20 minutes	35 minutes	1 slice

2 cups all-purpose flour

1 tsp. baking powder

½ tsp. baking soda

⅔ cup milk

2 TB. lemon juice

1½ tsp. lemon zest

1½ tsp. orange zest

2 large eggs

¾ cup granulated sugar substitute

½ cup (1 stick) unsalted butter, melted

1 tsp. vanilla extract

¼ cup poppy seeds

1. Preheat the oven to 350°F. Lightly coat an 8- or 9-inch loaf pan with cooking spray.

2. In a large bowl, whisk together all-purpose flour, baking powder, and baking soda. Set aside.

3. In a small bowl, whisk together milk, lemon juice, lemon zest, and orange zest. Set aside.

4. In a medium bowl, and using an electric mixer on medium speed, beat together eggs and granulated sugar substitute for about 5 minutes or until well combined and pale yellow. Add melted unsalted butter and vanilla extract, and beat 1 more minute.

5. Add ½ of flour mixture to egg mixture, and beat on low speed just to combine. Add milk mixture, and beat on low speed for 1 minute. Add remaining flour mixture, and beat well to combine. Stir in poppy seeds.

6. Spoon batter into the prepared loaf pan, and bake for 30 to 35 minutes or until a toothpick inserted in the center comes out clean and the top is lightly golden.

7. Cool on a wire rack for 10 minutes before removing from the pan. Serve warm, toasted, or at room temperature.

SWEET SECRET

Poppy seeds come from the opium poppy plant and have been harvested for medicinal purposes since ancient times. Eating a lot of poppy seeds has been known to give a false positive in tests for opiate use.

Chunky Chocolate Banana Bread

Naturally sweet, ripe bananas and dark, delicious chocolate are perfect companions in this mouthwatering muffinlike bread that's full of sensationally sweet flavor.

Yield:	Prep time:	Cook time:	Serving size:
1 (9×5-inch) loaf	15 minutes	45 to 50 minutes	1 (1-inch) slice

2 cups all-purpose flour

1 tsp. baking soda

½ tsp. salt

2 large eggs

½ cup granulated brown sugar substitute

1 or 2 medium ripe bananas, peeled and mashed (1 cup)

¼ cup canola oil

⅓ cup milk

1 tsp. vanilla extract

¾ cup sugar-free (not unsweetened) dark chocolate chunks, or sugar-free chocolate (not unsweetened) broken into pieces

1. Preheat the oven to 350°F. Lightly coat a 9×5-inch loaf pan with cooking spray.

2. In a medium bowl, whisk together all-purpose flour, baking soda, and salt.

3. In a large bowl, and using an electric mixer on high speed, beat together eggs and granulated brown sugar substitute for 1 minute.

4. Add banana, canola oil, milk, and vanilla extract, and beat on medium speed until well blended.

5. Add ½ of flour mixture into wet mixture, and beat on medium speed until just combined. Repeat with remaining flour mixture. Stir in sugar-free dark chocolate chunks, and pour into the prepared loaf pan.

6. Bake for 45 to 50 minutes or until golden and a toothpick inserted in the center comes out clean.

7. Cool on a wire rack for 10 minutes before loosening the edges and removing bread from the pan. Slice with a serrated knife, and serve.

SWEET SECRET

Vanilla enhances the flavor of chocolate. That's why chocolate candy manufacturers always add vanilla or vanillin (an artificial flavor) to their chocolaty products.

Corny Blueberry Muffins

It's corny but true: when cornbread and blueberries get together, they make for a super-moist and delicious muffin, loaded with toasty corn flavor and studded with sweet fruity berries.

Yield:	Prep time:	Cook time:	Serving size:
12 muffins	10 minutes	20 to 25 minutes	1 muffin

1½ cups all-purpose flour

¾ cup yellow cornmeal

¾ cup granulated sugar substitute

1½ tsp. baking powder

½ tsp. baking soda

¼ tsp. salt

½ cup (1 stick) unsalted butter, softened

1 large egg

1 cup buttermilk

1 tsp. vanilla extract

1½ cups fresh or frozen no-sugar-added blueberries

1. Preheat the oven to 350°F. Lightly coat a 12-cup muffin tin with cooking spray.

2. In a large bowl, whisk together all-purpose flour, yellow cornmeal, granulated sugar substitute, baking powder, baking soda, and salt.

3. In another large bowl, and using an electric mixer on high speed, beat unsalted butter for 3 minutes or until light and fluffy.

4. Add egg, and beat for 1 more minute. Add buttermilk and vanilla extract, and beat until well combined.

5. Add flour mixture to wet mixture in 2 batches, beating on medium speed just until combined. Do not overbeat. Stir in no-sugar-added blueberries.

6. Scoop batter into prepared muffin tin, and bake for 20 to 25 minutes or until a toothpick inserted in center of muffin comes out clean.

7. Cool muffins in the tin for 5 minutes. Loosen the edges, and turn out muffins onto a wire rack to cool completely before serving.

HONEY DON'T!

Beware of using prepackaged cornbread and muffin mixes. They often contain good amounts of added sugar.

Pineapple Coconut Crumb Muffins

The aroma of piña coladas will lull you into tropical heaven when you bake these super-moist muffins flavored with sweet ripe pineapple and exotic toasted coconut.

Yield:	Prep time:	Cook time:	Serving size:
12 muffins	20 minutes	20 to 25 minutes	1 muffin

1⅔ cups all-purpose flour

3 TB. plus ½ cup granulated sugar substitute

1 cup unsweetened flaked coconut

3 TB. unsalted butter, softened

1½ tsp. baking powder

¼ tsp. salt

2 large eggs, beaten

½ cup canola oil

1 cup chopped fresh pineapple

1. Preheat the oven to 375°F. Lightly coat a 12-cup muffin tin with cooking spray.

2. In a small bowl, combine ⅓ cup all-purpose flour, 3 tablespoons granulated sugar substitute, ½ cup coconut, and unsalted butter with a fork. Set aside.

3. In a medium bowl, whisk together remaining 1⅓ cups all-purpose flour, remaining ½ cup granulated sugar substitute, baking powder, and salt. Stir in remaining ½ cup coconut. Add eggs and canola oil, and beat by hand until just combined. Stir in pineapple.

4. Pour batter into the prepared muffin tin, and top each muffin with a little crumb mixture. Bake for 20 to 25 minutes or until lightly browned and a toothpick inserted in center of muffin comes out clean.

5. Cool muffins in the tin for 5 minutes. Carefully turn out muffins onto a wire rack to cool completely before serving.

TASTY TIP

By using unsweetened coconut in place of sweetened coconut, you can save between 2 and 3 grams sugar per tablespoon!

Glazed Applesauce Raisin Muffins

Flavorful and fruity applesauce and plump, juicy raisins provide most of the natural sweetness in these good-for-you morning muffins featuring an added "sugary" glaze for good measure.

Yield:	Prep time:	Cook time:	Serving size:
12 muffins	15 minutes	20 to 25 minutes	1 muffin

1½ cups all-purpose flour

1½ tsp. baking powder

½ tsp. baking soda

¼ tsp. salt

1 tsp. ground cinnamon

2 large eggs

½ cup granulated brown sugar substitute

½ cup (1 stick) unsalted butter, melted

1 cup unsweetened applesauce

¾ cup raisins

1 cup granulated sugar substitute

2½ TB. cornstarch

3 or 4 tsp. water

1. Preheat the oven to 375°F. Lightly coat a 12-cup muffin tin with cooking spray.

2. In a medium bowl, whisk together all-purpose flour, baking powder, baking soda, salt, and cinnamon.

3. In a large bowl, using an electric mixer on medium speed, beat eggs and granulated brown sugar substitute until well combined. Slowly add melted unsalted butter, and beat until incorporated. Add unsweetened applesauce, and beat in on low. Add flour mixture, and beat just until combined. Stir in raisins.

4. Pour batter into the prepared muffin tin, and bake for 20 to 25 minutes or until lightly browned and a toothpick inserted in center of muffin comes out clean.

5. Cool muffins in the tin for 5 minutes. Carefully turn out muffins onto a wire rack.

6. In a blender, purée granulated sugar substitute, cornstarch, and water until smooth. (Add more water to make pourable if necessary.) Spoon glaze over muffins while they're still warm.

SWEET SECRET

Cooked apples, such as those in applesauce, offer greater amounts of healthy pectin, a soluble fiber good for digestion and lowering cholesterol levels.

Whole-Wheat Bran Muffins

Hearty yet moist, these not-too-sweet muffins with just a hint of maple and brown sugar are ideal for breakfast.

Yield:	Prep time:	Cook time:	Serving size:
12 muffins	20 minutes	25 minutes	1 muffin

2 cups sugar-free bran cereal

1 cup milk

¾ cup unsweetened applesauce

¼ cup vegetable oil

1 large egg

1 tsp. maple extract

1 cup all-purpose flour

½ cup whole-wheat flour

½ cup granulated brown sugar substitute, firmly packed

2 tsp. baking powder

½ tsp. salt

¼ tsp. baking soda

1. Preheat the oven to 400°F. Lightly coat a 12-cup muffin pan with cooking spray.

2. In a medium bowl, combine sugar-free bran cereal, milk, applesauce, vegetable oil, egg, and maple extract. Let stand for 10 minutes.

3. In another medium bowl, whisk together all-purpose flour, whole-wheat flour, granulated brown sugar substitute, baking powder, salt, and baking soda.

4. Add dry ingredients to bran mixture, and stir just until combined. Divide among muffin cups, and bake for about 25 minutes or until tops are golden brown and a toothpick inserted in the middle comes out clean.

5. Cool on a wire rack for 5 minutes, gently remove from the pan, and store muffins in an airtight container for 3 to 5 days.

> **TASTY TIP**
>
> Freeze extra muffins by cooling them completely, wrapping them tightly in plastic, and storing them in a zipper-lock freezer bag. Defrost at room temperature overnight for breakfast.

Classically British Tea Scones

Every proper Englishman knows that perfect scones need very little sweetening (until you add your sugar-free jam, of course!), as these rich and buttery versions show.

Yield:	Prep time:	Cook time:	Serving size:
10 scones	25 minutes	12 to 15 minutes	2 scones

1½ cups *self-rising flour*
1 TB. granulated sugar substitute
Dash salt

3 TB. unsalted butter, diced
⅔ cup milk

1. Preheat the oven to 400°F. Line a baking sheet with parchment paper.

2. In a medium bowl, whisk together self-rising flour, granulated sugar substitute, and salt.

3. Add unsalted butter, and using a fork or pastry blender, work butter into flour mixture until it resembles sand.

4. Stir in milk a little at a time, blending only just to combine.

5. Turn out dough onto a lightly floured surface, and roll into a ¾-inch circle. Using a 2-inch biscuit cutter or the open end of a drinking glass, cut out 10 scones and place on the prepared pan. Reroll and cut as necessary to use up dough.

6. Bake for 12 to 15 minutes or until scones are golden on top and a toothpick inserted in the center comes out clean. Transfer to a wire rack to cool completely, or serve warm.

DEFINITION

Self-rising flour is flour that contains a leavener such as baking powder. It's available as all-purpose flour for general baking as well as cake flour and pastry flour versions.

Agave Whole-Wheat Drop Scones

These American-style scones get their sweet, earthy flavor from agave nectar and wholesome whole grains, while a hint of cinnamon completes the taste experience.

Yield:	Prep time:	Cook time:	Serving size:
8 scones	20 minutes	15 to 20 minutes	1 scone

½ cup whole-wheat flour
½ cup all-purpose flour
1½ tsp. baking powder
½ tsp. ground cinnamon
Dash salt

1 large egg
1 TB. unsalted butter, melted
2 TB. amber agave nectar
2 TB. milk

1. Preheat the oven to 400°F. Line a baking sheet with parchment paper.

2. In a medium bowl, whisk together whole-wheat flour, all-purpose flour, baking powder, cinnamon, and salt.

3. In another medium bowl, beat together egg, unsalted butter, amber agave nectar, and milk.

4. Add flour mixture to wet ingredients all at once, and stir just to combine.

5. Drop dough by rounded spoonfuls onto the prepared baking sheet, and smooth tops slightly with your fingers. Bake for 15 to 20 minutes or until nicely browned and a toothpick inserted in the center comes out clean. Transfer to a wire rack to cool, or serve warm.

TASTY TIP

Whole-wheat flours are best stored in a cool, dry place or even in the refrigerator. The bran and germ oils they contain make them susceptible to going rancid at warmer temperatures.

Jams, Jellies, and Syrups

In This Chapter

- Preserving flavor without fuss
- Making use of nature's sweetness
- Easy recipes for jams and jellies
- Pouring sugar-free syrup alternatives

Many breakfast selections, from simple toast to stacks of pancakes, require a finishing touch to make them complete. Whether it's a tablespoon of jam or jelly or a quick pour of maple syrup, a variety of morning delights are even more delightful when topped off with a sweet flourish.

But these treats usually contain a lot of unwanted sugar, so we may feel if sugar free is our aim that it's better to simply go without.

Jammin' Good Flavor

If commercial sugar-free jams, jellies, preserves, and marmalades have been your only choice up to now and left you less than satisfied, you're in for a real surprise when you try the fruitful spreads in this chapter. Loaded with great flavor from natural ingredients, you won't be missing the sugar any longer when you start spreading these easy-to-make versions.

If you're not a canner or preserver, there's no need to worry. All these recipes are simply cooked and refrigerated or frozen for later enjoyment.

Sensational Syrups

When topping off your unadorned stack of hotcakes, waffles, or French toast, there will be no hesitation when you've got the healthy syrups offered in this chapter. Whether blueberry is your passion or traditional maple is your syrup of choice, you'll be happy to know you can pour without guilt or worry and enjoy sensational taste as your reward.

Sweet Strawberry Preserves

This quick and easy recipe will surprise you with its authentic strawberry flavor and consistency. Using sweet seasonal and locally picked strawberries produces the best result, but you can substitute frozen berries in a pinch.

Yield:	Prep time:	Cook time:	Serving size:
3 cups	20 minutes	10 minutes	1 tablespoon

1 pt. fresh strawberries, stemmed and hulled	1 (3-oz.) pkg. sugar-free strawberry gelatin
1 cup water	

1. In a medium saucepan over medium heat, bring strawberries and water to a boil. Cook for 2 minutes, stirring often, and remove from heat.

2. Crush strawberries with a potato masher to desired consistency. While still hot, stir in sugar-free strawberry gelatin, and set aside to cool completely.

3. Stir well, and spoon into 3 (1-cup) jars. Refrigerate for up to 10 days, or freeze for up to 3 months.

SWEET SECRET

One cup of fresh strawberries contains only 45 calories and is an excellent source of vitamin C, fiber, and flavonoids—powerful antioxidants that fight free radicals and keep you healthy.

Quick Red Raspberry Jam

The sweet-tart taste of raspberries highlights this easy-to-make jam that gets an additional hint of flavor from orange oil.

Yield:	Prep time:	Cook time:	Serving size:
2½ cups	15 minutes	10 minutes	1 tablespoon

1½ cups fresh or frozen no-sugar-added raspberries

1 cup granulated sugar substitute

2 TB. no-sugar-needed pectin

Few drops orange oil, or ¼ tsp. orange extract

1. In a medium saucepan over medium heat, combine no-sugar-added raspberries, granulated sugar substitute, and pectin. Bring to a boil, reduce heat to low, and simmer for about 5 minutes or until berries have broken down and mixture has thickened.

2. Remove from heat and stir in orange oil. Cool slightly, transfer to airtight containers, and chill before serving. Keep refrigerated for up to 10 days.

TASTY TIP

Citrus oils are great for saving time and energy when intense flavoring is required in a recipe. Just a few drops have the flavor of 1 tablespoon of zest. You can find citrus oils for cooking and baking in specialty food stores or order them online.

Easy Stevia Summer Plum Jam

Concentrated stevia works particularly well in this "plum good" quick-cooking jam with the summery flavor of sweet, sugary plums and a hint of orange and cinnamon for an added level of terrific taste.

Yield:	Prep time:	Cook time:	Serving size:
2 cups	30 minutes	5 minutes	1 tablespoon

12 to 15 medium ripe plums

1 cup fresh orange juice

1 tsp. grated orange zest

½ tsp. ground cinnamon

1 TB. *no-sugar-needed pectin*

1 tsp. stevia powder, or more to taste

1. Using a sharp paring knife, carefully peel plums, remove pits, and roughly chop. Transfer, with any accumulated juices, to a medium saucepan over medium heat.

2. Stir in orange juice, orange zest, and cinnamon, and bring to a simmer, stirring occasionally.

3. Stir in no-sugar-needed pectin, and boil for 3 minutes. Remove from heat, and stir in stevia powder. Set aside to cool.

4. Stir well, and taste to see if more stevia is needed. Transfer to 2 (1-cup) jars. Refrigerate for up to 10 days, or freeze for up to 2 months.

DEFINITION

No-sugar-needed pectin is commercial pectin specifically designed for using in sugar-free jams and jellies. Regular pectin, which contains sugar, normally requires the addition of granulated sugar in order to thicken. Both can be found in your supermarket fruit or baking aisle.

Apple Grape Jelly

No-sugar-added juice is the surprising ingredient in this sweet spread that's full of fruity flavor.

Yield:	Prep time:	Cook time:	Serving size:
2 cups	5 minutes	10 minutes	1 tablespoon

2 cups no-sugar-added apple grape juice

4 tsp. unflavored gelatin

2 TB. granulated sugar substitute

1 TB. lemon juice

1. In a small bowl, combine ½ cup no-sugar-added apple grape juice and gelatin.

2. In a medium saucepan over medium-high heat, bring remaining 1½ cups no-sugar-added apple grape juice to a boil. Remove from heat.

3. Stir gelatin mixture into hot juice, stirring well until dissolved. Add granulated sugar substitute and lemon juice, and return to medium-high heat. Bring to a boil, and remove from heat to cool slightly.

4. Pour into 2 (1-cup) containers. Refrigerate for up to 1 month.

HONEY DON'T!

If you're a vegetarian or vegan, you might want to refrain from eating gelatin because it's derived from animal parts such as bone and cartilage. Instead, use agar, a thickener derived from seaweed. You can find it in most health food stores.

Bada-Bing Cherry Jelly

Tart cherry juice provides incredible cherry flavor in this terrific jelly that's just as tasty in a PB&J sandwich as it is for sweetening morning toast or muffins.

Yield:	Prep time:	Cook time:	Serving size:
2 cups	5 minutes	10 minutes	1 tablespoon

2 cups no-sugar-added tart cherry juice

4 tsp. unflavored gelatin

3 TB. granulated sugar substitute

2 tsp. lime juice

1. In a small bowl, combine $\frac{1}{2}$ cup no-sugar-added tart cherry juice with gelatin.

2. In a medium saucepan over medium-high heat, bring remaining $1\frac{1}{2}$ cups tart cherry juice to a boil. Remove from heat.

3. Stir in gelatin mixture until dissolved. Add granulated sugar substitute and lime juice, and return to medium-high heat. Bring to a full boil, remove from heat, and set aside to cool slightly.

4. Pour into 2 (1-cup) containers, and keep refrigerated for up to 1 month.

SWEET SECRET

Tart cherries, in addition to being delicious in pies, are known for their anti-inflammatory properties. They can help alleviate the pain of arthritis and other diseases caused by inflammation.

Short-Cut Orange Peach Marmalade

A snap to make, this great breakfast spread combines tangy citrus and sweet, juicy peaches, and gets an added kick from fresh ginger.

Yield:	Prep time:	Cook time:	Serving size:
2 cups	25 minutes	10 minutes	1 tablespoon

2 cups canned no-sugar-added peaches, with juice

1 TB. grated orange zest

2 tsp. peeled and grated fresh ginger

1 (1.75-oz.) pkg. no-sugar-needed pectin

½ cup granulated sugar substitute

1. In a food processor fitted with a steel blade, process no-sugar-added peaches with juice, orange zest, and ginger for about 1 minute or until smooth.

2. Transfer mixture to a medium saucepan over medium-high heat, and bring to a simmer. Gradually stir in no-sugar-needed pectin, and bring to a boil, stirring often. Boil for 1 minute, and remove from heat.

3. Stir in granulated sugar substitute, and set aside to cool slightly.

4. Stir well, and transfer to 2 (1-cup) jars or containers. Refrigerate for up to 10 days, or freeze for up to 3 months.

TASTY TIP

Use your sugar-free jams, jellies, and marmalades to glaze chicken when baking or grilling for a sweet, guilt-free treat.

Apple Cinnamon Syrup

Try this amazingly delicious syrup, slightly warmed, over waffles or pancakes for a fresh taste of ripe apples and aromatic cinnamon.

Yield:	Prep time:	Cook time:	Serving size:
2 cups	10 minutes	15 minutes	¼ cup

½ cup granulated brown sugar substitute, firmly packed

⅓ cup water

2 TB. unsalted butter

1 tsp. cornstarch

½ tsp. ground cinnamon

2 medium apples, peeled and finely chopped

1. In a medium saucepan over medium heat, combine granulated brown sugar substitute, water, unsalted butter, cornstarch, and cinnamon. Bring to a boil, and boil, stirring constantly, for 2 minutes or until thickened.

2. Reduce heat to low, stir in apples, and cook, stirring often, for 10 to 12 more minutes or until apples are tender.

3. Remove from heat, and serve warm. Store in an airtight container in the refrigerator for up to 3 days.

TASTY TIP

Homemade syrups should be reheated very gently, either on low power in the microwave or in a syrup bottle submerged in simmering water.

True Blueberry Pancake Syrup

What could be better on a stack of enticing blueberry pancakes than a truly intense blueberry flavored syrup? Use fresh blueberries when they're at the height of their sweet season if available; otherwise, frozen (no-sugar-added) berries can fill in quite nicely.

Yield:	Prep time:	Cook time:	Serving size:
1¼ cups	5 minutes	15 minutes	¼ cup

3 cups fresh blueberries, stemmed, or 3 cups frozen

½ cup water

1 tsp. lemon juice

½ cup granulated sugar substitute

1. In a medium saucepan over medium-high heat, bring blueberries, water, and lemon juice to a simmer. Cook for 5 minutes, stirring often, or until berries are broken down. Remove from heat.

2. Using a potato masher, mash blueberries. Return to medium-high heat, and boil for 1 more minute.

3. Remove from heat, and stir in granulated sugar substitute until dissolved. Syrup will thicken as it cools. Serve warm.

TASTY TIP

To make fruit syrups that are completely smooth without skin or seeds, strain them through a fine sieve, pushing any bits of fruit against the mesh. Doing so, however, reduces the amount of your finished syrup by half.

Sweet Pomegranate Syrup

Delicious over fruit, yogurt, pancakes, or waffles, this tasty syrup features the unique and exotic flavor of pomegranates.

Yield:	Prep time:	Cook time:	Serving size:
1 cup	1 minute	20 to 25 minutes	1 or 2 tablespoons

3 cups no-sugar-added
   pomegranate juice
¾ cup granulated sugar substitute

½ tsp. lemon juice
¼ cup fresh pomegranate seeds
   (optional)

1. In a medium saucepan over high heat, combine no-sugar-added pomegranate juice, granulated sugar substitute, and lemon juice. Bring to a boil, reduce heat to low, and simmer, stirring occasionally, for 20 to 25 minutes or until mixture is reduced by ⅔. Set aside to cool.

2. Stir in pomegranate seeds (if using), and pour into an airtight container. Store in the refrigerator for up to 1 week.

SWEET SECRET

Pomegranates are just as heart-healthy as red wine. They contain the same phytochemical, resveratrol, that's beneficial for lowering cholesterol and improving circulation.

"Maple" Walnut Syrup

Amber agave nectar's remarkable resemblance to maple syrup makes it the perfect foil for a low-glycemic, sugar-free pancake syrup, here embellished with the flavor of toasted walnuts.

Yield:	Prep time:	Cook time:	Serving size:
1½ cups	5 minutes	5 minutes	¼ cup

1½ cups amber agave nectar   ½ cup toasted chopped walnuts
1 tsp. maple extract

1. In a small saucepan over low heat, heat amber agave nectar. Do not boil.
2. Remove from heat, and stir in maple extract and walnuts. Serve warm.

TASTY TIP

To toast walnuts, place them in a dry skillet over medium-high heat, and cook, stirring often, for a few minutes or until lightly browned and fragrant. Use immediately, or store in an airtight container.

Light Fare and Go-Withs

The most dangerous times for sugar-free eaters can be during rushed lunches and in between meals when snack attacks hit. Nutritionally barren vending-machine fare and sugary snacks are too often reached for in a pinch, and the chapters in Part 3 provide some wonderfully satisfying alternatives that don't sacrifice flavor or pleasure. From quick salads to bowls of comfort-food soups, you'll have lunch and even snacks covered—all sugar free.

Part 3 also offers a collection of savory sauces and condiments whose commercially made counterparts contain a lot of added sugar. Ketchup, cranberry sauce, and chutney, to name a few, can add a lot of flavor to a dish, but they can also hike up the sugar and carb count. With the sugar-free versions in Part 3, you'll be able to savor the flavor—without guilt!

Finally, in this part I share some of my favorite sweet drinks and smoothies that are sure to please even the most intense sweet tooth. They're all pretty darn healthful, too—win-win!

Salads and Dressings

In This Chapter

- Refashioning old-fashioned salad favorites
- Tossing salads without sugar
- Utilizing natural flavors
- Whisking up sugar-free dressings

Many salads and especially salad dressings are loaded with sugar. Many of the classics, including coleslaw and spinach salad, can have more than a pinch of unwanted sugary sweetness when you're looking to control your intake and go sugar free.

In this chapter, we take a look at some of the traditional areas sugar lurks in salads and learn how to refashion some ingredients without altering any of the taste.

Sugar-Free Salad Ingredients

Much of the sweetness in the types of salads and dressings included in this chapter isn't from the actual addition of sugar. Other culprits often used in salad-making, such as prepared ingredients like ketchup and even peanut butter, come with their own added sugar.

Selecting versions of those ingredients that are reduced in sugar if not sugar free goes a long way in helping create the more healthful final dish you're after.

Less Is More

When adding sugary ingredients such as high-fructose corn syrup or heavily processed white sugar, food manufacturers can be very heavy handed. In reality, the amount of sugar needed to simply highlight flavor and taste in most products is much less than what's usually included.

As your taste buds adjust to eating less sugar, you'll find that you also *want* less sweetness—particularly in places where it doesn't necessarily belong. The salad bar is a perfect example. After you've tasted the recipes in this chapter, I think you'll agree.

Old-Fashioned Coleslaw

Traditional coleslaw gets a sugar-free makeover in this easy recipe that's got all the same great flavor you'd expect, thanks to sweet agave nectar and the addition of chewy, golden raisins.

Yield:	Prep time:	Serving size:
4 cups	15 minutes, plus 30 minutes chill time	½ cup

1 (16-oz.) pkg. shredded coleslaw cabbage

1 cup mayonnaise

1 TB. water

2 TB. light agave nectar

3 TB. apple cider vinegar

Dash salt, or more to taste

Freshly ground pepper

½ cup golden raisins

1. In a large bowl, place coleslaw cabbage.

2. In a medium bowl, whisk together mayonnaise, water, light agave nectar, apple cider vinegar, salt, and pepper. Pour over cabbage, and toss to coat.

3. Stir in golden raisins, and refrigerate for at least 30 minutes before serving.

SWEET SECRET

Cabbage is a great source of fiber. Fiber helps lower the glycemic effect of food during digestion—and that's especially important for diabetics.

New Waldorf Salad

This classic salad gets a pinch of concentrated sugar substitute to bring out the natural flavor and sweetness of the apples.

Yield:	Prep time:	Serving size:
2 cups	20 minutes	½ cup

½ cup mayonnaise

2 TB. milk

2 tsp. lemon juice

1 (1-g) pkt. concentrated sugar substitute

Dash salt, or more to taste

Dash ground nutmeg

Freshly ground pepper

1 large apple, cored and diced small

1 medium celery stalk, sliced ¼-in. thick

2 TB. chopped walnuts

1. In a small bowl, whisk together mayonnaise, milk, lemon juice, concentrated sugar substitute, salt, nutmeg, and pepper.

2. In a medium bowl, combine apple, celery, and walnuts.

3. Pour mayonnaise mixture over apple mixture, and toss well to coat. Cover and refrigerate for 30 minutes.

4. Taste to see if more salt and pepper are needed, and serve.

TASTY TIP

To prevent your diced apples from turning brown before you're ready to use them, sprinkle them with lemon juice and toss to coat lightly.

Thai Cucumber Salad

Your taste buds will love the combination of flavors from the mellow rice vinegar to the sultry *Thai basil* in this spicy and sweet salad.

Yield:	Prep time:	Serving size:
2 cups	25 minutes, plus 1 hour chill time	¼ cup

½ cup unseasoned rice vinegar

½ cup cold water

½ tsp. salt

2 (1-g) pkt. concentrated sugar substitute

1 large English cucumber, peeled and thinly sliced

2 scallions, trimmed and minced

1 TB. chopped fresh Thai basil

2 TB. chopped peanuts (optional)

1. In a medium bowl, whisk together rice vinegar, cold water, salt, and concentrated sugar substitute until granules are dissolved.

2. Add English cucumbers, scallions, and Thai basil, and toss well to coat. Refrigerate for 1 hour, occasionally tossing.

3. Serve chilled sprinkled with peanuts (if using).

DEFINITION

Thai basil is an Asian type of basil with purple stems and licorice-flavored leaves.

Sweet-and-Spicy Ginger Noodle Salad

This version of the popular Asian take-out salad, featuring tangy ginger, aromatic sesame oil, and the taste of hot red pepper flakes, has all the flavor of the restaurant version but none of the sugar.

Yield:	Prep time:	Cook time:	Serving size:
6 cups	30 minutes	10 minutes	1½ cups

8 oz. Chinese egg noodles

4 scallions, trimmed and cut into 1-in. pieces

½ medium red bell pepper, ribs and seeds removed, and cut into strips

1 medium carrot, peeled and shredded (½ cup)

½ cup smooth no-sugar-added peanut butter

3 TB. soy sauce

¼ cup warm water

1 TB. rice vinegar

1 TB. amber agave nectar

1 TB. toasted sesame oil

2 tsp. peeled and minced fresh ginger

¼ tsp. crushed red pepper flakes or to taste

2 TB. chopped peanuts

1. Cook Chinese egg noodles according to the package directions, and rinse under cold water.

2. In a large bowl, combine cooked Chinese egg noodles, scallions, red bell pepper, and carrot.

3. In a medium bowl, whisk together no-sugar-added peanut butter, soy sauce, warm water, rice vinegar, amber agave nectar, toasted sesame oil, ginger, and crushed red pepper flakes. Pour over noodle mixture, and toss to coat.

4. Sprinkle peanuts over salad, and serve at room temperature or chilled.

HONEY DON'T!

Be careful when purchasing rice vinegar. Some versions are seasoned and contain added sugar.

Crunchy Nutty Broccoli Salad

Health nuts will love this wholesome salad with a sweet side and the terrific flavor and crunch of bacon, walnuts, and sunflower seeds.

Yield:	Prep time:	Serving size:
4 cups	25 minutes, plus 1 hour chill time	½ cup

3½ cups small raw broccoli florets

½ medium red onion, diced small

3 TB. bacon bits

2 TB. chopped walnuts

2 TB. dried no-sugar-added cranberries

1 TB. sunflower seeds

½ cup mayonnaise

¼ cup low-fat plain yogurt

1 TB. apple cider vinegar

2 (1-g) pkt. concentrated sugar substitute

Dash salt, or more to taste

Freshly ground pepper

1. In a large bowl, combine broccoli florets, red onion, bacon bits, walnuts, no-sugar-added cranberries, and sunflower seeds.

2. In a medium bowl, whisk together mayonnaise, low-fat yogurt, apple cider vinegar, concentrated sugar substitute, salt, and pepper. Pour over broccoli mixture, and toss well to coat.

3. Chill for 1 hour. Taste to see if more salt and pepper are needed, and serve.

SWEET SECRET

Technically, the edible part of the sunflower seed is referred to as the *kernel*. That's where its concentrated nutritional value—vitamins E, B_1, and folate—is housed.

German-Style Potato Salad

This classic salad, usually served warm, goes sugar free but keeps its delicious sweet and savory flavor, thanks to maple-flavored agave and the salty taste of bacon.

Yield:	Prep time:	Cook time:	Serving size:
4 cups	20 minutes	30 minutes	$\frac{1}{2}$ cup

4 or 5 medium red-skinned
  potatoes
Pinch plus dash salt
6 slices bacon, cut into $\frac{1}{4}$-in. strips
1 TB. canola oil
1 medium yellow onion, chopped
1 tsp. all-purpose flour

$\frac{1}{2}$ cup water
$\frac{1}{3}$ cup apple cider vinegar
3 TB. amber agave nectar
Freshly ground pepper
2 TB. finely chopped fresh parsley

1. In a large saucepan over high heat, bring red-skinned potatoes, pinch of salt, and cold water to a boil. Reduce heat to medium, and cook for 15 to 20 minutes or until fork-tender. Drain and set aside.

2. While potatoes are still warm, remove skin with a paring knife, and slice potatoes into thick chunks.

3. In a large, nonstick skillet over medium-high heat, fry bacon, stirring occasionally, for 3 to 5 minutes or until nearly crisp. Using a slotted spoon, transfer bacon to a paper towel.

4. In the skillet over medium heat, combine canola oil with bacon drippings left in the skillet. Add yellow onion, and cook for 5 minutes or until softened.

5. Stir in all-purpose flour, and cook for 1 more minute.

6. In a small bowl, whisk together $\frac{1}{2}$ cup water, apple cider vinegar, and amber agave nectar. Pour into the skillet, and cook for 1 minute.

7. Add potatoes, dash of salt, and pepper, and stir well to combine and heat through.

8. Serve warm, sprinkled with chopped parsley.

SWEET SECRET

Germans have been eating potato salad warm since the early seventeenth century, when it was popular to serve potatoes sprinkled with sweet vinegar and spices at dinner.

Spinach Salad Dressing

This traditionally sweet dressing is no longer taboo for sugar-free eaters, thanks to this flavorful recipe featuring pungent garlic and mustard and a pinch of sugar substitute.

Yield:	Prep time:	Cook time:	Serving size:
¾ cup	10 minutes	15 minutes	2 tablespoons

6 slices bacon

¼ cup red wine vinegar

2 TB. water

2 TB. Dijon mustard

1 TB. granulated sugar substitute

1. In a large, nonstick skillet over medium-high heat, fry bacon for about 5 minutes or until crispy. Transfer to paper towels to cool. When cool, crumble into bits.

2. In a small saucepan over medium heat, whisk together ¼ cup bacon drippings, red wine vinegar, water, Dijon mustard, and granulated sugar substitute. Simmer for 1 minute, and remove from heat.

3. Stir in 2 tablespoons crumbled bacon, and serve warm over fresh spinach salad.

TASTY TIP

Spinach salad dressing is not just for spinach salad! Try it on tossed greens such as escarole, chicory, radicchio, and endive, or use as a marinade for chicken.

Raspberry Balsamic Pecan Dressing

Naturally sweet and fruity raspberries team up with balsamic vinegar and flavorful pecans for a great-tasting dressing that's perfect for any type of salad.

Yield:	Prep time:	Serving size:
1 cup	15 minutes	2 tablespoons

1 cup fresh or frozen no-sugar-added raspberries

1 (1-g) pkt. concentrated sugar substitute

¼ cup balsamic vinegar

½ tsp. mustard

Dash salt

Pinch freshly ground pepper

½ cup olive oil

¼ cup chopped pecans

1. In a blender or in a food processor fitted with a steel blade, purée no-sugar-added raspberries. Strain through a fine mesh sieve to remove seeds, and transfer seedless purée to a medium bowl.

2. Add concentrated sugar substitute, balsamic vinegar, mustard, salt, and pepper, and whisk well to combine.

3. Slowly whisk in olive oil until well blended. Stir in pecans.

4. Taste to see if more salt and pepper are needed. Keep refrigerated.

 HONEY DON'T!

Beware of using flavored vinegars like raspberry, pear, fig, and other varieties. They often contain added sugar.

Sugar-Free Catalina Dressing

This popular dressing is back on the menu, packed with tangy Worcestershire sauce and the flavor of bold paprika.

Yield:	Prep time:	Serving size:
1 cup	15 minutes	2 tablespoons

¼ cup Sugar-Free Ketchup (recipe in Chapter 10)

¼ cup red wine vinegar

¼ cup granulated sugar substitute

½ small yellow onion, grated

½ tsp. Worcestershire sauce

½ tsp. paprika

¼ tsp. salt

Freshly ground pepper

⅓ cup canola oil

1. In a medium bowl, whisk together Sugar-Free Ketchup, red wine vinegar, granulated sugar substitute, yellow onion, Worcestershire sauce, paprika, salt, and pepper.

2. Slowly whisk in canola oil, and continue whisking until well blended.

3. Taste to see if more salt and pepper are needed. Keep refrigerated.

TASTY TIP

Paprika comes in many different "flavors," including sweet, hot, and smoked. The latter is a particularly popular variety used in Spanish and other Latin cuisines.

Tangerine Mustard Citronette

You can whip up this dressing, tangy and full of delicious citrus flavor, in no time. It's perfect for dressing salads that contain bitter greens like escarole, radicchio, and arugula.

Yield:	Prep time:	Serving size:
1 cup	15 minutes	1 or 2 tablespoons

2 tsp. Dijon mustard

½ cup tangerine juice

1 tsp. lime juice

Dash onion powder

2 (1-g) pkt. concentrated sugar substitute

½ cup light olive oil

1 tsp. finely chopped fresh parsley

Salt

Freshly ground pepper

1. In a medium bowl, whisk together Dijon mustard, tangerine juice, lime juice, onion powder, and concentrated sugar substitute.

2. Slowly whisk in light olive oil to combine. Add parsley, salt, and pepper, and taste for seasoning. Keep in an airtight container for up to 1 week.

SWEET SECRET

Citronette dressings, made from citrus juices as opposed to vinaigrette dressings made primarily from vinegars, are popular in French cuisine and are often used on salads containing fruit, fish, or bitter greens.

Soups and Bisques

In This Chapter

- Discovering hidden sugar in soups
- Using sweeteners for subtle taste
- Blending a flavorful bowlful
- Enjoying sweet slurps guilt free

You might not think your soup bowl is one of the places you need to check for added sugar, but it is. Small amounts of sugar and syrups often make an appearance in soups and bisques to balance acidic tastes or add flavor to a less-than-vibrant spoonful.

Not to worry, however! There's a simple and sweet solution for every instance when sugar plays a role, and in this chapter, you'll discover how to sweeten your soups without sugar.

Flavorful Soups

Many soups made from naturally sweet vegetables such as squash, corn, sweet potato, red bell peppers, and even tomatoes often call for much less sugar than other types of soups to bring their flavor to the forefront. Creamy and rich varieties like butternut squash soup and corn chowder have so much remarkably sweet flavor on their own that sometimes only a teaspoon here or there of a sugar substitute is required. Letting nature's sugar bowl play a starring role in the flavor department often produces the best results, as you'll see by the recipes in this chapter.

On other occasions, when the terrain is less naturally sweet, a blend of mixed flavors from sweet to spicy to sour can result in the perfect combination. Typically, ethnic-based soups are the best examples of blended flavor. Think Thai coconut curry-based soups or cold and creamy avocado soup with a spicy Mexican kick.

No matter what its background, however, you'll be sure to enjoy these sugar-free selections and will no doubt be blending them up for your soup tureen on a regular basis.

Butternut White Bean Soup

Creamy and chunky, sweet and savory, and positively delicious, this hearty soup, with the taste of earthy spices like cinnamon and nutmeg and a flavorful hint of tarragon and thyme, is irresistible.

Yield:	Prep time:	Cook time:	Serving size:
6 cups	20 minutes	30 minutes	1½ cups

2 TB. olive oil	½ tsp. dried tarragon
1 small yellow onion, diced	½ tsp. dried thyme
1 medium carrot, peeled and diced	¼ tsp. ground cinnamon
Dash salt	⅛ tsp. ground nutmeg
Fresh ground pepper	2 TB. light agave nectar
4 cups low-sodium chicken or vegetable broth	1 (15-oz.) can white beans, drained and rinsed
1 medium butternut squash, cubed, peeled, and seeded (3 cups)	1 cup milk

1. In a heavy-bottomed soup pot over medium heat, heat olive oil. Add yellow onion, carrot, salt, and pepper, and cook for 5 minutes or until onion is softened.

2. Pour in chicken broth, and bring to a boil. Add butternut squash, tarragon, thyme, cinnamon, nutmeg, and light agave nectar, and return to a simmer. Cook, stirring occasionally, for 15 minutes or until squash is fork-tender.

3. Stir in white beans and milk, and bring to a simmer just to heat through. Remove from heat, and using a handheld immersion blender, pulse soup so it's slightly creamy but still chunky.

4. Taste to see if more salt and pepper are needed, and serve hot.

TASTY TIP

Handheld immersion blenders are fast and easy for sauce- and soup-making because you don't have to transfer the liquid to another container to purée. You can also use a blender or food processor if you don't have an immersion blender.

Curried Pumpkin Soup

The exotic flavor of curry spice highlights this creamy, rich, and warming soup that's sweetened with a little agave.

Yield:	Prep time:	Cook time:	Serving size:
3 cups	15 minutes	18 minutes	1½ cups

1 TB. olive oil

1 clove garlic, minced

1 medium carrot, chopped

1 (15-oz.) can unsweetened pumpkin

2 tsp. curry powder

1 tsp. ground ginger

¼ tsp. ground nutmeg

3 cups chicken or vegetable broth

1½ TB. light agave nectar

¼ cup light cream

Salt

Freshly ground pepper

Sour cream (optional)

1. In a medium heavy-bottomed saucepan over medium heat, heat olive oil. Add garlic, and cook, stirring often, for 1 minute. Do not brown.

2. Add carrot, and cook for 1 more minute.

3. Stir in pumpkin, curry powder, ginger, and nutmeg. Pour in chicken broth and light agave nectar, and bring to a boil. Reduce heat to low, and simmer, stirring occasionally, for 15 minutes.

4. Stir in light cream, and transfer mixture to a blender. Purée until smooth, and return to the saucepan that's been washed and dried.

5. Season with salt and pepper, and serve immediately with a dollop of sour cream (if using).

TASTY TIP

Adding cream at the end of the cook time warms it but ensures it won't boil and curdle in the soup or sauce.

Sweet Corn and Red Pepper Chowder

Naturally sweet corn off the cob and red bell peppers team up in this satisfying chowder that gets a flavor boost from fresh basil and a finishing kick for the taste buds from cayenne.

Yield:	Prep time:	Cook time:	Serving size:
6 cups	15 minutes	35 minutes	1½ cups

4 slices bacon

½ medium red onion, finely chopped

1 large red bell pepper, ribs and seeds removed, and diced

1 medium celery stalk, sliced

4 cups low-sodium chicken or vegetable stock

Kernels from 4 medium ears of corn, or 2 cups frozen

1 medium red-skinned potato, peeled and diced

¼ tsp. cayenne

1 TB. granulated sugar substitute

½ cup light cream

1 TB. cornstarch

Dash salt, or more to taste

1. In a heavy-bottomed soup pot over medium-high heat, fry bacon for 3 to 5 minutes or until crisp. Transfer to a paper towel to cool, crumble, and set aside.

2. In the soup pot over medium heat, combine bacon drippings with red onion, red bell pepper, and celery. Cook for 5 minutes or until softened.

3. Pour in chicken stock, and bring to a simmer.

4. Stir in corn, red-skinned potato, cayenne, and granulated sugar substitute. Reduce heat to medium-low, and cook for 20 minutes or until potato is fork-tender.

5. In a small bowl, stir together light cream and cornstarch until smooth. Pour into the soup pot, and cook, stirring constantly, for 5 minutes or until soup is thick and creamy.

6. Add salt and taste for additional seasoning. Serve hot, topped with crumbled bacon.

TASTY TIP

To remove corn kernels from the cob, you can use a corn husker, available at specialty kitchen stores, or simply hold the husked cob upright on a cutting board and slice down with a large knife to release the kernels. Turn the cob and continue to cut until cob is bare.

Coconut Curried Shrimp Soup

This popular Asian-style soup is easy to make when you have all the flavorful ingredients like sweet-tasting coconut milk, tangy ginger, and aromatic curry at hand. Sweetly flavored with a spicy flair, you'll love the results.

Yield:	Prep time:	Cook time:	Serving size:
4 cups	15 minutes	25 minutes	1 cup

2 TB. unsalted butter

1 small yellow onion, finely chopped

1 TB. peeled and finely chopped fresh ginger

1 medium garlic clove, minced

Dash salt

Freshly ground pepper

1 tsp. curry powder

4 cups low-sodium vegetable or chicken broth

1 tsp. hot sauce

1 small sweet potato, peeled and diced

½ small green bell pepper, ribs and seeds removed, and diced

1 cup frozen cooked baby salad shrimp, thawed

¼ cup frozen small peas, thawed

½ cup canned unsweetened coconut milk

2 TB. granulated sugar substitute

¼ cup light cream

2 TB. fresh cilantro leaves, roughly chopped

1. In a heavy-bottomed soup pot over medium heat, melt butter. Add yellow onion, ginger, garlic, salt, and pepper, and cook, stirring occasionally, for 3 minutes or until softened. Do not brown.

2. Stir in curry powder, and cook for 1 more minute.

3. Add vegetable broth and hot sauce, increase heat to medium-high, and bring to a simmer. Stir in sweet potato and green bell pepper, and simmer for 15 minutes or until potato is fork-tender.

4. Stir in baby salad shrimp, small peas, coconut milk, granulated sugar substitute, and light cream. Reduce heat to medium-low, and bring to a simmer. Cook for 3 minutes.

5. Taste to see if more salt is needed, and serve hot, topped with cilantro.

HONEY DON'T!

Always purchase unsweetened coconut milk, and add your own sweetener to taste. Sweetened coconut milk and coconut cream have large amounts of added sugar.

Sweet Pea Bisque with Mint

This delightfully creamy soup is delicious hot or cold. Fresh, fragrant mint provides the flavorful finish while black pepper adds a tasteful bite.

Yield:	Prep time:	Cook time:	Serving size:
4 cups	5 minutes	15 minutes	1 cup

1 TB. olive oil

1 medium *shallot,* minced

Dash salt

2 (10-oz.) pkg. frozen small peas

3 cups low-sodium vegetable broth or water

3 TB. granulated sugar substitute

¼ cup roughly chopped fresh mint leaves

⅓ cup light cream

Freshly ground black pepper

1. In a soup pot over medium heat, heat olive oil. Add shallot and salt, and cook for 3 minutes or until softened.

2. Add small peas, vegetable broth, granulated sugar substitute, and mint leaves, and bring to a simmer. Reduce heat to medium-low, and cook for 8 minutes or until reduced slightly.

3. Add light cream, and cook for 1 more minute.

4. Transfer soup to a blender, and, working in batches if necessary, purée until smooth. Season generously with black pepper, taste to see if more salt is needed, and serve hot or cold.

DEFINITION

Shallots are a variety of onion. They're mild-tasting and popularly used in gourmet cooking.

Italian Tomato Bisque

Smooth and comforting, this soup is full of authentic Italian flavor, thanks to *San Marzano tomatoes*, fresh basil, and a touch of rich mascarpone cheese.

Yield:	Prep time:	Cook time:	Serving size:
6 cups	15 minutes	25 minutes	1½ cups

2 TB. olive oil

1 medium yellow onion, diced

1 medium celery stalk, diced

Dash salt

2 (28-oz.) cans San Marzano plum tomatoes, with juice and crushed

2 cups low-sodium vegetable or chicken broth

3 TB. roughly chopped fresh basil leaves

Freshly ground pepper

2 tsp. granulated sugar substitute

¼ cup light cream

2 TB. mascarpone cheese

1. In a heavy-bottomed soup pot over medium heat, heat olive oil. Add yellow onion, celery, and salt, and cook, stirring occasionally, for 5 minutes or until onion is softened.

2. Add San Marzano plum tomatoes, vegetable broth, basil, pepper, and granulated sugar substitute, and bring to a simmer. Reduce heat to medium-low, and cook for 15 minutes or until slightly reduced.

3. Stir in light cream, and cook for 2 more minutes.

4. Transfer mixture to a blender and, working in batches if necessary, purée until smooth.

5. Taste to see if more salt is needed, and serve hot with ½ tablespoon mascarpone cheese swirled into each serving.

DEFINITION

San Marzano tomatoes are a variety of plum tomatoes grown near Naples, Italy. They're considered the most flavorful of all tomatoes used in Italian cooking and can be found in most supermarkets.

Creamy Avocado Soup

Packed with the enticing flavors found in guacamole—such as coriander, jalapeño, and lime—this cold soup is terrific on a hot day with a dollop of sour cream on top.

Yield:	Prep time:	Serving size:
3½ cups	25 minutes	½ cup

½ cup sweet onion such as Vidalia, chopped

1 medium tomato, cored and chopped

2 medium avocados, peeled, seeded, and diced

1 small jalapeño pepper, seeded and chopped

Juice of ½ lime

1 cup low-fat buttermilk

¾ cup low-sodium chicken or vegetable broth

2 tsp. light agave nectar

¼ tsp. ground coriander

Dash salt, or more to taste

1. In a blender, pulse sweet onion, tomato, avocados, jalapeño, and lime juice to chop well.

2. Add buttermilk, chicken broth, light agave nectar, coriander, and salt, and purée until smooth. Thin with additional broth if necessary.

3. Refrigerate until ready to serve. Taste to see if more salt is needed before serving.

TASTY TIP

Although avocados readily turn brown when exposed to the air, adding an acidic ingredient such as lime juice to a recipe they're in can delay this oxidation, or browning, process and keep your avocado dish green and appetizing.

Summer Strawberry Soup

Fruit soups can be just the ticket for hot summer days, and this delightfully fruity version, with its refreshing and not-too-sweet flavor, is no exception.

Yield:	Prep time:	Serving size:
4 cups	25 minutes, plus 1 hour chill time	1 cup

4 cups fresh strawberries, hulled and sliced

1/2 cup white wine or no-sugar-added white grape juice

1/2 cup no-sugar-added cranberry juice

1/2 tsp. orange zest

1/2 cup light strawberry yogurt

1/3 cup sour cream

2 TB. granulated sugar substitute

1. In a blender, purée 3 cups strawberries, white wine, no-sugar-added cranberry juice, orange zest, light strawberry yogurt, sour cream, and granulated sugar substitute until smooth. Thin with additional juice to desired consistency if necessary, and chill for 1 hour.

2. Stir soup well, ladle into bowls, top with remaining 1 cup sliced strawberries, and serve.

TASTY TIP

Cold fruit soups can also be served as elegant desserts, accompanied by short-bread or butter cookies.

Snacks and Appetizers

In This Chapter

- Whipping up guilt-free nibbles
- Dipping into healthful delights
- Curbing hunger with appetizing favorites
- Trading sugar for true satisfaction

Many of the snacks we enjoy on a regular basis have varying amounts of hidden and not-so-hidden sugar in their ingredient lists. Nut mixes, crunchy delights, delectable dips and spreads, and other common snack foods get much of their flavor from sugar. Believe it or not, however, it's pretty darn easy to sweep away the sugar when you know how, and in this chapter, you learn about the methods and ingredients you need to do just that.

Sugar-free snacking will become a true pleasure when you've mastered the simple recipes in this chapter.

Snack Attack Rescue

One of the most difficult things sugar-free eaters must face is the initial longing for nibbles and treats. Many of us have succumbed to the temptation the sugar snacks contain and fallen off our regimen with a forbidden snack or two.

Well, consider yourself rescued from any further snack attacks! Dive into these great-tasting sweet treats with confidence—and no guilt!

Sweet Candied Nuts

Crunchy, sugar-coated nuts are often a snacker's favorite munch, and here they make a sugar-free splash with a hint of cinnamon.

Yield:	Prep time:	Cook time:	Serving size:
2 cups	10 minutes	25 to 30 minutes	¼ cup

1 cup lightly salted peanuts

½ cup pecan halves

½ cup whole *blanched* almonds

1 large egg white, slightly beaten

½ cup granulated sugar substitute

¼ tsp. ground cinnamon

1. Preheat the oven to 300°F. Line a rimmed baking sheet with parchment paper.

2. In a medium bowl, combine peanuts, pecan halves, and almonds. Pour beaten egg white over nuts, and stir well to coat.

3. In a small bowl, stir together granulated sugar substitute and cinnamon. Sprinkle over nut mixture, and gently stir. Pour nuts onto the prepared baking sheet, and spread into an even layer.

4. Bake for 25 to 30 minutes, stirring occasionally, or until nut coating is golden and crisp. Cool, and store in an airtight container.

DEFINITION

Here, **blanched** refers to nuts that have had their skins removed.

Nibbler's Spicy Sweet Mix

Can't decide between spicy or sweet? No problem, with this easy-to-make flavorful snack mix that offers the bite of hot cayenne while providing a guilt-free sweet-tasting finish.

Yield:	Prep time:	Cook time:	Serving size:
5 cups	10 minutes	20 to 25 minutes	½ cup

2 cups no-sugar-added crispy wheat cereal squares

1 cup miniature pretzels

1 cup oyster crackers

1 cup unsalted mixed nuts

1 large egg white, slightly beaten

2 tsp. Worcestershire sauce

½ cup granulated sugar substitute

¼ tsp. cayenne

1. Preheat the oven to 300°F. Line a rimmed baking sheet with parchment paper.

2. In a medium bowl, combine no-sugar-added crispy wheat cereal squares, miniature pretzels, oyster crackers, and mixed nuts.

3. In a small bowl, stir together egg white and Worcestershire sauce. Pour over cereal mixture, and stir well to coat.

4. In another small bowl, stir together granulated sugar substitute and cayenne. Sprinkle over cereal mixture, and gently stir. Pour onto the prepared baking sheet, and spread into an even layer.

5. Bake for 20 to 25 minutes, stirring occasionally, or until toasted and lightly golden. Cool, and store in an airtight container.

SWEET SECRET

Worcestershire sauce was first made in 1837 by two English chemists named John Lea and William Perrins in the town of Worcester, England. It's based on a Roman condiment made from fermented fish and was intended for flavoring meats and fish.

Cream Cheese Vanilla Nut Spread

Great for a snack on crackers or bagels, this agave-sweetened spread, highlighted by the alluring flavors of vanilla and cinnamon, rivals the taste of any purchased sweetened cream cheese.

Yield:	Prep time:	Serving size:
1 cup	5 minutes	2 tablespoons

8 oz. cream cheese, softened

1/4 cup light agave nectar

1/2 tsp. vanilla extract

1/4 cup chopped walnuts

Dash ground cinnamon

1. In a medium bowl, and using an electric mixer on medium speed, beat cream cheese and light agave nectar for 1 or 2 minutes or until well combined.

2. Beat in vanilla extract, walnuts, and cinnamon, and transfer to an airtight container. Keep refrigerated.

TASTY TIP

When softening cream cheese or other smooth-textured ingredients like butter or margarine, remove it from the wrapping while it's still cold and firm to prevent it from sticking to the foil or paper it comes in when softened.

Creamy Fruity Fruit Dip

Perfect for dipping slices of fresh fruit or graham crackers, you'll love the variety of fruity flavors in this healthy snack when the urge for light, sweet munching arises.

Yield:	Prep time:	Serving size:
2 cups	15 minutes	2 tablespoons

1 cup nonfat or low-fat plain Greek yogurt	2 TB. sugar-free raspberry jam
½ cup whipped cream cheese	2 TB. finely chopped dried apricots
¼ cup light agave nectar	2 TB. finely chopped golden raisins

1. In a medium bowl, and using an electric mixer on medium speed, combine Greek yogurt, whipped cream cheese, and light agave nectar for 1 to 2 minutes or until smooth and creamy.

2. Stir in sugar-free raspberry jam, apricots, and golden raisins just to combine, leaving little streaks of raspberry jam swirled in mixture. Serve chilled.

TASTY TIP

Prevent sticking when chopping dried fruits by dusting lightly with flour and tossing to coat.

Sweet Santa Fe Salsa

Enjoy the combination of sweet and spicy in this terrific salsa featuring sweet onion, orange, and corn, with the bite of jalapeño.

Yield:	Prep time:	Serving size:
2 cups	20 minutes, plus 1 hour chill time	½ cup

4 medium plum tomatoes, cored, seeded, and diced

1 large seedless orange, peeled and diced

1 medium sweet or *Vidalia* onion, peeled and diced

½ cup canned sweet corn kernels, drained

1 medium jalapeño pepper, seeded and minced

Juice of ½ lime

1 (1-g) pkt. concentrated sugar substitute

1 TB. chopped fresh cilantro leaves

Salt

Freshly ground pepper

1. In a medium bowl, gently stir together plum tomatoes, orange, sweet onion, corn, and jalapeño pepper.

2. Squeeze lime juice over top, and sprinkle with concentrated sugar substitute and cilantro. Fold mixture to combine, and season with salt and pepper.

3. Refrigerate for 1 hour before serving.

DEFINITION

Vidalia is a type of sweet onion grown in Georgia. It's prized for its crisp and flavorful, sweet taste.

Tropical Blast Salsa

When served with Sugar-Free Cinnamon Sugar Chips (recipe later in this chapter), this sweet yet tangy kicked-up pineapple and mango salsa will keep them coming back for the exotic and satisfying taste of the tropics.

Yield:	Prep time:	Serving size:
3 cups	30 minutes	¼ cup

1½ cups mango, diced small

1½ cups pineapple, diced small

¼ cup finely chopped red onion

1 small jalapeño pepper, finely chopped

¼ cup chopped fresh cilantro leaves

Juice of ½ lime

2 TB. light agave nectar

1. In a large bowl, combine mango, pineapple, red onion, jalapeño, and cilantro. Stir just to combine.

2. Add lime juice and light agave nectar, and toss gently to coat. Refrigerate until ready to serve.

HONEY DON'T!

Be careful when chopping jalapeño peppers! Rubbing your eyes or face afterward can cause burning and stinging. Wear latex or rubber gloves, or wash your hands thoroughly immediately after to prevent the transfer of the pepper's hot oil.

Sweet Red Pepper Hummus

Traditional savory Middle Eastern hummus made with chickpeas gets a sweet side from the addition of red bell peppers and a drizzle of tasty agave.

Yield:	Prep time:	Cook time:	Serving size:
2 cups	15 minutes	5 minutes	¼ cup

1 TB. olive oil	1 TB. lemon juice
1 large red bell pepper, ribs and seeds removed, and diced	½ tsp. salt
	¼ tsp. ground cumin
1 (16-oz.) can chickpeas, drained and rinsed	1½ TB. amber agave nectar

1. In a nonstick skillet over medium heat, heat olive oil. Add red bell pepper, and cook, stirring often, for 5 minutes or until softened.

2. Transfer to a food processor fitted with a steel blade. Add chickpeas, lemon juice, salt, cumin, and amber agave nectar, and purée for 3 to 5 minutes or until very smooth, occasionally stopping to scrape the sides of the processor bowl.

3. Transfer to a bowl, and refrigerate until ready to serve.

TASTY TIP

Sautéing red bell peppers releases their natural sweet flavor, making them a terrific addition for sweetening pasta sauces, soups, and other dishes.

Quickie Bread-and-Butter Pickles

You'll love this "short and sweet" version of this sweet snacking pickle. It's full of tangy flavor and gets a bite from ginger and mustard seed.

Yield:	Prep time:	Cook time:	Serving size:
3 cups	2 hours	5 minutes	about 6 pickles

1 lb. Kirby or English cucumbers, unpeeled and cut into ¼-in.-thick slices

2 TB. coarse kosher salt

2 cups ice cubes

1 cup apple cider vinegar

½ cup granulated sugar substitute

2 tsp. yellow mustard seeds

½ tsp. celery seeds

½ tsp. black peppercorns

½ tsp. ground turmeric

¼ tsp. ground ginger

1. Place cucumbers in a large, wide bowl, and evenly sprinkle with kosher salt. Cover with ice cubes, and set aside for 1½ hours. Drain, and rinse cucumbers under cold water.

2. In a medium saucepan over medium-high heat, combine apple cider vinegar, granulated sugar substitute, yellow mustard seeds, celery seeds, peppercorns, turmeric, and ginger. Bring to a simmer, and stir well.

3. Add cucumber slices, bring to a boil, and cook for 2 minutes. Remove from heat, and allow to cool slightly, stirring occasionally.

4. Transfer mixture to 2 (12-ounce) jars, cover, and refrigerate for at least 10 days before opening. Once opened, pickles will keep for up to 3 weeks.

SWEET SECRET

Bread-and-butter pickles got their name during the 1930's depression in America because they became a steady part of the everyday diet—along with bread and butter.

Southern Pickled Peppers

These easy peppers, which get a kick from hot pepper flakes and a hint of sweetness from sugar substitute, are great with sandwiches or in salad.

Yield:	Prep time:	Serving size:
1 pint	30 minutes	3 or 4 pepper strips

½ cup water

4 or 5 medium green bell peppers, ribs and seeds removed, and cut into ½-in. strips

2 TB. *pickling spice*

Dash red pepper flakes

Pinch salt

1 (1-g) pkt. concentrated sugar substitute

1¼ cups apple cider vinegar

1. Pour water into a 1-pint pickling jar. Add green bell pepper strips, a little at a time, pressing firmly to fill spaces.

2. Add pickling spice, red pepper flakes, salt, and concentrated sugar substitute, and top with apple cider vinegar.

3. Close lid and shake gently. Place in the refrigerator for 1 week before opening and eating. Pickles will keep chilled up to 3 months.

DEFINITION

Pickling spice is a combination of herbs and spices including bay leaf, coriander, peppercorns, and dill. You can find it in the spice section of most supermarkets.

Sugar-Free Cinnamon Sugar Chips

Crunchy and flavorful with a hint of saltiness and the taste of cinnamon sugar, these chips go great with fruit salsas—or are great for snacking just on their own!

Yield:	Prep time:	Cook time:	Serving size:
36 chips	20 minutes	15 to 20 minutes	6 chips

6 (8-in.) corn tortillas	½ cup granulated sugar substitute
Cooking spray	2 TB. ground cinnamon
½ tsp. coarse *kosher salt*	

1. Preheat the oven to 350°F. Lightly spray 2 rimmed baking sheets with cooking spray.

2. Stack tortillas on top of each other, and cut through to make 6 stacks of triangles. Arrange in a single layer on the prepared pans.

3. Spray a little more cooking spray over tortillas, and sprinkle with kosher salt. Bake, turning once, for 15 to 20 minutes or until toasted and lightly golden.

4. Meanwhile, in a lunch-size brown paper bag, combine granulated sugar substitute and cinnamon. While chips are still warm, shake them in batches in the bag to lightly coat. Transfer chips to a wire rack to cool. Store in a zipper-lock bag.

DEFINITION

Kosher salt is the salt of choice for most chefs because its flavor is untainted by preservatives and its consistency is easy to feel when seasoning. Its name derives from its original use in "koshering," or salting meats according to religious law. Coarse sea salt makes a good cooking substitute.

Best Cinnamon Applesauce

Here, Golden Delicious apples provide terrific flavor and texture in this easy applesauce featuring just a hint of sugar substitute and a bold cinnamon taste.

Yield:	Prep time:	Cook time:	Serving size:
3 cups	15 minutes	25 minutes	½ cup

4 medium Golden Delicious apples, peeled, cored, and diced

1 cup water

¼ cup granulated sugar substitute

1 tsp. lemon juice

1 tsp. ground cinnamon

Dash salt

1. In a large saucepan over medium-high heat, bring Golden Delicious apples, water, granulated sugar substitute, lemon juice, cinnamon, and salt to a simmer. Cook, stirring frequently, for 15 to 20 minutes or until apples are tender and have partially broken down.

2. Remove from heat, and allow to cool before refrigerating in an airtight container.

TASTY TIP

For smooth applesauce, run your cooked apples through a food mill or processor when slightly cooled.

Sauces and Condiments

Chapter 10

In This Chapter

- Making the sweet switch on sauces
- Whipping up delicious sweet condiments
- Creating sugar-free staples
- Enjoying a bit of "sweet" with the savory

When it comes to bottled sauces and condiments, you might be alarmed when you actually take a look at the ingredient list. We all know barbecue sauce has *some* sugar, but must it be the main ingredient?—yikes! Condiment lovers face a true dilemma when it comes to going sugar free.

Or do they?

Flavor Subs for Sugar

There's no denying that a bit of sweet can be the perfect partner for savory dishes. Think of sweet tomato ketchup with french fries, or cranberry sauce with turkey. Somehow they work well together and please our palates to no end.

You don't have to break up that happy partnership when you substitute the terrifically flavored sugar-free versions in this chapter. From "honey" mustard to chutney, you'll be reaching for these subs on every possible occasion.

Easy Does It

You'll also find how easy it really is to make these types of staples we all use so frequently. Once you taste the difference in flavor over store-bought, you'll probably ease right into homemade condiment-making without blinking an eye.

There are so many possibilities for using them, so let's get into the kitchen and start getting saucy!

Sweet and Smoky Barbecue Sauce

Commercial barbecue sauce can be drowning in sugar or high-fructose syrup, but in this version, you'll find all the same sweet flavor you desire, along with an enticing smoky aroma and a tangy and exciting taste.

Yield:	Prep time:	Cook time:	Serving size:
2 cups	15 minutes	25 minutes	2 tablespoons

2 TB. canola oil

1 small yellow onion, minced

2 small garlic cloves, minced

Dash salt, or more to taste

1 cup tomato sauce

1 (6-oz.) can tomato paste

¼ cup apple cider vinegar

¼ cup water

2 tsp. Worcestershire sauce

½ tsp. *liquid smoke*

¼ cup granulated sugar substitute

½ tsp. prepared mustard

½ tsp. paprika

Dash cayenne, or more to taste

1. In a medium saucepan over medium-high heat, heat canola oil. Add yellow onion, and cook, stirring often, for 3 minutes or until onion is somewhat softened.

2. Add garlic and salt, and cook for 1 more minute.

3. Stir in tomato sauce, tomato paste, apple cider vinegar, water, Worcestershire sauce, liquid smoke, granulated sugar substitute, mustard, paprika, and cayenne. Bring to a simmer, reduce heat to low, and cook, covered, stirring occasionally, for 15 to 20 minutes or until thickened.

4. Remove from stove. Sauce will continue to thicken. Taste to see if more salt is needed before serving. Keep refrigerated.

DEFINITION

Liquid smoke is a seasoning that consists of flavored wood-chip smoke that's been dissolved in water and made through a distillation process. You can find it in the condiment aisle of most grocery stores.

Soy and Sesame Sauce

You can use this savory sauce with a hint of sweetness to stir-fry or simply as a dipping sauce for pot stickers or other Asian appetizers.

Yield:	Prep time:	Serving size:
1 cup	10 minutes	2 tablespoons

2½ TB. soy sauce

2 TB. unseasoned rice vinegar

2 TB. peanut oil

1 TB. sugar-free creamy peanut butter

2 TB. water

1 TB. vegetable or chicken broth

2 TB. *tahini*

2 tsp. peeled and chopped fresh ginger

1 large clove garlic, minced

2 TB. granulated sugar substitute

1 tsp. sesame seeds

1. In a blender, purée soy sauce, rice vinegar, peanut oil, sugar-free peanut butter, water, vegetable broth, tahini, ginger, garlic, and granulated sugar substitute until smooth.

2. Transfer to an airtight container or serving bowl, and stir in sesame seeds.

3. Serve immediately or refrigerate for up to 2 weeks.

DEFINITION

Tahini is a paste made from sesame seeds used to flavor many Middle Eastern and Asian recipes.

Creamy Orange Ginger Sauce

You'll love this slightly sweet and powerfully fragrant sauce on fish such as grilled salmon or even steamed vegetables.

Yield:	Prep time:	Cook time:	Serving size:
1 cup	15 minutes	20 minutes	¼ cup

1 (2-in.) piece peeled and roughly chopped fresh ginger

2 cups orange juice

½ cup granulated sugar substitute

¼ cup (½ stick) unsalted butter, diced

½ cup half-and-half

1 tsp. cornstarch

Salt

Freshly ground pepper

1. In a medium saucepan over medium heat, combine ginger, orange juice, and granulated sugar substitute. Bring to a boil, stirring often, and boil for about 12 minutes or until reduced to about ½ cup.

2. Remove from heat, and whisk in unsalted butter.

3. In a small bowl, combine half-and-half with cornstarch. Slowly whisk into sauce mixture. Return the saucepan to medium heat, and bring to a boil, whisking constantly. Cook for 2 minutes, season with salt and pepper, and remove from heat.

4. Serve warm over fish, chicken, or vegetables.

HONEY DON'T!

Never reheat butter sauces in the microwave because they're likely to break and curdle. Always reheat over very low heat.

Sugar-Free Ketchup

Unlike any other sugar-free ketchup you may have tried, this version is full of tomato flavor and spicy taste with a sweet kick of agave nectar.

Yield:	Prep time:	Serving size:
2 cups	15 minutes	1 tablespoon

2 (6-oz.) cans tomato paste

½ cup water

¼ cup light agave nectar

¼ cup apple cider vinegar

1 tsp. salt

1 tsp. dry mustard

½ tsp. onion powder

½ tsp. garlic powder

¼ tsp. ground cumin

Dash ground cloves

1. In a blender, purée tomato paste, water, light agave nectar, apple cider vinegar, salt, dry mustard, onion powder, garlic powder, cumin, and cloves until smooth.

2. Taste to see if more seasoning is needed, and keep refrigerated in an airtight container for 1 month.

SWEET SECRET

Up until the late nineteenth century, most American households made their own version of ketchup (or catsup, as it's also called) with varied ingredients such as mushrooms, fermented fish, and walnuts.

Whole-Grain Agave "Honey" Mustard

For dipping or spreading on sandwiches, sweet mustard has become a popular condiment, and here it gets an agave makeover and added flavor from whole mustard seeds as well as a zing from *Colman's dry mustard*.

Yield:	Prep time:	Cook time:	Serving size:
1 cup	15 minutes, plus overnight chill time	3 minutes	1 tablespoon

2 TB. whole brown mustard seeds

1/4 cup Colman's dry mustard or other dry mustard

1/2 cup white wine vinegar

1/2 cup light agave nectar

1/2 tsp. salt or more to taste

1. In a nonstick skillet over medium-high heat, cook brown mustard seeds for several minutes, shaking seeds as they pop, being careful not to burn. When finished popping, transfer seeds to a medium bowl and allow to cool.

2. Whisk in Colman's dry mustard, white wine vinegar, light agave nectar, and salt. Refrigerate overnight.

3. Stir well, and taste to see if more salt is needed before serving.

DEFINITION

Colman's dry mustard is the gold standard of mustards in England and most chefs' kitchens because of its fine, pure, and zesty flavor. It's generally found in the condiment aisle of your supermarket. You can substitute another hot mustard powder in its place.

Chunky Orange Cranberry Sauce

You won't be giving up your favorite cranberry sauce with turkey any longer after you've tasted this delicious sugar-free version full of tart juicy cranberries and the sweet flavor of orange.

Yield:	Prep time:	Cook time:	Serving size:
3 cups	10 minutes	15 minutes	2 tablespoons

3 cups fresh or frozen no-sugar-added cranberries

1 large navel orange, peeled, seeded, and chopped

1 tsp. grated orange zest

1 cup granulated sugar substitute

½ cup fresh orange juice

1 tsp. cornstarch

1. In a medium saucepan, combine no-sugar-added cranberries, orange, orange zest, and granulated sugar substitute. Stir well.

2. In a small bowl, combine orange juice and cornstarch, and stir until cornstarch is dissolved. Pour into the saucepan, and stir well.

3. Set the saucepan over medium-high heat, and bring contents to a simmer, stirring often. Cook for 5 to 8 minutes or until berries begin to pop and mixture thickens. Stir to prevent sticking.

4. Set aside to cool, and refrigerate until ready to serve.

TASTY TIP

Use homemade sugar-free cranberry sauce to make gelatin salads and desserts or to baste roasted or grilled poultry.

Gingered Mango Chutney

Sweet, hot, and sour traditional chutney—an Indian condiment—can contain a lot of added sugar, but here, agave nectar provides the subtle sweetness, while fresh herbs offer a further flavor enhancement.

Yield:	Prep time:	Cook time:	Serving size:
1 cup	25 minutes	25 minutes	1 tablespoon

½ cup light agave nectar

½ cup apple cider vinegar

¼ cup water

1 (2-in.) piece fresh ginger, peeled and grated

1 small jalapeño pepper, cored and minced

2 medium ripe mangoes, peeled, pitted, and diced

1 tsp. chopped fresh cilantro

1 tsp. chopped fresh mint

1. In a medium saucepan over medium heat, bring light agave nectar, apple cider vinegar, and water to a simmer, stirring often. Stir in ginger and jalapeño, and simmer for 2 minutes.

2. Add mangoes, and stir well to combine. Cover, reduce to low, and cook, stirring occasionally, for 15 minutes or until mangoes are fork-tender and mixture is thick.

3. Stir in cilantro and mint, and cook, uncovered, for 2 more minutes or until almost all liquid has evaporated.

4. Remove from heat and allow to cool before transferring to an airtight container and refrigerating. Stir well before serving.

SWEET SECRET

Major Grey's Chutney, perhaps the most famous of chutneys, was reputedly created by a British major in colonial India and traditionally, in addition to mango, contains tamarind and raisins.

Sweet Drinks and Smoothies

In This Chapter

- Serving up sweet sippers
- Cool and creamy blender favorites
- Filling up on fantastic flavor
- Refreshing sugar-free beverages

If ever in the past you've been attempting to go sugar free, at least in part, you're probably already aware of what's on offer in the beverage aisle of your supermarket. "Diet" and "lite" sodas and drinks have been around for a long time, but they don't ever seem to get better tasting and always make us feel as if we're really missing something. All that comes to an end now.

Flavor Alternatives

In this chapter, you'll find some classic drinks like soda and iced tea that, although they are sugar free, taste like no other versions you've tried. Full of flavor and without missing a single bit of taste, these alternatives will become your go-to recipes for go-with beverages and quaffs.

With these alternatives at your fingertips, your taste buds will once again find delight.

Sweeteners Blend In

Similarly, when you're itching for a sweet and substantial treat like a smoothie or milkshake, you've no doubt been disappointed with the choices before you. Here, however, sugar-free sweeteners blend in perfectly with a number of tasty ingredients, from berries to chocolate to coffee, and fit the bill for just the right level of flavor you're after.

So pull out your blender, and let's create some terrific-tasting sugar-free delights!

Agave Ginger Ale

You've never tasted ginger ale like this, with authentic flavor thanks to fresh ginger and a smooth, sweet taste from agave.

Yield:	Prep time:	Cook time:	Serving size:
4 cups	1 hour	5 minutes	1 cup

½ cup peeled and chopped fresh ginger

½ cup water

½ cup light agave nectar

1 TB. vanilla extract

Juice of 2 limes

1 (32-oz.) bottle club soda, chilled

1. In a small saucepan over medium-high heat, bring ginger and water to a boil. Reduce heat to low, and simmer for 3 minutes. Set aside to cool for at least 45 minutes.

2. Strain ginger water through a fine mesh strainer into a large pitcher. Add light agave nectar, vanilla extract, and lime juice, and stir well to combine.

3. Add club soda, stir, and serve.

SWEET SECRET

Fresh ginger ale can be a great medicinal drink for upset stomachs, nausea, and morning sickness.

Iced Citrus Green Tea

"Diet" iced tea takes on a whole new level of taste in this easy-to-make refreshing beverage made by the glass, with the tangy flavor of orange and lemon.

Yield:	Prep time:	Cook time:	Serving size:
about 1 cup	10 minutes	3 minutes	about 1 cup

1 cup water

1 green tea bag

1 (1-g) pkt. concentrated sugar substitute

¼ cup no-sugar-added orange juice

1 tsp. lemon juice

Ice cubes

1. In a small saucepan over high heat, bring water to a boil. Remove from heat, and add green tea bag. Steep for 3 minutes, remove tea bag, and set tea aside to cool for 5 minutes.

2. Add concentrated sugar substitute, no-sugar-added orange juice, and lemon juice, and stir to combine.

3. Place ice cubes in a tumbler, and pour in citrus tea. Serve immediately.

TASTY TIP

To prevent your iced tea from diluting, make ice cubes from juice or tea and use them to cool your drink. They will add flavor as they melt!

Muddled Pomegranate Julep

A Southern favorite gets a modern, sugar-free twist with flavorful and tangy pomegranate juice in this mocktail-type drink that can be kicked up with a shot of bourbon if you like.

Yield:	Prep time:	Serving size:
1 cup	5 minutes	1 cup

1 lemon slice, cut into quarters

2 TB. roughly chopped fresh mint leaves

1 (1-g) pkt. concentrated sugar substitute

1 cup no-sugar-added pomegranate juice

Ice cubes

1. In a heavy tumbler or cocktail shaker, and using a *muddler* or the back of a wooden spoon, crush together lemon pieces, mint leaves, and concentrated sugar substitute.

2. Pour in no-sugar-added pomegranate juice, and stir well. Strain into an ice-filled glass, and serve.

DEFINITION

A **muddler** is a bartender's tool shaped like a pestle that's used to crush drink ingredients like fruit, spices, and herbs to release their essential flavors.

Multi-Berry Slurper

Mixed berries provide a delicious sweet and fruity flavor while a bit of sugar-free frozen yogurt offers a luxurious slurp sensation to this dessertlike smoothie that's sure to please.

Yield:	Prep time:	Serving size:
2 cups	5 minutes	1 cup

1 cup frozen no-sugar-added
   mixed berries

½ cup low-fat plain yogurt

½ cup no-sugar-added frozen
   vanilla yogurt

¼ cup milk

2 TB. granulated sugar substitute

1. In a blender, purée no-sugar-added mixed berries, yogurt, no-sugar-added frozen yogurt, milk, and granulated sugar substitute until smooth.

2. Pour into 2 (8-ounce) glasses, and serve immediately.

TASTY TIP

Make your own package of frozen mixed berries by placing fresh blueberries, raspberries, and hulled strawberries on a rimmed baking sheet and freezing them until solid. Transfer to a zipper-lock bag, and keep frozen.

Creamy Orange Smoothie

You'll love the sweet citrus flavor and delicious smooth texture of this good-for-you smoothie with a hint of fragrant vanilla and nutmeg.

Yield:	Prep time:	Serving size:
1½ cups	3 minutes	1½ cups

1 cup low-fat plain yogurt

1 cup no-sugar-added orange juice

1 tsp. vanilla extract

1 (1-g) pkt. concentrated sugar
   substitute

Dash nutmeg

¼ cup ice cubes

1. In a blender, purée yogurt, no-sugar-added orange juice, vanilla extract, concentrated sugar substitute, and nutmeg just until combined.

2. Add ice cubes, and purée for 30 seconds or until completely smooth. Serve immediately.

TASTY TIP

Eliminate most of the ice in smoothie-making by freezing some of the ingredients ahead of time. If your smoothie contains fruit or their juices, for example, freeze those in small sandwich bags until you're ready to use them.

Chocolate Banana Soy Smoothie

Enjoy this healthy and delicious smoothie, featuring the flavor of deep chocolate and the sweet taste of ripe banana, any time of day.

Yield:	Prep time:	Serving size:
2 cups	5 minutes	2 cups

1 medium banana, peeled and diced, preferably frozen

1 cup unsweetened soy milk

2 TB. unsweetened cocoa powder

2 TB. granulated sugar substitute

½ tsp. vanilla extract

1. In a blender, purée banana, soy milk, unsweetened cocoa powder, granulated sugar substitute, and vanilla extract until smooth.

2. Serve immediately.

HONEY DON'T!

To avoid added sugar, always purchase unsweetened soy milk. Plain soy milk, as well as other plain milk alternatives like almond and coconut, actually has some sweetening added to improve its taste.

Mocha Fudge Frappé

Who can resist the yummy combination of chocolate and coffee, especially when whipped up into a cool and refreshing frappé? Enjoy the intense and heavenly flavor as you sip this incredible treat.

Yield:	Prep time:	Serving size:
1½ cups	3 minutes	1½ cups

¼ cup warm strong-brewed coffee

2 TB. unsweetened cocoa powder

1 (1-g) pkt. concentrated sugar substitute

1 cup no-sugar-added chocolate fudge ice cream

½ cup milk

1. In a blender, puré warm coffee, unsweetened cocoa powder, and concentrated sugar substitute for 30 seconds or until well combined.

2. Add no-sugar-added chocolate fudge ice cream and milk, and purée until smooth. Serve immediately.

SWEET SECRET

The term *frappé* comes from the French word *frapper,* which means "to whip," and is commonly used to refer to whipped or blended drinks like milkshakes and smoothies.

Mexican Hot Chocolate

You'll love this rich and creamy hot chocolate with a hint of cinnamon and a dash of spice.

Yield:	Prep time:	Cook time:	Serving size:
2 cups	5 minutes	3 minutes	1 cup

3 TB. unsweetened cocoa powder

6 (1-g) pkt. concentrated sugar substitute

¼ tsp. ground cinnamon

Dash cayenne

2 cups milk

1. In a medium saucepan over medium-high heat, whisk together cocoa powder, concentrated sugar substitute, cinnamon, and cayenne.

2. Slowly whisk in milk to a smooth consistency, and heat, whisking often, until hot and frothy. Serve immediately.

TASTY TIP

When whisking for volume or froth, always use the largest whisk you have. The whisking will go faster, and you'll get maximum volume.

Marvelous Mulled Apple Cider

Terrific on a chilly night or whenever you're in the mood, this fragrant quaff is sure to delight, with its subtly spiced flavor and sweet apple finish.

Yield:	Prep time:	Cook time:	Serving size:
4 cups	10 minutes	30 minutes	1 cup

4 cups unsweetened apple cider	2 (3-in.) cinnamon sticks
¼ cup granulated sugar substitute	Juice of ½ lemon
8 whole cloves	8 thin "wagon wheel" slices *clementine* oranges
3 whole allspice	

1. In a medium saucepan over high heat, combine apple cider, granulated sugar substitute, cloves, allspice, cinnamon sticks, and lemon juice. Stir well, and bring to a boil. Reduce heat to low, and simmer for 30 minutes.

2. Using a slotted spoon, remove spices. Add clementine orange slices, stir gently, and serve.

DEFINITION

Clementine oranges are a type of mandarin orange. They're small, easy to peel, usually seedless, and generally very sweet. In this recipe, cut them *across* the segments so the resulting slices look like wagon wheels, with the spokes visible.

Dinner Entrées and Side Dishes

Who knew sugar could sneak its way onto the dinner table so easily? Favorite entrées you've enjoyed for years may have actually been sabotaging your sugar-free goals. In Part 4, you see how many common selections, from teriyaki beef to whipped sweet potatoes, all traditionally call for more than a pinch of sugar. But with sugar-free cooking as our focus, I share tons of tips for revamping your favorites so you can enjoy them without added sugar.

Even vegetarian dishes can contain hidden sugar, added to bring out the flavor and natural sweetness of healthy ingredients like beans and vegetables. Worried about losing that punch of flavor? Don't be! I give you loads of options for adding flavor without sugar.

Main Course Meats

Chapter 12

In This Chapter

- Getting to the meat of sugar-free entrées
- Pairing sugar substitutes with beef and pork
- Switching out sugar for sweet fruit fiber
- Enjoying favorites without sugar

Sugar can keep company with some of the most unsuspecting ingredients, and main course meats are no exception. A quick glance at some of your all-time favorite entrées featuring beef and pork reveals how close this relationship has been and where added sugar has crept its way into some very standard and popular recipes. From teriyaki to tenderloin, don't be surprised to find at least a bit of sugar lurking in the ingredient list. Is it really all necessary, and is there anything you can do to reduce its presence without noticing?

Downplay Sugar's Role

The combination of sweet and savory is nothing new. However, the addition of sugar to many meat entrées is often found in the accompanying sauce or marinade as part of a flavor combo.

Reducing the role sugar plays won't drastically alter the outcome of most recipes if other flavorful ingredients are there to begin with. Substituting with a subtle sugar enhancement while highlighting herbs and aromatics goes a long way in creating an outstanding remake of your once-sugar-laden favorites.

In addition, making use of sugar-free ingredients such as ketchup and peanut butter can help downplay sugar's prominent role in many classic recipes like peanut satay or stuffed cabbage and allow the real flavors to come through.

Fruity Fiber to the Rescue

Instead of so-called fruit-flavored sauces we often see in Asian dishes as well as many American dishes—which are nothing more than sugary sweet syrups—let the fruit itself rescue the recipe by adding authentic, not artificial, flavor.

Using fresh juices and zest can be a great way to heighten taste, while whole fruit and dried fruit can add healthy fiber as well, reducing the impact of fruit's natural sugars on blood glucose for diabetics and dieters. All in all, it's a win-win situation for meat eaters who love a hint of sweet even before the sweets are served.

Tangy Tangerine Beef

Loaded with tons of terrific tangy flavor, you'll love this sugar-free version of the popular Chinese dish that's subtly sweet but powerfully delicious with the taste of fresh ginger, tangerine, and chili.

Yield:	Prep time:	Cook time:	Serving size:
4 cups	25 minutes	5 minutes	1 cup

1 lb. flank or sirloin steak, sliced thinly

6 TB. soy sauce

2 tsp. cornstarch

2 TB. amber agave nectar

1 TB. chili sauce

1 TB. rice vinegar

⅓ cup tangerine juice

2 tsp. tangerine zest

2 TB. canola oil

1 TB. peeled and minced fresh ginger

4 scallions, trimmed and cut into 1-in. pieces

1. Place flank steak in a medium bowl, and sprinkle with 3 tablespoons soy sauce. Add cornstarch, and stir well to coat. Set aside.

2. In a small bowl, whisk together remaining 3 tablespoons soy sauce, amber agave nectar, chili sauce, rice vinegar, tangerine juice, and tangerine zest. Set aside.

3. In a large, nonstick skillet or wok over high heat, heat canola oil. Add ginger and beef, and stir-fry for 2 minutes or until beef is no longer pink.

4. Pour in tangerine juice mixture, and add scallions. Stir-fry for 2 more minutes or until sauce is thickened and ingredients are piping hot. Remove from heat and serve immediately over rice or Chinese noodles, if desired.

Teriyaki Beef and Broccoli

Quick and easy, this version of the classic Japanese dish cuts way back on sugar but not on flavor, thanks to pungent garlic, zesty ginger, and a splash of sweetness from an unexpected source—pineapple juice.

Yield:	Prep time:	Cook time:	Serving size:
4 cups	30 minutes	10 minutes	1 cup

½ cup soy sauce

⅓ cup pineapple juice

1 (1-in.) piece fresh ginger, peeled and chopped

1 large garlic clove, chopped

3 TB. granulated brown sugar substitute

8 oz. beef tenderloin, sliced thinly

1 TB. canola oil

2 cups small broccoli florets

1. In a shallow bowl, combine soy sauce, pineapple juice, ginger, garlic, and granulated brown sugar substitute. Stir well until sugar substitute is dissolved.

2. Add sliced beef tenderloin, stir to coat, and set aside for 15 minutes.

3. In a large, nonstick skillet or wok over high heat, heat canola oil. Drain beef, reserving any remaining liquid, and add to the skillet. Stir-fry for 2 minutes or until beef is no longer pink and is slightly browned on the edges. Using a slotted spoon, remove beef to a clean bowl. Set aside.

4. Add broccoli florets and any reserved liquid to the skillet, and stir. Reduce heat to low, cover, and cook for 2 minutes or until broccoli is just fork-tender.

5. Return beef to the skillet, stir well to heat through, and serve immediately.

Skewered Beef Kebabs with Peanut Sauce

Rich, creamy peanut sauce gets a sugar-free makeover in this dish full of fabulous flavor and spicy sweetness.

Yield:	Prep time:	Cook time:	Serving size:
8 skewers	15 minutes	6 minutes	2 skewers

⅓ cup sugar-free peanut butter

¼ cup unsweetened coconut milk, or more to thin

¼ cup soy sauce

2 (1-g) pkt. concentrated sugar substitute

Dash hot sauce, or to taste

1 lb. beef sirloin, cut into bite-size pieces

Dash salt

Freshly ground pepper

1. Preheat an indoor or outdoor grill to medium-high.

2. In a small saucepan over medium-low heat, combine sugar-free peanut butter, coconut milk, soy sauce, concentrated sugar substitute, and hot sauce. Cook, stirring often, for 3 minutes or until creamy and smooth. Set aside in a warm place.

3. Thread beef sirloin pieces onto 8 metal or bamboo skewers, and season with salt and pepper. Grill beef, turning skewers to cook evenly, for 3 minutes or until browned for medium-rare. Continue to grill 1 or 2 more minutes for more doneness, if desired.

4. Place skewers on a serving platter, pour peanut sauce into a dipping bowl, and serve immediately.

SWEET SECRET

Thai-inspired dishes tend to contain less sugar than Chinese and Japanese dishes. Most of the characteristic flavor comes from fresh ingredients like chile peppers, herbs, and unsweetened coconut milk.

Slow and Easy German Sauerbraten

Grab your slow cooker for this hearty fix-and-forget-it entrée that's full of sweet-and-sour flavor and is scrumptious served with potatoes or traditional *spaetzle*.

Yield:	Prep time:	Cook time:	Serving size:
6 cups	20 minutes	7 or 8 hours	1 cup

2 lb. stewing beef, trimmed of fat and cut into 1-in. pieces

1 large yellow onion, diced

1 medium celery stalk, diced

2 large carrots, diced

1 cup beef broth

1 cup apple cider vinegar

1 bay leaf

½ cup finely crushed sugar-free gingersnaps

2 TB. granulated brown sugar substitute

Chopped parsley

1. In a 3- or 4-quart slow cooker, combine stewing beef, yellow onion, celery, carrots, beef broth, apple cider vinegar, and bay leaf. Stir well to combine, cover, and cook on low heat for 7 hours or until beef is fork-tender.

2. Using a slotted spoon, transfer beef to a warm bowl. Pour remaining liquid into a medium saucepan.

3. Add sugar-free gingersnaps and granulated brown sugar substitute to the saucepan, and set over medium heat. Cook, stirring often, for 10 minutes or until mixture is thickened and bubbly.

4. Taste to see if more salt and pepper are needed, remove bay leaf, and pour over beef. Sprinkle with chopped parsley, and serve immediately.

DEFINITION

Spaetzle is a small, soft-textured type of egg noodle popular in German and Austrian cuisine. It's traditionally made by forcing dough through a fine sieve.

Blazin' Braised Short Ribs

Tenderly cooked in a spicy tomato sauce and flavored with aromatic herbs and a hint of agave, these delicious short ribs will surely become a favorite.

Yield:	Prep time:	Cook time:	Serving size:
6 ribs	10 minutes	2½ hours	1 rib

6 large beef short ribs, bone-in (about 6 lb.)

Dash salt

Freshly ground pepper

1 TB. olive oil

1 large yellow onion, diced

1 (28-oz.) can tomato sauce

3 TB. Worcestershire sauce

½ cup reduced-sodium beef broth

3 TB. red wine vinegar

2 TB. amber agave nectar

2 TB. chopped fresh parsley leaves

1 TB. chopped fresh thyme leaves

1 small sprig rosemary

2 bay leaves

1 tsp. crushed red pepper flakes

1. Preheat the oven to 400°F.

2. Season short ribs with salt and pepper, and place in a large roasting pan. Cook ribs, turning once, for 30 minutes or until lightly browned and much of the fat has been rendered.

3. Meanwhile, in a large, heavy-bottomed pot over medium-high heat, heat olive oil. Add yellow onion, and cook, stirring occasionally, for 2 minutes or until slightly softened.

4. Add tomato sauce, Worcestershire sauce, reduced-sodium beef broth, red wine vinegar, amber agave nectar, parsley, thyme, rosemary, bay leaves, and crushed red pepper flakes, and stir well to combine. Bring to a simmer, reduce heat to medium, and cook for 5 minutes.

5. Using tongs, transfer ribs to the pot and submerge in braising liquid. Cover, reduce heat to medium-low, and cook, stirring occasionally, for 2 hours or until meat is fork-tender.

6. Carefully remove ribs from the pot, and serve with sauce, bay leaves removed, spooned over top.

TASTY TIP

Sugar is often added to tomato-based dishes to balance the high acidity of tomatoes. Sugar substitutes can easily perform the same task for sugar-free cooking.

Super Stuffed Cabbage Rolls

This slightly sweet, slightly sour version of stuffed cabbage gets its delicious flavor from a mix of ground meats and the resulting unique tomato sauce containing a hint of fragrant dill.

Yield:	Prep time:	Cook time:	Serving size:
10 cabbage rolls	30 minutes	1 hour	2 cabbage rolls

1 large head green cabbage (about 2 lb.)

1 lb. ground *meatloaf mix*

1 medium yellow onion, chopped

Dash salt, or more to taste

Freshly ground pepper

1 large garlic clove, minced

¼ cup Sugar-Free Ketchup (recipe in Chapter 10)

1 cup cooked white rice

1½ cups tomato juice

2 TB. apple cider vinegar

2 tsp. dried dill

1 TB. granulated sugar substitute

1. Bring a large pot of water to boil over high heat.

2. Using a sharp knife, cut out woody core of cabbage from the bottom. Drop cabbage head into the pot, and as leaves begin to soften, carefully remove them with tongs and transfer to paper towels to dry. Do this until you have 10 or 12 whole leaves. Reserve remaining cabbage for another use.

3. In a large, nonstick skillet over medium-high heat, cook ground meatloaf mix, yellow onion, salt, and pepper, breaking up any meat clumps that form, for 5 to 8 minutes or until no longer pink and slightly browned.

4. Stir in garlic, and cook for 1 more minute. Remove from heat, stir in Sugar-Free Ketchup and white rice until well combined. Set aside.

5. Preheat the oven to 375°F. Lightly coat a 13×9-inch baking dish with cooking spray.

6. In a medium saucepan over medium heat, combine tomato juice, apple cider vinegar, dill, and granulated sugar substitute. Bring to a simmer, stirring often. Set aside.

7. Place 1 cabbage leaf, curled side up, on a cutting board, and carefully cut away 1 inch of stem end, keeping leaf intact. Spoon about ¼ cup meat filling near stem end, and shape into a log. Fold up sides of cabbage leaf, gently roll up, and place roll seam side down in the baking dish. Repeat with remaining cabbage leaves and filling, fitting snugly in the baking dish.

8. Pour tomato juice mixture evenly over rolls, and add a little water to the edges of the pan to moisten. Cover and bake for 45 minutes.

9. Uncover, spoon resulting sauce over rolls, and bake for 10 more minutes or until sauce is thick and rolls are piping hot. Allow to rest for 10 minutes before serving.

> **DEFINITION**
>
> **Meatloaf mix,** sometimes referred to as meatball mix, is a package of equal parts ground beef, veal, and pork found in the meat section of the supermarket. When unavailable, any combination of these meats can be substituted.

Veal Scallops in Peach Sauce

Boneless pork *scallops* or medallions work equally well in this quick-cooking dish featuring the flavor of sweet peaches in a brown sugar glaze.

Yield:	Prep time:	Cook time:	Serving size:
8 scallops	10 minutes	15 minutes	2 scallops

2 TB. olive oil	½ cup all-purpose flour
1 TB. unsalted butter	1 cup canned diced no-sugar-added peaches, drained
8 medium veal scallops, pounded thin	¼ cup granulated brown sugar substitute
Salt	
Freshly ground pepper	

1. In a large, nonstick skillet over medium-high heat, melt olive oil and unsalted butter.

2. Season veal scallops with salt and pepper, and lightly dust with all-purpose flour. Add to the skillet, in batches if necessary, and fry for 2 minutes per side or until lightly browned and no longer pink inside. Transfer to a warm, clean serving platter.

3. Add no-sugar-added peaches to the skillet, and heat, stirring up skillet remains, for 2 minutes.

4. Stir in granulated brown sugar substitute and cook for about 3 minutes or until brown sugar is melted and peaches are coated. Serve on top of cooked veal.

> **DEFINITION**
>
> **Scallops,** also called scallopini, are thin, boneless cuts of meat—usually veal, pork, or beef—that are tender and quick-cooking.

Maple-Glazed Pork Chops

Agave's uncanny maple flavor is featured in this easy entrée that's sweetly glazed and full of rich, buttery flavor.

Yield:	Prep time:	Cook time:	Serving size:
8 pork chops	10 minutes	20 minutes	2 pork chops

8 thin cut pork loin chops, trimmed of fat	3 TB. unsalted butter
Dash salt	¼ cup apple cider vinegar
Freshly ground pepper	⅓ cup low-sodium chicken broth
1 TB. olive oil	⅓ cup amber agave nectar
	½ tsp. maple extract

1. Season both sides of pork chops with salt and pepper.

2. In a large, nonstick skillet over medium-high heat, melt olive oil and unsalted butter.

3. Place pork chops in the skillet in a single layer, and cook for 3 minutes per side or until lightly browned. Using tongs, transfer to a clean plate, and set aside.

4. Pour apple cider vinegar into the skillet, and reduce heat to medium. Cook, scraping up any browned bits, for 2 minutes or until vinegar is almost evaporated.

5. Stir in low-sodium chicken broth, amber agave nectar, and maple extract, and bring to a simmer.

6. Return pork chops to the skillet, cover, reduce heat to low, and cook for 5 to 8 minutes or until pork chops are no longer pink inside and liquid has thickened. Stir occasionally, and turn chops to prevent sticking.

7. Transfer chops to a serving platter, and spoon remaining glaze over all. Serve immediately.

TASTY TIP

If intense maple flavor is your passion, seek out one of the newer agave syrups already flavored with maple and use in any recipe as you would maple syrup.

Sliced Pork Tenderloin with Apricots

Sweet apricots complement the tender and subtle flavor of perfectly cooked pork tenderloin in this dish that also highlights the earthiness of fresh rosemary and a hint of exotic cumin.

Yield:	Prep time:	Cook time:	Serving size:
16 slices	15 minutes	30 minutes	4 slices

²/₃ cup dried apricots, chopped

¹/₂ cup orange juice

1 (1¹/₂- to 2-lb.) whole pork tender-loin, trimmed of fat

Dash salt

Freshly ground pepper

¹/₄ tsp. ground cumin

1 tsp. flour

2 TB. olive oil

1 medium shallot, minced

1 cup low-sodium chicken broth

1 small sprig rosemary

1. In a small bowl, combine apricots and orange juice. Set aside.

2. Season pork tenderloin with salt, pepper, and cumin, and dust lightly with flour.

3. In a large, nonstick skillet over medium-high heat, heat olive oil. Add tender-loin, and cook, turning to brown evenly, for 5 minutes. Using tongs, transfer to a clean plate.

4. Add shallot to the skillet, reduce heat to medium, and cook, stirring often, for 3 minutes or until softened.

5. Pour low-sodium chicken broth into the skillet, and add apricots with orange juice and rosemary. Bring to a simmer, stirring well.

6. Return tenderloin to the skillet, cover, and reduce heat to low. Cook, occasionally stirring, for about 20 minutes or until an instant-read thermometer reaches 150°F when inserted in the middle and sauce has thickened.

7. Transfer tenderloin to a cutting board to rest for 5 minutes before slicing. Taste pan sauce for additional salt and pepper, and keep warm. Spoon over slices and serve.

SWEET SECRET

Although dried fruits can often contain much concentrated natural sugar, their high fiber content makes them a healthy choice—in moderation—when eating sugar free.

Pan-Seared Lamb Chops with Minty Pomegranate Glaze

The flavor of lamb with mint is a classic, and here, a bit of sweet pomegranate highlights both in a flavorful and easy entrée that's sure to please.

Yield:	Prep time:	Cook time:	Serving size:
8 lamb chops	12 minutes	10 minutes	2 lamb chops

1 TB. olive oil	1 cup no-sugar-added pomegranate juice
8 thin lamb rib chops, trimmed of fat	¼ cup beef or chicken broth
Salt	2 (1-g) pkt. concentrated sugar substitute
Freshly ground pepper	1 TB. finely chopped fresh mint
1 medium shallot, minced	
1 clove garlic, minced	

1. In a large, nonstick skillet over medium-high heat, heat olive oil.

2. Season lamb rib chops with salt and pepper, and add to the skillet. Cook for about 3 minutes per side or until nicely browned and still medium in the middle. Transfer chops to a warm, clean plate, and cover with aluminum foil.

3. Add shallot and garlic to the skillet, reduce heat to medium, and cook, stirring occasionally, for 3 minutes or until softened.

4. Add no-sugar-added pomegranate juice, beef broth, and concentrated sugar substitute. Increase heat to high, and boil for about 2 minutes or until liquid is reduced by $\frac{1}{2}$.

5. Stir in mint, and return chops, with any accumulated juices on the plate, to the skillet. Cook for 1 more minute or until piping hot.

6. Serve lamb chops with glaze spooned over top.

SWEET SECRET

Mint has been a common accompaniment for meat entrées since ancient times, valued for its ability to aid in digestion and keep the breath fresh.

Chicken and Seafood Suppers

Chapter 13

In This Chapter

- Making over popular supper dishes without sugar
- Finding flavor in fruity combinations
- Using sugar substitutes tastefully
- Stirring up sweet sauces and glazes

Poultry and seafood recipes are often livened up with the addition of sweet syrups, jams, and pinches of pure sugar. Used to bring out the flavors of other ingredients or simply create accompanying sauces, sugar can be found in many obvious dishes such as sweet-and-sour chicken or sweet chili shrimp. It can also be lurking in not-so-obvious places, such as balsamic-flavored chicken or even meatballs.

Sweet, Natural Fruit

Sometimes a small amount of sugary flavor from naturally sweet fruit is all that's needed to substitute for and replicate the sweet taste we're after.

Pineapples, oranges, cherries, and other types of fruit are handy in the sugar-free kitchen. Often coupled with a bit of sugar substitute like agave or a granulated variety, much of the original sugar content can be removed without sacrificing flavor and overall taste.

Saucy Sweetness

Many entrées, especially chicken and shrimp, contain most of their sugar content in accompanying sauces or glazes meant to enhance the dining experience without dominating the palate. A surprisingly small amount of sugar substitute can go a long way in replicating the desired flavor and result in a simple hint of sweetness when appropriate. You'll see this deliciously evident in this chapter's dishes.

So without further ado, let's take a look at some remarkable suppers that are sugar free and super delicious!

Sensational Sweet-and-Sour Chicken

This classic Chinese entrée gets a sugar-free makeover in this easy recipe that features the tart tang of rice vinegar and the fruity sweetness of pineapple.

Yield:	Prep time:	Cook time:	Serving size:
4 cups	15 minutes	25 minutes	1 cup

½ cup pineapple juice

2 TB. soy sauce

1 garlic clove, minced

2 tsp. peeled and finely chopped fresh ginger

1 lb. chicken tenderloins, cut into bite-size pieces

Dash salt, or more to taste

Freshly ground pepper

¼ cup cornstarch

2 TB. canola oil

½ medium yellow onion, roughly chopped

½ medium green bell pepper, ribs and seeds removed, and roughly chopped

½ medium red bell pepper, ribs and seeds removed, and roughly chopped

½ cup Sugar-Free Ketchup (recipe in Chapter 10)

3 TB. granulated sugar substitute

¼ cup unseasoned rice vinegar

1 cup fresh pineapple chunks

1. In a shallow dish, combine pineapple juice, 1 tablespoon soy sauce, garlic, and ginger. Add chicken, and stir to coat. Set aside to marinate, stirring occasionally, for 20 to 30 minutes.

2. Using a slotted spoon, transfer chicken to a plate and pat dry with paper towels. Reserve marinade.

3. Season chicken with salt and pepper, and dust with cornstarch.

4. In a large, nonstick skillet or wok over high heat, heat 1 tablespoon canola oil. Add chicken, and stir-fry for 3 to 4 minutes or until no longer pink and beginning to brown. Transfer to a clean plate, and set aside.

5. Add remaining 1 tablespoon canola oil to the skillet, and when hot, add yellow onion, green bell pepper, and red bell pepper. Stir-fry for 2 minutes or until slightly softened.

6. Stir in reserved marinade, remaining 1 tablespoon soy sauce, Sugar-Free Ketchup, granulated sugar substitute, and unseasoned rice vinegar. Bring to a boil, and simmer, stirring often, for 1 minute.

7. Return chicken and any accumulated juices to the skillet along with pineapple chunks. Cook, stirring constantly, for 2 minutes or until sauce is thick and all ingredients are piping hot. Serve immediately over rice, if desired.

SWEET SECRET

Red bell peppers taste sweeter than green bell peppers simply because they've been left longer to ripen on the vine, which gives them more time to develop their natural sugars. All green peppers become red peppers eventually If allowed to fully ripen.

Creole Chicken Stew

The flavors of Louisiana abound in this slightly spicy one-dish meal that's great over rice or with garlic bread dipped into the tangy sauce.

Yield:	Prep time:	Cook time:	Serving size:
about 6 cups	20 minutes	30 minutes	1½ cups

2 TB. olive oil

1 small yellow onion, diced

Salt

Freshly ground pepper

½ medium red bell pepper, ribs and seeds removed, and diced

1 medium celery stalk, diced

1 cup canned chopped tomatoes, with juice

1 cup chicken broth

2 (1-g) pkt. concentrated sugar substitute

1 cup frozen corn kernels, thawed

3 (4-oz.) boneless, skinless chicken breasts, cut into bite-size pieces

2 tsp. *Creole seasoning*

Dash cayenne

4 scallions, trimmed and chopped

½ cup low-fat plain yogurt

1. In a medium, heavy-bottomed pot over medium-high heat, heat olive oil. Add yellow onion, season with salt and pepper, and cook, stirring occasionally, for 2 minutes or until slightly softened.

2. Stir in red bell pepper and celery, and cook for 2 minutes.

3. Pour in tomatoes, with juice, and chicken broth. Bring to a boil, reduce heat to medium-low, and stir in concentrated sugar substitute and corn.

4. Sprinkle chicken pieces with 1 teaspoon Creole seasoning, and set aside for 1 minute.

5. Meanwhile, add remaining 1 teaspoon Creole seasoning and cayenne to the pot, and stir well.

6. Add chicken pieces, and cook at a low simmer for 10 to 12 minutes or until chicken is no longer pink.

7. Add scallions and yogurt, stir well, and cook 1 more minute. Serve immediately.

DEFINITION

Creole seasoning is a blend of herbs and spices that generally contains paprika, a variety of peppers, and onion and garlic powder.

Sweet-Tart Lemon Chicken

Fresh ginger and garlic provide a delicious punch for the taste buds in this classic dish that's sweetened with the help of agave nectar and bursting with tart, lemony flavor.

Yield:	Prep time:	Cook time:	Serving size:
12 chicken pieces	12 minutes	20 minutes	3 chicken pieces

1 large egg, beaten

1 TB. water

¾ cup *panko breadcrumbs*

1 lb. (about 6) thin chicken cutlets, halved

Dash salt

Freshly ground pepper

3 TB. canola oil

⅓ cup fresh lemon juice

2 TB. cornstarch

½ cup low-sodium chicken broth

½ tsp. lemon zest

1 TB. soy sauce

¼ cup light agave nectar

1 large garlic clove, minced

1 tsp. peeled and finely chopped fresh ginger

1. In a shallow bowl, stir together egg and water.

2. In another shallow bowl, place panko breadcrumbs.

3. Season chicken pieces with salt and pepper. Dip each chicken piece in egg mixture, allowing excess to drip off, and dredge in breadcrumbs. Set each aside on parchment paper.

4. In a large, nonstick skillet over medium-high heat, heat canola oil. Add chicken, and cook in a single layer, in batches if necessary, for 2 minutes per side or until nicely browned. Set aside on clean plate, and keep warm.

5. In a small bowl, whisk together lemon juice and cornstarch. Add low-sodium chicken broth, lemon zest, soy sauce, and light agave nectar, and stir well to combine.

6. In the same skillet over medium heat, cook garlic and ginger for 1 or 2 minutes until fragrant. Do not brown.

7. Pour lemon mixture into the skillet, stir well, and bring to a simmer. Allow to bubble, stirring often, for about 3 minutes or until sauce is thickened.

8. Return cooked chicken to the skillet to coat in sauce for 1 minute. Transfer entire skillet contents to a warm platter, and serve immediately.

DEFINITION

Panko breadcrumbs are a Japanese variety of breadcrumbs that result in a light and crispy crust when used for frying. They can be found in Asian groceries and most supermarkets.

Best Balsamic Glazed Chicken

Deep-flavored, oaky balsamic vinegar teams up with soy sauce and sweet agave in this easy chicken recipe that will please the whole family.

Yield:	Prep time:	Cook time:	Serving size:
8 thighs	10 minutes	50 minutes	2 thighs

½ cup balsamic vinegar

½ cup amber agave nectar

¼ cup soy sauce

1 large garlic clove, minced

8 chicken thighs, skins removed

Dash salt

Freshly ground pepper

1. In a medium bowl, whisk together balsamic vinegar, amber agave nectar, soy sauce, and garlic.

2. Place chicken thighs in a single layer in a shallow dish, and pour vinegar mixture over. Marinate in the refrigerator, turning occasionally, for 30 minutes.

3. Preheat the oven to 400°F. Line a rimmed baking sheet with aluminum foil.

4. Remove chicken from marinade, and pat dry. Place on the prepared baking sheet, and season with salt and pepper. Bake for 45 to 50 minutes, turning occasionally, or until an instant-read thermometer inserted in the thickest part of thigh reaches 165°F.

5. Meanwhile, pour marinade into a small saucepan and set over medium-high heat. Simmer for 15 to 20 minutes or until thick.

6. Brush each cooked thigh with glaze, and let stand for 10 minutes before serving.

SWEET SECRET

Contrary to common belief, balsamic vinegar gets its name not from the type of wood barrels used in its production but rather from the Latin word *balsamum*, meaning "balsamlike," referring to its original restorative and curative use.

Chipotle Orange Grilled Chicken Breasts

Sweet citrus and smoky *chipotle chile* liven up this delicious and easy entrée that benefits from an overnight marinade to increase its flavor.

Yield:	Prep time:	Cook time:	Serving size:
4 breasts	10 minutes, plus overnight marinate time	8 minutes	1 breast

1 cup fresh squeezed orange juice

1 tsp. orange zest

2 large cloves garlic, minced

1 tsp. dried oregano

½ tsp. dried thyme

1 TB. chipotle chile powder

4 boneless, skinless chicken breasts (1 lb.)

Dash salt

Freshly ground pepper

1. In a small bowl, whisk together orange juice, orange zest, garlic, oregano, thyme, and chipotle chile powder. Pour into a large zipper-lock bag.

2. Add chicken breasts, and marinate in the refrigerator for a few hours or preferably overnight.

3. Heat an outdoor or indoor grill to medium-high.

4. Remove chicken from marinade, and pat dry. Season with salt and pepper.

5. Grill chicken for 12 to 15 minutes, turning occasionally, or until an instant-read thermometer inserted in the middle reaches 165°F.

6. Allow to rest for 5 minutes before serving.

> **DEFINITION**
>
> **Chipotle chile** peppers are red jalapeño peppers that have been dried and smoked. You can find them powdered, whole, or canned in a marinade or adobo sauce.

Oven-Roasted Cherry-Glazed Turkey Breast

Sweet cherries complement the savory flavor of roast turkey in this surprisingly easy recipe that also boasts a hint of sage and bold rosemary.

Yield:	Prep time:	Cook time:	Serving size:
12 slices	10 minutes	40 to 50 minutes	2 or 3 slices

1 (1½- to 2½-lb.) boneless or partially boned turkey breast

1 tsp. olive oil

Dash salt

Freshly ground pepper

2 sprigs fresh sage

1 sprig fresh rosemary

½ cup sugar-free cherry jam

¼ cup low-sodium chicken broth

Juice of ½ lemon

1 (1-g) pkt. concentrated sugar substitute

1. Preheat the oven to 400°F.

2. Rub turkey breast with olive oil, and season with salt and pepper. Place in a medium roasting pan, and tuck sage and rosemary sprigs underneath.

3. Roast turkey for 40 to 50 minutes or until nicely browned and an instant-read thermometer inserted in the thickest part reaches 165°F.

4. Meanwhile, in a small saucepan over medium heat, combine sugar-free cherry jam, low-sodium chicken broth, lemon juice, and concentrated sugar substitute. Bring to a simmer.

5. While turkey is roasting, brush on some cherry mixture every 10 minutes to form a glaze.

6. Pour any remaining mixture over turkey after it's removed from the oven, and allow turkey to rest for 10 minutes before slicing and serving.

SWEET SECRET

Cherries contain an antioxidant called anthocyanin, which is responsible for their red pigment and has been associated with reducing pain and inflammation in the body.

Turkey Meatballs in Sweet Vinegar Sauce

Slightly sweet with a fruity side, these tasty meatballs also have a slightly sour side that's just perfect for ground turkey but would also be delicious with ground chicken.

Yield:	Prep time:	Cook time:	Serving size:
12 meatballs	20 minutes	40 minutes	2 or 3 meatballs

1 lb. lean ground turkey

1 large egg

1 small yellow onion, finely chopped

1 large garlic clove, minced

½ tsp. salt

Freshly ground pepper

¼ cup Sugar-Free Ketchup (recipe in Chapter 10)

¾ cup plain breadcrumbs

1 TB. olive oil

2 cups tomato purée

¼ cup no-sugar-added grape juice

¼ cup red wine vinegar

1 TB. lemon juice

2 TB. tomato paste

2 TB. sugar-free grape jelly

½ tsp. garlic salt

¼ tsp. ground allspice

⅛ tsp. ground cloves

1 (1-g) pkt. concentrated sugar substitute

1. Preheat the oven to 350°F.

2. In a large mixing bowl, combine ground turkey, egg, yellow onion, garlic, salt, pepper, Sugar-Free Ketchup, and breadcrumbs. Stir until well combined.

3. Form mixture into 12 meatballs, and place on a rimmed baking sheet. Bake, shaking the pan occasionally, for 20 to 25 minutes or until lightly browned.

4. Meanwhile, in a large pot over medium-high heat, combine olive oil, tomato purée, no-sugar-added grape juice, red wine vinegar, lemon juice, tomato paste, sugar-free grape jelly, garlic salt, allspice, cloves, and concentrated sugar substitute. Bring to a simmer, and cook, stirring often, for 3 to 5 minutes.

5. Transfer meatballs to the pot, stir carefully, and cook, stirring often to prevent sticking, for 15 more minutes or until meatballs are firm and sauce is somewhat thickened.

6. Serve over rice or noodles with sauce spooned over top.

TASTY TIP

Adding a spoonful of sugar-free jam to subtly sweet sauces and gravies helps thicken the consistency, thanks to its pectin content, while adding another layer of flavor.

Coconut-Breaded Shrimp with Orange Sauce

This sugar-free makeover of the popular restaurant dish will leave you wanting more, thanks to its delectably sweet and crunchy coating and deliciously simple dipping sauce.

Yield:	Prep time:	Cook time:	Serving size:
about 24 shrimp	10 minutes	10 minutes	about 6 shrimp

⅓ cup all-purpose flour

Dash salt

Dash cayenne

2 large eggs, beaten

2 TB. unsweetened coconut milk

¼ cup panko breadcrumbs

½ cup unsweetened shredded coconut

1 (1-g) pkt. concentrated sugar substitute

1 lb. jumbo raw shrimp, shelled, deveined, and tail on

½ cup sugar-free orange marmalade

2 TB. orange juice

Canola oil

1. In a small bowl, stir together all-purpose flour, salt, and cayenne.

2. In another small bowl, combine eggs and coconut milk.

3. In a third small bowl, combine panko breadcrumbs, coconut, and concentrated sugar substitute.

4. One at a time, lightly coat shrimp with flour mixture, dip into egg mixture, coat well with coconut mixture, and transfer to parchment paper.

5. In a dipping bowl, combine sugar-free orange marmalade and orange juice. Refrigerate until ready to serve.

6. Fill a skillet with enough canola oil to come about $\frac{1}{2}$ inch up the side. Set over medium-high heat, and bring to a temperature of between 350°F and 360°F.

7. Add coated shrimp, without crowding, and fry for 1 or 2 minutes per side or until golden. Transfer to paper towels to drain.

8. Serve shrimp on a platter with dipping sauce on the side.

TASTY TIP

When frying these shrimp, or any other large number of items, always let the oil return to the appropriate temperature in between batches to prevent a greasy result.

Sweet Spicy Chili Shrimp

Delightfully delicious with the flavor of hot chili and the sweet addition of agave, this shrimp dish is full of layers of flavor, with a hint of paprika and a finish of fresh cilantro.

Yield:	Prep time:	Cook time:	Serving size:
about 24 shrimp	15 minutes	20 minutes	about 6 shrimp

2 TB. olive oil

$\frac{1}{2}$ small yellow onion, finely chopped

$\frac{1}{2}$ cup finely chopped red bell pepper

$\frac{1}{2}$ cup chili sauce

$\frac{1}{4}$ cup light agave nectar

1 lb. (about 24) jumbo raw shrimp, shelled, tailed, and deveined

Dash paprika

Dash salt

Freshly ground pepper

2 tsp. finely chopped cilantro leaves

1. In a medium saucepan over medium heat, heat 1 tablespoon olive oil. Add yellow onion and red bell pepper, and cook, stirring often, for 3 minutes or until softened.

2. Add chili sauce and light agave nectar, bring to a simmer, reduce heat to low, and cook, stirring often, for 5 to 8 minutes or until thickened. Set aside in a warm place.

3. Season shrimp with paprika, salt, and pepper.

4. In a large, nonstick skillet over medium-high heat, heat remaining 1 tablespoon olive oil. Add shrimp, and cook for 2 minutes per side or until pink.

5. Pour in sauce mixture, stir well, reduce heat to medium-low, and simmer for 2 or 3 minutes or until piping hot and shrimp is nicely coated with sauce.

6. Transfer to a warm serving bowl, sprinkle with cilantro, and serve immediately over rice, if desired.

TASTY TIP

For a further reduction in sugar grams, look for bottles of reduced-sugar or no-sugar-added chili sauce.

Lemon-Baked Sea Scallops

A hint of maple-flavored agave adds a delicious layer of flavor in this easy scallop dish with the enticing taste of *Old Bay Seasoning* and lots of tangy lemon.

Yield:	Prep time:	Cook time:	Serving size:
15 to 20 scallops	10 minutes	20 minutes	4 or 5 scallops

1 lb. (15 to 20) large sea scallops, rinsed and patted dry

¼ tsp. Old Bay Seasoning

1 TB. olive oil

1 TB. finely chopped shallot

1 small garlic clove, minced

2 TB. lemon juice

1 TB. amber agave nectar

Dash salt

Freshly ground pepper

1 tsp. finely chopped fresh parsley leaves

1. Preheat the oven to 350°F. Lightly spray a baking dish with cooking spray.

2. Place scallops in a single layer in the prepared dish, and sprinkle with Old Bay Seasoning. Bake for 10 minutes or until just beginning to turn opaque.

3. Meanwhile, in a small saucepan over medium heat, heat olive oil. Add shallot, and cook, stirring often, for 3 minutes or until softened.

4. Add garlic and cook 1 more minute.

5. Add lemon juice, amber agave nectar, salt, and pepper, and bring to a simmer.

6. Drizzle lemon mixture over scallops, and return them to the oven to cook 8 to 10 more minutes or until firm and opaque and sauce has formed a glaze.

7. Remove scallops from the oven, sprinkle with parsley, and serve immediately from the baking dish.

DEFINITION

Old Bay Seasoning is a classic blend of herbs and spices created in the 1940s for flavoring crab, shrimp, and other shellfish. It includes mustard, paprika, celery seed, bay leaf, black and red pepper, cinnamon, cloves, allspice, nutmeg, cardamom, salt, mace, and ginger.

Roasted Salmon with Mustard and Dill

Succulent salmon fillets paired with roasted sliced potatoes get a boost of additional flavor from sweet, whole-grain mustard and the fragrant aroma of fresh dill.

Yield:	Prep time:	Cook time:	Serving size:
2 (4-ounce) pieces salmon	15 minutes	40 minutes	1 (4-ounce) piece salmon

2 medium red-skinned potatoes, skin on, and cut into ¼-in. slices

2 TB. canola oil

Dash salt

Freshly ground pepper

2 (4-oz.) salmon fillets, skin and all bones removed

1 TB. whole-grain mustard

2 TB. granulated brown sugar substitute

1 TB. chopped fresh dill

1. Preheat the oven to 375°F.

2. In a medium bowl, combine red-skinned potatoes, 1 tablespoon canola oil, salt, and pepper, and toss to coat. Transfer to a medium roasting pan, and place in a single layer. Roast for 15 minutes, turning once, or until just beginning to brown.

3. Shift potatoes to the edge of the pan, and place salmon fillets in the middle.

4. In a small bowl, stir together remaining 1 tablespoon canola oil, whole-grain mustard, granulated brown sugar substitute, and dill, and spread on top of salmon.

5. Roast, occasionally turning potatoes, for 25 to 30 minutes or until salmon is firm to the touch and potatoes are browned and crispy.

6. To serve, mound ½ of potatoes on a dinner plate and top with 1 salmon fillet.

TASTY TIP

If you're uncomfortable skinning the salmon, ask the fishmonger to do it for you when you buy it. And always check for pin bones—the small, sharp bones that appear up and down the center of the fillet—even if the piece has already been deboned. One or two can linger in the flesh.

Fried Fish Fillets with Kicked-Up Tomato Sauce

If you like the combination of spicy and sweet, you'll love this terrific dish featuring flaky fish fillets topped with a flavorful hot sauce of sweet tomatoes and the heat of Tabasco.

Yield:	Prep time:	Cook time:	Serving size:
8 fillets	20 minutes	20 minutes	2 fillets

1 cup tomato sauce	Freshly ground pepper
1 TB. tomato paste	8 (2-oz.) catfish, cod, or haddock fillets
1 tsp. Tabasco sauce	
2 TB. granulated sugar substitute	1 cup all-purpose flour
1 TB. lemon juice	1 tsp. hot paprika
2 tsp. apple cider vinegar	Canola oil
Salt	

1. In a small saucepan over medium heat, combine tomato sauce, tomato paste, Tabasco sauce, granulated sugar substitute, lemon juice, and apple cider vinegar. Bring to a simmer, stirring often, and cook for 10 minutes or until very thick. Season with salt and pepper, and set aside.

2. Season catfish fillets with salt and pepper.

3. In a shallow dish, combine all-purpose flour and hot paprika.

4. Dredge fish in flour mixture, and place on a wire rack.

5. Meanwhile, heat about ¼ inch canola oil in a large, heavy skillet over medium-high heat. When hot (365°F), add fish fillets, and fry for 2 or 3 minutes per side or until golden and no longer opaque inside. Remove fish from the skillet, and set aside on paper towels to drain.

6. Serve fillets with hot sauce spooned over top or on the side.

TASTY TIP

If you don't have a thermometer to check the oil temperature, you can do the bread test. Simply drop a small piece of bread into the hot oil. If it immediately sizzles and browns, the oil is ready for frying.

Vegetarian Entrées

In This Chapter

- Sugar-free meat-free dinners
- Eighty-sixing the sugar in popular main dishes
- Finding bold flavor in spices
- Enjoying naturally sweet taste

Just like any entrée you may come across, the chances of finding added sugar in some form or another are very high, even when dining vegetarian. From the unwanted addition of sugary ingredients like ketchup or Asian condiments to the actual dip into the sugar bowl, going sugar free requires just as much attention and vigilance in the savory meatless kitchen as it does in the bake shop.

In many ways, adjusting to sugar-free cooking and the resulting taste sensations should be no problem for most vegetarian eaters who have already eliminated meat, chicken, fish, and perhaps even some dairy from their diet. Subtle changes, like the ones made in the entrées in this chapter, will hardly be noticeable to those who are already primed for true authentic flavor.

Spice It Up

The inclusion of bold and flavorful spices like paprika and cayenne can go a long way in compensating for the absence of sweetness here and there. Still, there is no deprivation—not while you have terrific sugar substitutes with in your cooking arsenal!

Let's step into the vegetarian kitchen and start preparing some really flavorful (and healthy!) dishes for you to savor and enjoy.

Very Veggie Chili

Oodles of yummy vegetables highlight this flavorful chili featuring a hint of sweetness and a touch of balsamic vinegar.

Yield:	Prep time:	Cook time:	Serving size:
6 cups	20 minutes	30 minutes	1 or 2 cups

1 TB. olive oil

1 small yellow onion, diced

$\frac{1}{2}$ medium green bell pepper, ribs and seeds removed, and diced

$\frac{1}{2}$ medium red or yellow bell pepper, ribs and seeds removed, and diced

1 medium carrot, diced

Salt

Freshly ground pepper

1 medium jalapeño pepper, seeded and minced

1 TB. chili powder

1 tsp. paprika

$\frac{1}{2}$ tsp. ground cumin

Dash cayenne

1 (15-oz.) can crushed tomatoes, with juice

$\frac{1}{2}$ cup water

2 TB. granulated sugar substitute

1 TB. balsamic vinegar

1 (15-oz.) can red kidney beans, drained and rinsed

1 cup canned black beans, drained and rinsed

1 cup canned cannellini beans, drained and rinsed

1 cup frozen corn kernels, thawed

1. In a heavy-bottomed pot over medium-high heat, heat olive oil. Add yellow onion, green bell pepper, red bell pepper, and carrot, and season with salt and pepper. Reduce heat to medium, and cook, stirring occasionally, for 6 minutes or until softened.

2. Add jalapeño, and cook for 1 minute.

3. Stir in chili powder, paprika, cumin, and cayenne, coating vegetables well. Add tomatoes with juice, water, granulated sugar substitute, and balsamic vinegar, and bring to a boil. Reduce heat to low, and cook, stirring occasionally, for 10 to 12 minutes until slightly thickened.

4. Stir in red kidney beans, black beans, cannellini beans, and corn, and simmer for 10 more minutes until thick and piping hot.

5. Season with additional salt and pepper, if necessary, and serve immediately.

TASTY TIP

Chili of all kinds freezes extremely well and continues to become more flavorful. Make an extra batch, and freeze in 1-cup containers for school or work lunches on the go.

Divine Noodle Kugel

This slightly sweet, creamy, and rich Jewish holiday dish becomes a healthy meal in itself for vegetarian diners, with a hint of cinnamon and the natural sweetness of golden raisins.

Yield:	Prep time:	Cook time:	Serving size:
6 cups	15 minutes	40 minutes	1 cup

8 oz. medium egg noodles

½ cup reduced-fat sour cream

½ cup low-fat cottage cheese

3 TB. cream cheese

¼ cup granulated sugar substitute

1 large egg

1 large egg white

½ tsp. vanilla extract

¼ tsp. ground cinnamon

⅔ cup golden raisins

1. Cook egg noodles according to the package directions. Drain, rinse under cold water, and set aside.

2. Preheat the oven to 350°F. Lightly coat the bottom and sides of a 2-quart casserole dish with cooking spray.

3. In a large bowl, and using an electric mixer on medium-high speed, beat together reduced-fat sour cream, low-fat cottage cheese, cream cheese, and granulated sugar substitute until smooth.

4. Add egg, egg white, vanilla extract, and cinnamon, and beat for 2 minutes or until well combined.

5. Add golden raisins and drained noodles, and stir well. Transfer to the prepared casserole, and smooth out evenly. Bake for 40 to 45 minutes or until top is lightly browned and kugel is firmly set.

6. Cool slightly on a wire rack before cutting and serving.

SWEET SECRET

Although today most kugels are baked in square or rectangular pans, the name comes from the German *kugel,* meaning "round" or "spherical." That was the traditional shape of pan used for these types of dishes.

Loads of Beans Casserole

Slow baked and full of sweet and tangy flavor, this dish made from four different beans is sure to please every vegetarian in the house as well as baked bean lovers.

Yield:	Prep time:	Cook time:	Serving size:
8 cups	15 minutes	2 or 3 hours	1½ cups

1 TB. olive oil

1 medium yellow onion, finely chopped

Dash salt, or more to taste

Freshly ground pepper

1 (15-oz.) can red kidney beans, drained and rinsed

1 (15-oz.) can butter beans, drained and rinsed

1 (15-oz.) can lima beans, drained and rinsed

1 (15-oz.) can vegetarian no-sugar-added baked beans, with liquid

1 (8-oz.) can tomato sauce

½ cup Sugar-Free Ketchup (recipe in Chapter 10)

¼ cup apple cider vinegar

1 tsp. dry mustard

½ cup granulated brown sugar substitute

1. Preheat the oven to 300°F. Lightly coat a 13×9-inch casserole dish with cooking spray.

2. In a large, nonstick skillet over medium-high heat, heat olive oil. Add yellow onion, salt, and pepper, and cook, stirring often, for 3 minutes or until onion is softened but not browned.

3. Add red kidney beans, butter beans, and lima beans, and stir well to combine. Transfer to the prepared casserole dish.

4. In the same skillet, combine vegetarian no-sugar-added baked beans, tomato sauce, Sugar-Free Ketchup, apple cider vinegar, dry mustard, and granulated brown sugar substitute. Reduce heat to medium, and cook, stirring often, for 3 minutes or until bubbly and hot.

5. Transfer mixture to the casserole dish, and stir well to combine with beans and onion. Bake for 2 or 3 hours, stirring every 20 minutes, until beans are thick, tender, and bubbly. Allow to cool for 15 minutes before serving.

TASTY TIP

Acidic ingredients like vinegar help lower the glycemic impact of foods that tend to raise glucose levels quite high such as refined white flour breads and many fruits.

Plum-Good Tofu Stir-Fry

Stir-fries often benefit from a little sweetness in the form of fruit sauces or pastes, and here, a not-too-sweet plum jam complements the robust flavor of fresh ginger and garlic.

Yield:	Prep time:	Cook time:	Serving size:
4 cups	20 minutes	15 minutes	1 cup

1 lb. extra-firm tofu, halved and cut into chunks

Dash salt, or more to taste

Freshly ground pepper

1 TB. canola oil

½ medium red bell pepper, ribs and seeds removed, and sliced

1 bunch scallions, trimmed and cut into 2-in. pieces

1 large garlic clove, minced

1 cup baby corn

½ cup sliced water chestnuts

½ cup vegetable broth

½ cup sugar-free plum jam

1 TB. peeled and finely chopped fresh ginger

1 TB. lemon juice

1 TB. soy sauce

1 (1-g) pkt. concentrated sugar substitute

1. Press tofu chunks between paper towels to remove all excess liquid. Season with salt and pepper.

2. In a large, nonstick skillet or wok over high heat, heat canola oil. Carefully add tofu to the skillet, and brown lightly, turning occasionally, for 1 or 2 minutes. Using a slotted spoon, remove tofu and set aside.

3. Add red bell pepper and scallions to the skillet, increase heat to high, and cook, stirring constantly, for about 2 minutes or until somewhat softened.

4. Add garlic, baby corn, and water chestnuts, and cook for 1 more minute.

5. Pour in vegetable broth, and return browned tofu slices to the skillet. Reduce heat to low, cover, and cook for 2 minutes.

6. Meanwhile, in a small bowl, whisk together sugar-free plum jam, ginger, lemon juice, soy sauce, and concentrated sugar substitute.

7. Uncover skillet and add plum jam mixture, gently stirring to coat tofu and vegetables. Cook for 1 or 2 more minutes until thick and bubbly. Taste to see if more salt and pepper are needed, transfer to a bowl, and serve immediately with rice, if desired.

HONEY DON'T!

Refrain from using traditional plum sauce or "duck sauce" in your cooking. They're notoriously high in sugar and often contain high-fructose corn syrup as the main ingredient.

Pad Thai Noodle Wraps

You'll love the addition of sweet agave when you roll up these hot and spicy Thai-inspired wraps fragrant with cilantro and deliciously satisfying with a sprinkling of roasted peanuts.

Yield:	Prep time:	Cook time:	Serving size:
6 wraps	30 minutes	10 minutes	2 wraps

1 (14-oz.) pkg. thin *rice noodles*

1 TB. canola oil

1 large garlic clove, minced

¼ cup unseasoned rice vinegar

¼ cup light agave nectar

3 TB. Sugar-Free Ketchup (recipe in Chapter 10)

1 TB. soy sauce

1 TB. chili sauce

1 TB. lime or lemon juice

⅔ cup shredded carrots

3 scallions, trimmed and cut into 2-in. pieces

1½ cups fresh bean sprouts

Dash salt

Freshly ground pepper

6 large vegetarian sandwich wraps, warmed

3 TB. chopped fresh cilantro leaves

⅓ cup chopped lightly salted roasted peanuts

1. Cook rice noodles according to the package directions. Drain, rinse under cold water, and set aside.

2. In a large, nonstick skillet over medium-high heat, heat canola oil. Add garlic, and cook, stirring, for 1 minute.

3. Add cooked rice noodles, and stir-fry for 2 minutes or until heated through.

4. In a small bowl, whisk together unseasoned rice vinegar, light agave nectar, Sugar-Free Ketchup, soy sauce, chili sauce, and lime juice. Pour over noodles, and cook for 3 minutes, stirring often, or until noodles are completely transparent.

5. Add carrots, scallions, and bean sprouts, and stir-fry for 2 or 3 minutes or until heated through. Season with salt and pepper, and remove from heat.

6. Mound noodle mixture into center of wraps, sprinkle with cilantro and peanuts, and roll up by folding over sides of wrap and then rolling away from you to form a thick log. Cut each wrap into 2, if desired, and serve immediately.

DEFINITION

Rice noodles are a popular alternative to flour-based noodles in Eastern and Southeast Asian cuisine. Usually made from rice flour and water, they become chewy and transparent when cooked. You can find them dried in most supermarkets.

Great Garden Goulash

Traditional Hungarian goulash often contains at least a small amount of sugar in some form. In this vegetarian version, a brown sugar substitute fills the bill, providing a slightly sweet side to this bold and flavorful dish.

Yield:	Prep time:	Cook time:	Serving size:
6 cups	20 minutes	45 minutes	1½ cups

1 TB. olive oil

3 TB. unsalted butter

1 medium yellow onion, chopped

1 large carrot, diced

Dash salt, or more to taste

Freshly ground pepper

1 garlic clove, minced

2 cups low-sodium vegetable broth

1 TB. Hungarian paprika

Dash cayenne

¾ cup Sugar-Free Ketchup (recipe in Chapter 10)

1 TB. granulated brown sugar substitute

½ tsp. dry mustard

1 cup diced butternut squash

1 medium white turnip, diced

10 baby red potatoes

1 cup cauliflower florets

½ cup frozen peas

2 TB. all-purpose flour

¼ cup water

1. In a large, heavy-bottomed pot over medium-high heat, melt olive oil and unsalted butter. Add yellow onion, carrot, salt, and pepper, and cook, stirring occasionally, for 4 minutes or until vegetables are somewhat softened.

2. Add garlic, and cook for 1 more minute.

3. Pour in vegetable broth, and bring to a simmer.

4. Add Hungarian paprika, cayenne, Sugar-Free Ketchup, granulated brown sugar substitute, and dry mustard, and stir well to combine. Simmer for 2 minutes.

5. Add butternut squash, white turnip, and red potatoes, and stir well. Cover, reduce heat to medium-low, and cook, stirring occasionally, for 12 minutes or until vegetables are nearly fork-tender.

6. Uncover and stir in cauliflower florets and peas. Cook, stirring to prevent sticking, for about 5 more minutes or until all vegetables are tender.

7. In a small bowl, whisk together all-purpose flour and water. Stir into goulash, increase heat to medium-high, and bring to a low boil, stirring constantly, for 1 or 2 minutes or until mixture is very thick.

8. Remove from heat, taste to see if more salt and pepper are needed, and serve immediately over noodles or rice, if desired.

SWEET SECRET

The word *goulash* comes from the Hungarian word *gulyás,* which means "herd." The dish was often made by cattle herdsman over an open fire when they stayed with their animals in the hills overnight.

Bowties with Sweet Kasha

Delicious, nutty-flavored kasha, or *buckwheat groats,* combine beautifully with sweet, caramelized onions and pasta in this traditional dish that's perfect as a main course.

Yield:	Prep time:	Cook time:	Serving size:
4 cups	10 minutes	25 minutes	1 or 2 cups

¾ cup medium-grain kasha

1 large egg, slightly beaten

1 TB. vegetable oil

1 TB. unsalted butter

1 medium yellow onion, halved and thinly sliced

1 cup shredded carrots

1 TB. granulated sugar substitute

Dash salt

Freshly ground pepper

1½ cups low-sodium vegetable broth

1½ cups dry bowtie pasta

1. In a medium bowl, place kasha. Stir in egg, being sure to coat each grain. Set aside.

2. In a large, nonstick skillet over medium-high heat, melt vegetable oil and unsalted butter. Add yellow onion and carrots, sprinkle with granulated sugar substitute, and season with salt and pepper. Cook, stirring often, for about 5 minutes or until vegetables are softened and slightly browned.

3. Add kasha to the skillet, and cook, breaking up any clumps with the back of a fork, for 3 or 4 minutes or until egg has dried and kasha begins to toast.

4. Pour in low-sodium vegetable broth, bring to a boil, reduce heat to low, cover, and cook for 10 to 15 minutes or until kasha is tender.

5. Meanwhile, cook bowtie pasta according to the package directions. Drain, rinse under cold water, and set aside.

6. Add bowties to the skillet, stir to combine well, and cook for 3 or 4 more minutes or until piping hot. Taste to see if more salt and pepper are needed, and serve immediately.

> **DEFINITION**
>
> **Buckwheat groats,** also called kasha, are the hulled grains of buckwheat cereal, a popular grain in Eastern European cooking, often made as a porridge. It's become more popular in the United States recently because it's a safe alternative for people who are gluten intolerant.

Creamy Red Pepper Pasta

Roasted red peppers add a smoky layer of flavor to this vegetarian pasta dish while goat cheese adds a luxuriously rich texture.

Yield:	Prep time:	Cook time:	Serving size:
6 cups	10 minutes	20 minutes	2 cups

8 oz. penne pasta

2 (12-oz.) jars roasted red peppers, drained

2 cloves garlic, chopped

1 TB. olive oil

¼ tsp. paprika

½ cup tomato sauce

1 TB. tomato paste

1 (1-g) pkt. concentrated sugar substitute

1 (3-oz.) log plain goat cheese, crumbled

Salt

Freshly ground pepper

1 TB. chopped fresh basil leaves

1. Cook penne pasta according to the package directions. Drain.

2. Meanwhile, in a food processor fitted with a steel blade or a blender, purée roasted red peppers, garlic, olive oil, paprika, tomato sauce, tomato paste, and concentrated sugar substitute until smooth.

3. Transfer to a medium saucepan over medium-high heat, and heat, stirring often, for about 3 minutes or until just bubbly.

4. Add goat cheese, reduce heat to medium, and cook, stirring often, for about 5 minutes until cheese has melted and blended into sauce.

5. Season with salt and pepper, and stir in basil. Toss with hot penne, and serve immediately.

TASTY TIP

Goat cheese has a slightly sour and salty taste, so always refrain from seasoning with additional salt until after it's added to a dish.

Quick Vegetarian Spaghetti Sauce

You'll marvel at the flavor of this easy-to-make tomato-based pasta sauce that features Italian herbs and piquant olives.

Yield:	Prep time:	Cook time:	Serving size:
2 cups	15 minutes	30 minutes	½ cup

2 TB. olive oil

½ medium yellow onion, finely diced

Salt

Freshly ground pepper

2 cloves garlic, minced

1 (28-oz.) can chopped tomatoes, with juice

1 (8-oz.) can tomato sauce

2 TB. tomato paste

2 TB. granulated sugar substitute

2 tsp. dried oregano

2 tsp. dried basil

1 tsp. dried parsley

Dash crushed red pepper flakes

1 bay leaf

½ cup chopped ripe black olives

1 TB. grated romano cheese

1. In a heavy-bottomed pot over medium-high heat, heat olive oil. Add yellow onion, season with salt and pepper, and cook, stirring often, for 3 minutes or until softened. Do not brown.

2. Add garlic, and cook for 1 more minute.

3. Stir in tomatoes with juice, tomato sauce, tomato paste, granulated sugar substitute, oregano, basil, parsley, crushed red pepper flakes, and bay leaf. Bring to a simmer, stirring often. Reduce heat to very low, and cook simmer for 20 minutes or until flavorful and thickened.

4. Stir in black olives and romano cheese, and cook for 2 more minutes.

5. Remove bay leaf, and serve immediately over cooked spaghetti or another pasta.

HONEY DON'T!

Commercial spaghetti sauces can have added sugar, and even though they may be meatless, they could be flavored with chicken or beef stock as well. Always read labels carefully.

On the Side

In This Chapter

- Delicious accompaniments for main meals
- Putting sugar to the side
- Finding flavor in naturally sweet vegetables
- Cutting back on unnecessary sweetness

Many side dishes have a sweet side, which is why we like to add them to the array of food on our dinner plate. Somehow, something a little sweet can be just the thing to bring out the flavor of our savory selections. Whether it be just a taste, or occasionally quite a lot, side dishes can be heavily laden with sugar without our realizing it.

Sweet on Veggies

You may wonder why vegetables that already possess their own natural sweetness would need further sweetening. The answer lies in complementary flavors.

Carrots and sweet potatoes taste even sweeter when drenched in corn syrup or sprinkled with white sugar. But with a little clever substituting, we can eliminate the sugar without compromising the taste. In this chapter, you see how it's done.

Eliminating Excess

In a dish like traditional candied yams, would a good recipe really suffer if it didn't have gobs of brown sugar and half a gallon of dark corn syrup? Surely not. The proof, however, is in the pudding (in this chapter, the corn pudding as well as the baked beans and glazed carrots).

So let's start sampling some terrific sides that demonstrate how less is more when it comes to sugar.

Agave-Glazed Baby Carrots

Tender baby carrots benefit from a hint of sweetness, and here, they find a perfect foil in agave nectar with an aromatic hint of cinnamon and nutmeg.

Yield:	Prep time:	Cook time:	Serving size:
3 cups	5 minutes	15 minutes	½ cup

1 lb. pkg. baby carrots
2 TB. unsalted butter
⅓ cup light agave nectar
Freshly ground pepper

½ tsp. ground cinnamon
¼ tsp. ground nutmeg
Dash salt

1. Bring a large pot of salted water to a boil over high heat. Add carrots, return to a boil, and cook for 7 to 10 minutes or until fork-tender. Drain carrots, and set aside.

2. Add unsalted butter, light agave nectar, pepper, cinnamon, and nutmeg to the pot. Reduce heat to low, and stir for 1 minute.

3. Add carrots, and carefully stir to coat with glaze. Continue cooking on low, stirring often, for 2 minutes or until carrots are nicely glazed.

4. Remove from heat, season with salt, and serve immediately.

TASTY TIP

Carrots sometimes get a bad rep from diets based on the glycemic index because their number, on a scale from 1 to 100, is relatively high—up to 90 depending on whether they're raw or cooked. However, in order for carrots to have that sort of effect, you'd need to eat more than 2 pounds of them in one sitting with nothing else! On average, a serving of carrots is closer to 45, a perfectly acceptable GI number.

Not-So-Traditional Candied Sweet Potatoes

Move over, dark corn syrup and brown sugar! This sugar-free version is delicately sweet and wonderfully flavorful, thanks to brown sugar substitute and a touch of agave.

Yield:	Prep time:	Cook time:	Serving size:
4 cups	15 minutes	1 hour, 15 minutes	½ cup

4 medium orange-flesh sweet potatoes	¼ cup amber agave nectar
½ cup (1 stick) unsalted butter	Dash salt
½ cup granulated brown sugar substitute	Freshly ground pepper
	½ cup sugar-free marshmallows (optional)

1. Preheat the oven to 375°F. Line a baking sheet with aluminum foil.

2. Place sweet potatoes on the prepared baking sheet, and bake for 35 to 45 minutes or until fork-tender. Remove from the oven, and set aside to cool slightly.

3. Spray the bottom and sides of a 13×9-inch casserole with cooking spray.

4. When sweet potatoes are cool enough to handle but still quite warm, carefully remove the ends and skin with a sharp paring knife. Cut into quarters, and lay flat side down in the casserole dish as snugly as possible.

5. In a medium saucepan over medium heat, melt unsalted butter, granulated brown sugar substitute, amber agave nectar, salt, and pepper. Cook, stirring often, for 3 minutes or until bubbly. Pour evenly over sweet potatoes.

6. Bake, occasionally spooning liquid over sweet potatoes, for 30 to 35 minutes or until well glazed and bubbly around the edges.

7. Top with sugar-free marshmallows (if using), and bake for 3 more minutes or until marshmallows are melted. Allow to cool somewhat before serving.

TASTY TIP

When sweet potatoes are baked or roasted, their flesh begins to caramelize. This enhances their natural sweetness.

Sweet-as-Can-Be Whipped Sweet Potatoes

Sweet potatoes offer up their natural sweetness in this creamy and delicious side dish that's full of cinnamon and spice and a hint of tangy orange.

Yield:	Prep time:	Cook time:	Serving size:
5 or 6 cups	20 minutes	1 hour, 30 minutes	½ cup

4 medium orange-flesh sweet potatoes

⅔ cup granulated sugar substitute

2 TB. unsalted butter, melted

1 large egg, beaten

1 tsp. ground cinnamon

½ tsp. ground ginger

Dash ground nutmeg

¼ tsp. orange zest

½ tsp. salt

Freshly ground pepper

½ cup coarsely chopped pecans

1 TB. granulated brown sugar substitute

1. Preheat the oven to 375°F. Line a baking sheet with aluminum foil.

2. Place sweet potatoes on the prepared baking sheet, and bake for 35 to 45 minutes or until fork-tender. Remove from the oven, and set aside to cool slightly.

3. Spray the bottom and sides of a 1½-quart casserole dish with cooking spray.

4. When sweet potatoes are cool enough to handle but still quite warm, carefully remove the ends and skin with a sharp paring knife. Cut into chunks, and place in a large bowl.

5. Using an electric mixer on medium-high speed, beat in granulated sugar substitute, melted unsalted butter, egg, cinnamon, ginger, nutmeg, orange zest, salt, and pepper until smooth and creamy. Transfer sweet potato mixture to the prepared casserole dish, and smooth out evenly.

6. In a small bowl, stir together pecans and granulated brown sugar substitute. Sprinkle over top of sweet potato mixture.

7. Bake for 45 to 55 minutes or until topping is browned and sweet potatoes are piping hot. Allow to cool for 10 minutes before serving.

SWEET SECRET

Sweet potatoes actually belong to the same botanical family as morning glory flowers. Yams, however, are related to lilies and grasses.

Apple Butternut Casserole

The natural sweetness of apples and butternut squash complement each other in this delicious dish fragrant with fall spice and flavored with sweet agave.

Yield:	Prep time:	Cook time:	Serving size:
6 cups	30 minutes	45 to 55 minutes	$\frac{1}{2}$ cup

1 large butternut squash, peeled, seeded, and cut into $\frac{1}{4}$-in. slices

2 large apples, peeled, cored, and cut into $\frac{1}{4}$-in. slices

$\frac{1}{4}$ cup ($\frac{1}{2}$ stick) unsalted butter, diced

Salt

Freshly ground pepper

$\frac{1}{4}$ tsp. ground *mace*

2 TB. amber agave nectar

1. Preheat the oven to 375°F. Lightly coat a 13×9-inch casserole dish with cooking spray.

2. Layer butternut squash on the bottom of the prepared casserole dish, and arrange apple slices evenly on top. Dot with unsalted butter, and sprinkle with salt, pepper, and mace. Drizzle amber agave nectar over all.

3. Cover with aluminum foil, and bake for 45 to 55 minutes or until squash and apples are fork-tender.

4. Remove the foil, and allow to cool somewhat before serving.

DEFINITION

Mace is a seasoning derived from the red covering of the nutmeg fruit seed. It's similar in taste to nutmeg, with a bit more pungency.

Oven-Glazed Acorn Squash

Delightfully sweet and full of earthy flavor, this side dish is the perfect foil for poultry dishes, especially roast turkey.

Yield:	Prep time:	Cook time:	Serving size:
8 pieces	10 minutes	50 minutes	2 pieces

2 medium acorn squash, cut into quarters and seeded

Salt

Freshly ground pepper

4 tsp. unsalted butter

8 tsp. granulated brown sugar substitute

2 TB. chopped pecans (optional)

1. Preheat the oven to 375°F. Line a rimmed baking sheet with aluminum foil, and coat lightly with cooking spray.

2. Sprinkle acorn squash pieces with salt and pepper, and place cut side down on the prepared baking sheet. Bake for 30 minutes, turning after 15 minutes.

3. Turn squash pieces cut sides up, place $\frac{1}{2}$ teaspoon unsalted butter in each cavity, and sprinkle 1 teaspoon granulated brown sugar substitute on top of butter. Bake for 20 more minutes, occasionally brushing flesh of squash with a pastry brush to coat with butter and sugar mixture, until squash is nicely glazed and fork-tender.

4. Transfer to a platter, sprinkle with pecans (if using), and serve.

SWEET SECRET

Acorn squash belong to the winter squash family. Butternut, buttercup, and turban squashes are part of the winter squash family, too. They are high in beta-carotene, dietary fiber, and potassium.

Triple-Delight Corn Pudding

If you enjoy the flavor and texture of sweet corn on the cob, you'll love this triple-whammy side dish that's full of corny sweetness and a hint of chives.

Yield:	Prep time:	Cook time:	Serving size:
4 or 5 cups	10 minutes	45 to 55 minutes	½ cup

¼ cup milk

1 large egg

1 (8.5-oz.) pkg. sugar-free corn muffin mix

¼ cup granulated sugar substitute

3 TB. unsalted butter, melted

Dash salt

1 (14.75-oz.) can creamed corn

1 cup canned or frozen white corn

2 tsp. finely chopped fresh chives

1. Preheat the oven to 350°F. Spray the bottom and sides of an 8×8-inch-square baking dish with cooking spray.

2. In a large bowl, using an electric mixer on medium-high speed, beat together milk, egg, sugar-free corn muffin mix, granulated sugar substitute, melted unsalted butter, and salt for about 1 minute or until well combined.

3. Pour in creamed corn, and beat for 1 more minute.

4. Stir in white corn and chives, and transfer to the prepared baking dish. Spread out evenly.

5. Bake for 45 to 55 minutes or until lightly browned on the edges and a toothpick inserted in the center comes out clean. Allow to cool for 10 minutes before cutting into pieces and serving.

TASTY TIP

You can freeze fresh, uncooked corn on the cob right in its husk in freezer-safe bags to enjoy when out of season.

Southern Sautéed Greens

Every good Southern cook knows that a pinch or more of sugar helps balance the bitterness of traditional greens. Here, with the help of sweet apples and hint of agave, sautéed greens are ready to serve in no time!

Yield:	Prep time:	Cook time:	Serving size:
4 cups	30 minutes	25 minutes	1 cup

2 slices bacon, diced

1 lb. fresh collard greens, washed, stems removed, and leaves cut into 1-in.-wide ribbons

Dash salt, or more to taste

Freshly ground pepper

1 medium Golden Delicious apple, peeled, cored, and diced

1 cup low-sodium chicken broth

1 TB. apple cider vinegar

2 TB. amber agave nectar

1. In a large, heavy-bottomed pot over medium-high heat, fry bacon for 2 minutes or until just beginning to crisp. Using a slotted spoon, transfer bacon to a paper towel.

2. Immediately add collard greens to the pot, season with salt and pepper, and cook, stirring often, for 2 or 3 minutes or until greens begin to wilt.

3. Stir in Golden Delicious apple, and cook for 1 more minute.

4. Pour in low-sodium chicken broth, bring to a simmer, reduce heat to low, and cook, covered, for 15 to 18 minutes or until collards are tender.

5. Uncover and stir in apple cider vinegar and amber agave nectar. Cook for 2 more minutes or until piping hot.

6. Stir in bacon bits, taste to see if more salt and pepper are needed, and serve immediately.

SWEET SECRET

On June 2, 2011, collard greens were named the official vegetable of South Carolina. Governor Nikki Haley signed the law.

Sweet and Smoky Baked Beans

This version of the American classic side dish will become your standard go-to recipe after you taste the bold and smoky flavor of its sauce coupled with a hint of cayenne.

Yield:	Prep time:	Cook time:	Serving size:
2 cups	10 minutes	45 minutes	½ cup

1 TB. canola oil

1 medium yellow onion, finely chopped

1 (16-oz.) can pork and beans, drained

2 TB. Sugar-Free Ketchup (recipe in Chapter 10)

2 TB. granulated brown sugar substitute

1 tsp. Worcestershire sauce

½ tsp. mustard

¼ tsp. liquid smoke

Dash cayenne, or to taste

1. Preheat the oven to 350°F.

2. In a large, nonstick skillet over medium-high heat, heat canola oil. Add yellow onion, and cook, stirring often, for 5 minutes or until softened.

3. Stir in pork and beans, Sugar-Free Ketchup, granulated brown sugar substitute, Worcestershire sauce, mustard, liquid smoke, and cayenne. Cook for 2 minutes, stirring often, until heated through.

4. Transfer to a 1-quart casserole dish, and bake, stirring occasionally, for 35 to 40 minutes or until thickened and bubbly around the edges. Cool briefly before serving.

TASTY TIP

To cut back on sugar even further in recipes that call for pork and beans, look for canned beans that say "reduced sugar" or "no added sugar" and adjust your recipe by adding a touch more sugar substitute.

Chinese Stir-Fried Green Beans

A delightful side for any type of meat or poultry, this quick green bean dish features the vibrant flavor of ginger and the sweetness of soy and brown sugar.

Yield:	Prep time:	Cook time:	Serving size:
3 cups	10 minutes	15 minutes	$\frac{1}{2}$ cup

1 lb. green beans, ends trimmed

2 TB. peanut oil

1 clove garlic, minced

1 tsp. peeled and chopped fresh ginger

Salt

Freshly ground pepper

3 TB. soy sauce

2 TB. granulated brown sugar substitute

1 tsp. toasted sesame oil

1. Fill a large saucepan with salted water, and bring to a boil over high heat. Add green beans, and cook for 6 to 8 minutes or until fork-tender. Drain and set aside.

2. Meanwhile, in a large, nonstick skillet over medium-high heat, heat peanut oil. Add garlic and ginger, sprinkle with salt and pepper, and cook, stirring constantly, for 1 minute.

3. Add green beans, and stir-fry quickly to heat and coat with oil mixture.

4. In a small bowl, combine soy sauce and granulated brown sugar substitute. Pour over green beans, and stir-fry until piping hot.

5. Drizzle with toasted sesame oil, taste for additional seasoning, and serve immediately.

 HONEY DON'T!

Watch out for added sugar in commercial stir-fry sauces and other Chinese condiments. High-fructose corn syrup is often the main ingredient.

Bakery Favorites

From cookies to cakes to pies and cobblers, sugar plays a leading role in baked goods. But they can be made without sugar and without losing their delectable flavor and sweetness, as you'll find out in the chapters in Part 5. You're sure to find many of your favorites here, from chocolate-chip cookies to apple pie. Even better? Sugar-free sugar cookies! What more could a sweet tooth ask for?

In addition, you'll discover that many fruit-based desserts like pies and tarts can actually carry their own terrific sweet flavor without much tampering, as long as your ingredients are ripe and ready. Too often commercial bakers add sugar to compensate for the lack of flavor in such items, but thanks to perfectly sweet and delicious ingredients in these recipes, you won't need the extra sugar. So put on your baker's hat, and get out your rolling pin. It's time to bake!

Cookies, Bars, and Brownies

Chapter 16

In This Chapter

- Baking morsels of sweetness
- Making over favorite classics
- Opening up to flavorful ingredients
- Whipping up guilt-free treats

What more obvious place to find sugar in the kitchen than in the proverbial cookie jar? From chocolate chip to oatmeal to plain old-fashioned sugar cookies, is it possible to create satisfying sugar-free versions of all your favorites without feeling like something is definitely amiss?

The answer is a resounding "Yes!" as you'll see by the recipes in this chapter. You'll find batches of delicious treats that eliminate most of, if not all, the sugar and still taste wonderful.

Even More Flavor

Believe it or not, sometimes just cutting back a little on sugar content helps you enjoy and appreciate the other flavors and tastes going on in your food. Delicious flavors like peanut butter, cinnamon, lemon, and of course, chocolate burst forth with real taste without being sugar laden. You'll see what I mean when you discover that each recipe is more flavorful than the last.

It might be hard to pick a favorite, but why bother when you can make them all, guilt free? Go ahead and indulge while you enjoy the surprising results of sugar-free baking.

Sugar-Free Sugar Cookies

These sweet and satisfying cookies taste as good as the classic with the great flavor of vanilla and a hint of lemon.

Yield:	Prep time:	Cook time:	Serving size:
4 dozen cookies	20 minutes, plus 1 hour chill time	10 to 12 minutes	1 cookie

1 cup (2 sticks) unsalted butter, softened

1 cup granulated sugar substitute

1 large egg

2 tsp. vanilla extract

1 tsp. lemon juice

1½ cups all-purpose flour

1½ cups cake flour

1 tsp. baking soda

¼ tsp. salt

1. In a large bowl, and using an electric mixer on medium speed, beat together unsalted butter and granulated sugar substitute for 2 minutes or until light and fluffy.

2. Add egg, vanilla extract, and lemon juice, and beat for about 1 minute or until well combined.

3. In another large bowl, whisk together all-purpose flour, cake flour, baking soda, and salt.

4. Add flour mixture to butter mixture in 3 batches, beating on low speed until dough forms. Do not overbeat.

5. Transfer dough to a floured work surface. Form into 2 discs and wrap in plastic. Refrigerate for 1 hour.

6. Preheat the oven to 350°F. Line cookie sheets with parchment paper.

7. Roll out dough to ¼-inch thickness, cut into 2-inch circles or other shapes, and transfer to the prepared cookie sheet. Bake for 10 to 12 minutes or until bottoms are lightly golden.

8. Cool cookies on wire racks, and store in an airtight container.

TASTY TIP

Cake flour isn't just for baking cakes. Substituting fine cake flour for all-purpose flour in recipes like cookies can create a softer, melt-in-your-mouth consistency.

Chewy Chocolate-Chip Cookies

The sweet, rich flavor of brown sugar highlights these ultimate cookie favorites loaded with delicious semisweet chocolate.

Yield:	Prep time:	Cook time:	Serving size:
2 or 3 dozen cookies	10 minutes	9 to 12 minutes	1 cookie

1 cup granulated brown sugar substitute

1 cup (2 sticks) unsalted butter, melted

2 large eggs

1 TB. vanilla extract

2 cups all-purpose flour

1 tsp. baking soda

1 tsp. baking powder

¼ tsp. salt

2 cups sugar-free chocolate chips

1. Preheat the oven to 375°F. Line cookie sheets with parchment paper.

2. In a large bowl, stir together granulated brown sugar substitute and melted unsalted butter until blended.

3. Add eggs, 1 at a time, and vanilla extract. Beat by hand for 1 minute.

4. In another large bowl, whisk together all-purpose flour, baking soda, baking powder, and salt.

5. Add flour mixture to egg mixture in 2 batches, beating well to combine. Fold in sugar-free chocolate chips.

6. Drop by rounded tablespoons onto the prepared cookie sheets. Bake for 9 to 11 minutes or until lightly browned around the edges but still soft in the middle.

7. Cool cookies on wire racks, and store in an airtight container.

TASTY TIP

Look for reduced-sugar and sugar-free chocolate chips at health food stores or online. These are often sweetened with sugar alcohols or stevia instead of sugar.

Oatmeal Walnut Raisin Cookies

Studded with sweet raisins and crunchy walnuts, these cookies, full of the goodness of oats, will become a sugar-free favorite in your house.

Yield:	Prep time:	Cook time:	Serving size:
2 dozen cookies	15 minutes	10 to 12 minutes	1 cookie

1 cup (2 sticks) unsalted butter, softened

1 cup granulated sugar substitute

1 large egg

2 TB. amber agave nectar

1 tsp. vanilla extract

1 cup all-purpose flour

1 tsp. baking soda

½ tsp. ground cinnamon

1½ cups old-fashioned oats

¾ cup raisins

⅔ cup chopped walnuts

1. Preheat the oven to 350°F. Line cookie sheets with parchment paper.

2. In a large bowl, and using an electric mixer on medium speed, beat together unsalted butter and granulated sugar substitute for 2 minutes or until fluffy.

3. Add egg, amber agave nectar, and vanilla extract, and beat on low speed for 1 minute or until well combined.

4. In a medium bowl, whisk together all-purpose flour, baking soda, and cinnamon.

5. Add flour mixture to egg mixture in 2 batches, beating until just combined.

6. Stir in old-fashioned oats, raisins, and walnuts.

7. Drop by rounded tablespoons onto the prepared cookie sheets, and bake for 10 to 12 minutes or until lightly browned.

8. Cool cookies on wire racks, and store in an airtight container.

HONEY DON'T!

Do not use quick-cooking oats in place of old-fashioned oats in this recipe. They can overcook and add a mushy consistency to the finished cookie.

Chocolaty Peanut Butter Cookies

Who doesn't love the great combination of peanut butter and chocolate? Rich in chocolate and full of peanut flavor, you'll enjoy every bite of these yummy cookies.

Yield:	Prep time:	Cook time:	Serving size:
2 dozen cookies	20 minutes	7 to 9 minutes	1 cookie

¼ cup unsalted butter, softened

1 cup sugar-free creamy peanut butter

1 large egg

2 TB. light agave nectar

1 tsp. vanilla extract

1 cup granulated sugar substitute

1½ cups all-purpose flour

½ tsp. baking soda

¼ tsp. salt

⅔ cup sugar-free dark chocolate pieces

1. Preheat the oven to 350°F. Line cookie sheets with parchment paper.

2. In a large bowl, and using an electric mixer on medium speed, beat together unsalted butter and sugar-free peanut butter for 2 minutes or until well combined.

3. Add egg, light agave nectar, and vanilla extract, and beat for 1 minute.

4. Add granulated sugar substitute, and beat on medium speed for 1 minute or until well blended.

5. In another large bowl, whisk together all-purpose flour, baking soda, and salt.

6. Add flour mixture to peanut butter mixture in 2 batches, beating just until blended.

7. Stir in sugar-free dark chocolate pieces.

8. Form tablespoons of dough into balls, and place 2 inches apart on the prepared cookie sheets. Flatten slightly with a fork, and bake for 7 to 9 minutes or until edges are golden.

9. Cool cookies on wire racks, and store in an airtight container.

HONEY DON'T!

Refrain from using natural peanut butter in this recipe. It can separate during baking and make your cookies greasy.

Cinnamon Snickerdoodles

Fragrant and tasty ground cinnamon highlights these delicious cookies that are full of old-fashioned flavor.

Yield:	Prep time:	Cook time:	Serving size:
1 dozen cookies	15 minutes	7 to 9 minutes	1 cookie

1 cup (2 sticks) unsalted butter, softened

1½ cups plus 2 TB. granulated sugar substitute

2 large eggs

1 tsp. vanilla extract

2¾ cups all-purpose flour

1 tsp. baking soda

2 tsp. *cream of tartar*

1 TB. ground cinnamon

1. Preheat the oven to 375°F. Line a cookie sheet with parchment paper.

2. In a large bowl, and using an electric mixer on medium-high speed, beat together unsalted butter and 1½ cups granulated sugar substitute for 3 minutes or until well blended.

3. Add eggs, 1 at a time, and vanilla extract, and beat for 1 minute.

4. In another large bowl, whisk together all-purpose flour, baking soda, and cream of tartar.

5. Add flour mixture to butter mixture in 3 batches, beating well to combine.

6. In a small bowl, stir together remaining 2 tablespoons granulated sugar substitute and cinnamon.

7. Form dough into walnut-size balls, and roll in cinnamon-sugar mixture. Place cookies 2 inches apart on the prepared cookie sheet, and bake for 7 to 10 minutes or until just lightly brown.

8. Cool cookies on wire racks and store in an airtight container.

DEFINITION

Cream of tartar is an acidic powder used in cooking to activate baking soda, stabilize egg whites, and prevent crystallization of sugar syrups.

Perfect Pumpkin Bars

Moist, rich, and full of autumn spice flavors, these bars, topped with sweet crunchy pecans, will delight your taste buds.

Yield:	Prep time:	Cook time:	Serving size:
18 bars	12 minutes	20 to 25 minutes	1 bar

1 cup canned unsweetened pumpkin purée

2 large eggs

¼ cup unsalted butter, melted

¾ cup amber agave nectar

½ tsp. vanilla extract

1¾ cups all-purpose flour

1 tsp. baking powder

1 tsp. baking soda

¾ tsp. salt

½ tsp. ground cinnamon

½ tsp. ground nutmeg

⅛ tsp. ground cloves

¼ cup chopped pecans

1. Preheat the oven to 325°F. Grease and flour a 9×9-inch-square baking pan.

2. In a large bowl, and using an electric mixer on low speed, beat together pumpkin purée and eggs.

3. Add unsalted butter, amber agave nectar, and vanilla extract, and beat for 30 seconds or until well combined.

4. In another large bowl, whisk together all-purpose flour, baking powder, baking soda, salt, cinnamon, nutmeg, and cloves.

5. Add flour mixture to pumpkin mixture in 2 batches, and beat on medium speed just until combined. Pour batter into the prepared baking pan, and spread evenly to the edges. Sprinkle pecans over the top.

6. Bake for 20 to 25 minutes or until a toothpick inserted in the center comes out clean and edges are lightly browned.

7. Cool completely before cutting and removing from the pan.

TASTY TIP

To keep unused chopped nuts fresh, place them in an airtight zipper-lock bag and store in the freezer.

Luscious Lemon Bars

Rich, creamy, and full of the delicious tang of fresh lemon, these bars, surrounded by a sweet and tender crust, will satisfy the biggest sweet tooth around.

Yield:	Prep time:	Cook time:	Serving size:
16 bars	10 minutes	30 to 35 minutes	1 bar

1⅓ cups all-purpose flour

2 TB. plus 1¼ cups granulated sugar substitute

Pinch salt

6 TB. unsalted butter, diced

½ cup light cream

3 large eggs

1 large egg yolk

½ cup fresh lemon juice

1 TB. lemon zest

1. Preheat the oven to 350°F. Coat an 8- or 9-inch-square baking pan with cooking spray.

2. In a medium bowl, combine 1 cup all-purpose flour, 2 tablespoons granulated sugar substitute, and salt.

3. Add unsalted butter, and, using a pastry blender or fork, combine into a coarse meal.

4. Press mixture into the bottom of the prepared baking pan, and bake for 15 to 20 minutes or until crust is lightly browned.

5. Meanwhile, in a medium bowl, whisk together light cream, eggs, and egg yolk. Add remaining ⅓ cup all-purpose flour and 1¼ cups granulated sugar substitute, and whisk to combine. Stir in lemon juice and lemon zest, and pour into hot crust.

6. Bake for 12 to 15 minutes or until center is set and edges are lightly golden.

7. Cool completely before slicing and removing from the pan.

TASTY TIP

To get the most juice out of your lemon, heat it in the microwave for 5 to 10 seconds before cutting and squeezing it.

Deep, Dark Chocolate Brownies

Decadently flavored with extra-dark chocolate, these chewy and delicious brownies are a dream come true for any chocolate fan.

Yield:	Prep time:	Cook time:	Serving size:
16 brownies	20 minutes	22 to 28 minutes	1 brownie

½ cup (1 stick) unsalted butter

¼ cup unsweetened cocoa powder

¼ cup sugar-free dark chocolate (70 percent cacao), chopped

2 large eggs

1 cup granulated sugar substitute

¾ cup all-purpose flour

½ tsp. baking soda

⅛ tsp. salt

¼ cup buttermilk

1. Preheat the oven to 350°F. Grease and flour an 8-inch-square baking pan.

2. In a small saucepan over low heat, melt unsalted butter, unsweetened cocoa powder, and sugar-free dark chocolate, whisking to combine. Set aside to cool slightly.

3. In a large bowl, whisk together eggs and granulated sugar substitute. Slowly add chocolate mixture, whisking constantly until well blended.

4. In another large bowl, whisk together all-purpose flour, baking soda, and salt.

5. Add flour mixture to wet mixture, and beat to combine.

6. Pour in buttermilk, and beat by hand for 1 minute.

7. Pour into the prepared baking pan, smooth out to the edges, and bake for 22 to 28 minutes or until a toothpick inserted 1 inch from the middle comes out clean.

8. Cool brownies before cutting and removing from the pan.

SWEET SECRET

When looking for deep chocolate flavor, select chocolate bars that boast more than 60 percent cacao, the amount of actual cocoa essence in the product. Darker chocolate also generally contains less added sugar.

Chocolate Pecan Agave Brownies

Tasty pecans and a hint of cinnamon complement light and amber agave sweeteners in these moist and flavorful brownies made with healthy whole-wheat flour.

Yield:	Prep time:	Cook time:	Serving size:
24 brownies	15 minutes	35 to 40 minutes	1 or 2 brownies

1 cup whole-wheat flour

½ cup unsweetened cocoa powder

½ tsp. salt

½ tsp. baking soda

¼ tsp. ground cinnamon

4 large eggs

⅔ cup light agave nectar

⅔ cup amber agave nectar

2 tsp. vanilla extract

1 cup (2 sticks) unsalted butter, melted

1 cup chopped pecans

1. Preheat the oven to 350°F. Lightly coat a 13×9-inch baking pan with cooking spray.

2. In a medium bowl, whisk together whole-wheat flour, cocoa powder, salt, baking soda, and cinnamon.

3. In a large bowl, and using an electric mixer on high speed, beat eggs until light and fluffy. Beat in light agave nectar, amber agave nectar, and vanilla extract, and continue to beat for 2 minutes on medium speed. Slowly beat in melted unsalted butter until well combined.

4. Add dry ingredients to egg mixture in 2 batches, beating just to combine each time. Stir in pecans.

5. Transfer to prepared pan, spread evenly, and bake for 35 to 40 minutes or until edges begin to pull away from the pan and top becomes crackly.

6. Cool completely on a wire rack before cutting and serving.

TASTY TIP

Freeze 1 or 2 brownies in sandwich bags, stash a bag in your lunchbox in the morning, and by noon, the brownies will be defrosted and ready to eat!

Chewy Butterscotch Blondies

You'll love these moist and chewy cousins to brownies, brimming with delicious brown sugar, buttery flavor, and white chocolate.

Yield:	Prep time:	Cook time:	Serving size:
36 blondies	10 minutes	25 to 30 minutes	1 blondie

1 cup (2 sticks) unsalted butter, softened

¾ cup granulated brown sugar substitute

1 TB. vanilla extract

2 large eggs

2 cups all-purpose flour

1 tsp. baking powder

¼ tsp. salt

1½ cups sugar-free white chocolate chips

½ cup chopped nuts (optional)

1. Preheat the oven to 350°F. Lightly spray a 13×9-inch baking pan with cooking spray.

2. In a large bowl, and using an electric mixer on medium-high speed, beat together unsalted butter and granulated brown sugar substitute for 2 minutes or until well combined.

3. Add vanilla extract and eggs, and beat for 1 more minute.

4. In another large bowl, whisk together all-purpose flour, baking powder, and salt.

5. Add flour mixture to wet mixture in 2 batches, stirring just to combine.

6. Stir in sugar-free white chocolate chips and nuts (if using).

7. Transfer to the prepared baking pan, spread to the edges, and bake for 25 to 30 minutes or until a toothpick inserted 1 inch from the center comes out clean.

8. Cool blondies completely before cutting and removing from the pan.

SWEET SECRET

White chocolate isn't really chocolate at all. It contains no chocolate solids from chocolate liquor—only cocoa butter (which contains little chocolate flavor) combined with sugar, milk, and other flavorings. Be sure to opt for the sugar-free version.

Classic Cakes, Cupcakes, and Cheesecakes

In This Chapter

- Baking layers of sweet, guilt-free goodness
- Classic makeovers to enjoy
- Amazing sugar-free cupcakes
- Rich and creamy cheesecakes

If you often pass on delicious desserts like layer cakes, snack cakes, cupcakes, and cheesecakes because you know the sugar content is far beyond what you're allowed, you'll love this chapter.

In the following pages, I share delicious cake recipes guaranteed not to disappoint. From basic yellow and chocolate cakes, to exceptionally creamy and rich cheesecakes, you'll find it all here, no matter what the occasion. Even better, some are so easy that they don't even require baking, and many make use of prepared ingredients that are a snap to find and even quicker to use.

Incredible Cupcakes

If cupcakes are more your style, you'll find what you're after here. I give you a standard vanilla cupcake recipe that's moist and delicious. If red velvet cupcakes are your favorite, I have you covered here, too, with a huge reduction in added sugar. Be sure to try the Triple-Chocolate Mini Cupcakes. They'll send any chocoholic to the moon and back after just one bite.

Cheesecake Lovers Unite!

No longer is rich, delectable cheesecake off the menu, thanks to the amazingly delicious recipes in this chapter. From simple, classic creations to marvelous no-bake versions, they're all here to enjoy.

Easy Yellow Layer Cake

When you're looking for a versatile yellow cake recipe, look no further than this delicious, not-too-sweet version with the light taste of vanilla and the rich taste of real butter.

Yield:	Prep time:	Cook time:	Serving size:
1 (8-inch) layer cake	15 minutes	35 to 40 minutes	$\frac{1}{12}$ of cake

3 cups cake flour

1 cup granulated sugar substitute

2 tsp. baking powder

$\frac{1}{2}$ tsp. baking soda

$1\frac{1}{4}$ cups unsalted butter, diced

$1\frac{1}{4}$ cups buttermilk

2 large eggs, beaten

2 tsp. vanilla extract

1. Preheat the oven to 350°F. Butter and flour 2 (8-inch) cake pans.

2. In a large bowl, whisk together cake flour, granulated sugar substitute, baking powder, and baking soda.

3. Add unsalted butter, and using an electric mixer on low speed, beat together to a crumblike consistency. Add $\frac{1}{4}$ cup buttermilk, and beat well to combine.

4. In a small bowl, combine remaining 1 cup buttermilk, eggs, and vanilla extract. Add to flour mixture in 2 batches, beating well each time until smooth and well blended.

5. Divide batter between the prepared pans, and bake for 35 to 40 minutes or until a toothpick inserted in the center comes out clean.

6. Cool on wire racks, remove cakes from the pans, and frost as desired.

TASTY TIP

Freeze unfrosted cake layers by individually wrapping cooled cakes securely in plastic wrap and placing in a large freezer bag. Allow to defrost in the refrigerator before using.

Rich Chocolate Layer Cake

Everybody needs a great basic chocolate cake recipe. You'll love the deep chocolate flavor that's not overly sweet.

Yield:	Prep time:	Cook time:	Serving size:
1 (8-inch) layer cake	20 minutes	35 to 40 minutes	$\frac{1}{12}$ of cake

¾ cup unsalted butter, softened	1 cup unsweetened cocoa powder
1½ cups granulated sugar substitute	1 tsp. baking powder
3 large eggs	1 tsp. baking soda
1 tsp. vanilla extract	2 TB. cold coffee
2½ cups all-purpose flour	1½ cups whole or reduced-fat milk

1. Preheat the oven to 350°F. Butter and flour 2 (8-inch) cake pans.

2. In a large bowl, and using an electric mixer on medium-high speed, beat together unsalted butter and granulated sugar substitute for 2 minutes or until creamy. Beat in eggs 1 at a time, add vanilla extract, and beat to combine.

3. In a medium bowl, whisk together all-purpose flour, cocoa powder, baking powder, and baking soda. Add to egg mixture in 2 batches, and beat on medium speed until well combined.

4. Add cold coffee and whole milk, and beat on low speed (batter will be thin) until smooth and well combined.

5. Divide batter between the prepared pans, and bake for 35 to 40 minutes or until a toothpick inserted in the center comes out clean.

6. Cool on wire racks, remove cakes from the pans, and frost as desired.

TASTY TIP

A small amount of coffee in chocolate desserts brings out more of the true chocolate flavor—and doesn't make the whole dish taste like coffee.

Easy One-Layer Carrot Cake

This moist and delicious version of the popular bakery creation gets a healthy make-over with sweet golden raisins, crunchy walnuts, and even a tasty sugar-free cream cheese frosting.

Yield:	Prep time:	Cook time:	Serving size:
1 (8-inch) square cake	25 minutes	30 to 40 minutes	$\frac{1}{16}$ of cake

2 large eggs

$\frac{3}{4}$ cup canola oil

$1\frac{1}{2}$ cups granulated sugar substitute

1 cup all-purpose flour

1 tsp. baking soda

1 tsp. ground cinnamon

$\frac{1}{2}$ tsp. ground ginger

$\frac{1}{2}$ tsp. salt

1 cup grated carrots

$\frac{1}{2}$ cup golden raisins

$\frac{1}{2}$ cup chopped walnuts

1 (3-oz.) pkg. cream cheese, softened

2 tsp. milk

$\frac{1}{2}$ tsp. lemon juice

1. Preheat the oven to 350°F. Lightly coat an 8-inch-square baking pan with cooking spray.

2. In a medium bowl, and using an electric mixer on medium speed, beat together eggs, canola oil, and $\frac{3}{4}$ cup granulated sugar substitute for 2 minutes.

3. In another medium bowl, whisk together all-purpose flour, baking soda, cinnamon, ginger, and salt.

4. Add $\frac{1}{2}$ of flour mixture to egg mixture, and beat on low speed until well combined. Add remaining flour mixture, and beat on medium speed for 2 minutes.

5. Stir in carrots, golden raisins, and walnuts.

6. Pour batter into the prepared pan, and bake for 30 to 40 minutes or until a toothpick inserted in the center comes out clean and edges of cake are lightly browned. Cool on a wire rack.

7. Meanwhile, in a medium bowl, and using an electric mixer on medium speed, beat together cream cheese, remaining $\frac{3}{4}$ cup granulated sugar substitute, milk, and lemon juice until very smooth. Chill until ready to use.

8. When cake is completely cooled, decoratively spread frosting on top, slice, and serve.

TASTY TIP

Carrots contain a good amount of natural sweetness, so cakes, muffins, and cookies made with them often require less sugar.

Velvety Cream Cheese Pound Cake

Rich and delicious, this classic cake can be sliced and served in all different ways, but you might just want to savor its sweet and smooth flavor all on its own.

Yield:	Prep time:	Cook time:	Serving size:
12 slices	15 minutes	50 to 55 minutes	1 slice

¾ cup (1½ sticks) unsalted butter, softened

1 (3-oz.) pkg. cream cheese, softened

1½ cups granulated sugar substitute

1½ cups all-purpose flour

½ tsp. salt

1 tsp. baking powder

5 large eggs

1 tsp. vanilla extract

1. Preheat the oven to 350°F. Lightly coat a 9×5-inch loaf pan with cooking spray.

2. In a large bowl, and using an electric mixer on high speed, beat together unsalted butter and cream cheese until light and fluffy.

3. Beat in granulated sugar substitute until well combined.

4. In a medium bowl, whisk together all-purpose flour, salt, and baking powder. Add to butter mixture in 2 batches, beating well each time. Mixture will be thick.

5. Beat in eggs, 1 at a time, until well incorporated. Beat in vanilla extract.

6. Spoon batter into prepared loaf pan, and bake for 50 to 55 minutes or until a toothpick inserted in the center comes out clean and top is lightly golden.

7. Cool for 10 minutes before turning cake out of the pan and cooling completely on a wire rack. Slice and serve.

SWEET SECRET

Although many variations exist today, traditional pound cake always consisted of 1 pound each butter, sugar, flour, and eggs.

Maple Spice Snack Cake

When you're looking for just a little something sweet, you'll be delighted with this easy-to-make spice cake featuring the flavors of maple, cinnamon, and ginger and a hint of fruity sweetness from natural applesauce.

Yield:	Prep time:	Cook time:	Serving size:
1 (8-inch) square cake	15 minutes	25 to 30 minutes	$\frac{1}{16}$ of cake

$\frac{1}{2}$ cup (1 stick) unsalted butter, softened

$\frac{1}{4}$ cup amber agave nectar

2 large eggs

1 tsp. vanilla extract

1 TB. pure maple syrup

$\frac{1}{2}$ cup unsweetened applesauce

1 cup granulated sugar substitute

1 cup all-purpose flour

1 tsp. baking powder

$\frac{1}{2}$ tsp. baking soda

$1\frac{1}{2}$ tsp. ground cinnamon

$\frac{1}{2}$ tsp. ground ginger

1. Preheat the oven to 350°F. Lightly coat an 8-inch-square baking pan with cooking spray.

2. In a medium bowl, and using an electric mixer on medium speed, beat together unsalted butter and amber agave nectar until well combined.

3. Beat in eggs 1 at a time. Add vanilla extract, pure maple syrup, and applesauce, and beat for 1 minute.

4. In another medium bowl, whisk together granulated sugar substitute, all-purpose flour, baking powder, baking soda, cinnamon, and ginger.

5. Add flour mixture to wet mixture in 2 batches, beating well to combine after each addition.

6. Spread batter evenly in the prepared pan, and bake for 25 to 30 minutes or until a toothpick inserted in the center comes out clean.

7. Cool on a wire rack before cutting and serving.

SWEET SECRET

Native Americans were the first to tap maple trees for the spring sap and reduce it into a syrup—a practice they taught the first European settlers when they arrived.

Vanilla Cupcakes with Strawberry Frosting

One bite of these sugar-free cupcakes and you'll be in heaven. Full of dense, moist vanilla flavor with a light, satisfying strawberry frosting, you'll be licking your fingers in no time.

Yield:	Prep time:	Cook time:	Serving size:
18 cupcakes	20 mInutes	12 to 15 minutes	1 cupcake

¾ cup unsalted butter, softened

1 cup granulated sugar substitute

3 large eggs

2 tsp. vanilla extract

¾ cup buttermilk

2¾ cups cake flour

2 tsp. baking powder

¾ tsp. baking soda

¼ tsp. salt

1 (8-oz.) tub sugar-free vanilla frosting

1 tsp. strawberry extract

1 cup diced fresh strawberries

1. Preheat the oven to 350°F. Line 18 muffin cups with paper liners.

2. In a large bowl, and using an electric mixer on medium-high speed, beat together unsalted butter and granulated sugar substitute for 2 minutes or until creamy. Beat in eggs 1 at a time.

3. Add vanilla extract and buttermilk, and beat for 1 minute.

4. In another large bowl, whisk together cake flour, baking powder, baking soda, and salt. Add to buttermilk mixture in 2 batches, beating well each time to combine.

5. Divide batter among 18 muffin cups, and bake for 12 to 15 minutes or until a toothpick inserted in the center comes out clean.

6. Cool for 10 minutes, and transfer cupcakes to a wire rack to cool completely.

7. Meanwhile, in a medium bowl, stir together sugar-free vanilla frosting, strawberry extract, and diced strawberries.

8. When cupcakes are cool, decoratively spread frosting on top, and serve. Keep any leftovers refrigerated.

Red Velvet Cupcakes

These popular bakery offerings are deliciously adapted for a sugar-free diet but retain their signature deep cocoa flavor and are topped with a sweet and creamy icing.

Yield:	Prep time:	Cook time:	Serving size:
12 cupcakes	20 minutes	12 to 15 minutes	1 cupcake

3 TB. unsweetened cocoa powder

1½ TB. red food coloring

1½ tsp. vanilla extract

½ cup unsalted butter, softened

⅝ cup plus 3 TB. granulated sugar substitute

2 large egg yolks, beaten

2 large egg whites

½ cup buttermilk

1 tsp. white vinegar

¼ tsp. salt

1 cup plus 2 TB. cake flour

½ tsp. baking powder

¾ tsp. baking soda

1 (8-oz.) pkg. cream cheese, softened

2 TB. cup milk

1. Preheat the oven to 350°F. Line 12 muffin cups with paper liners.

2. In a small bowl, whisk together cocoa powder, red food coloring, and 1 teaspoon vanilla extract. Set aside.

3. In a large bowl, and using an electric mixer on medium speed, beat together ¼ cup unsalted butter and ⅝ cup granulated sugar substitute until creamy. Beat in egg yolks for 1 minute until smooth.

4. In another large bowl, and using an electric mixer with clean beaters on high speed, beat egg whites until soft peaks form. Set aside.

5. In a small bowl, combine buttermilk, white vinegar, and salt.

6. In another large bowl, whisk together cake flour, baking powder, and baking soda. Alternating between buttermilk mixture and flour mixture, beat into butter mixture just to combine.

7. Scrape in cocoa mixture, and beat for 1 more minute.

8. Fold in beaten egg whites, maintaining as much volume as possible.

9. Divide batter among 12 muffin cups, and bake for 12 to 15 minutes or until a toothpick inserted in the center comes out clean. Cool for 5 minutes, and transfer to a wire rack to cool completely.

10. Meanwhile, in a medium bowl and using an electric mixer on medium-high speed, beat together cream cheese, remaining ¼ cup unsalted butter, remaining ½ teaspoon vanilla extract, remaining 3 tablespoons granulated sugar substitute, and milk until smooth and creamy.

11. When cupcakes are cool, decoratively spread frosting on top, and serve. Keep any leftovers refrigerated.

SWEET SECRET

When added to red velvet cake batter, the combination of buttermilk and vinegar enhances the red color of the cocoa and food coloring.

Triple-Chocolate Mini Cupcakes

Triple your chocolate pleasure! These dense and delicious mini cakes are drizzled with melted chocolate and topped off with a light chocolate-flavored whipped cream.

Yield:	Prep time:	Cook time:	Serving size:
12 to 18 mini cupcakes	30 minutes	20 to 30 minutes	1 cupcake

1 TB. cornstarch

2 tsp. unsweetened cocoa powder

6 oz. bittersweet chocolate, chopped

2 TB. unsalted butter, diced

3 TB. sour cream

2 cups granulated sugar substitute

3 large egg yolks

1 TB. water

4 large egg whites

4 oz. sugar-free chocolate, chopped and melted

½ batch Luscious Chocolate Whipped Cream (recipe in Chapter 20)

1. Preheat the oven to 250°F. Line 12 to 18 mini muffin cups with paper liners.

2. In a small bowl, whisk together cornstarch and cocoa powder. Set aside.

3. In the top of a double boiler over medium heat, combine bittersweet chocolate, unsalted butter, and sour cream. Cook, stirring often, until melted and smooth. Remove from heat, and set aside.

4. In a medium bowl, and using an electric mixer on medium speed, beat together granulated sugar substitute, egg yolks, and water until light and thickened.

5. In another medium bowl, and using an electric mixer with clean beaters on high speed, beat egg whites until soft peaks form.

6. Add cocoa powder mixture to warm chocolate mixture, and whisk well. Slowly add egg yolk mixture, whisking constantly until well combined and smooth.

7. Fold in egg whites, trying to maintain as much volume as necessary.

8. Spoon into cupcake cups, and bake for 20 to 30 minutes or until a toothpick inserted in the center comes out clean. Cool in pans on a wire rack for 10 minutes, and transfer to a serving platter to cool completely.

9. Drizzle a little melted sugar-free chocolate over each cake, and refrigerate for 20 minutes.

10. Just before serving, dollop or decoratively pipe Luscious Chocolate Whipped Cream on each cake, and serve immediately. Keep any leftovers refrigerated.

TASTY TIP

You can find disposable pastry piping bags at most bakery shops and online. A medium-size star tip is ideal for decorative piping. A plastic zipper-lock bag with the corner snipped off also works well if you don't want the trouble and expense of the piping bag and tip.

New York–Style Cheesecake

Fans of authentic New York cheesecake will relish this recipe with its rich and creamy taste, sweet graham cracker crust, and faint hint of lemon.

Yield:	Prep time:	Cook time:	Serving size:
1 (10-inch) cheesecake	15 minutes, plus 4 hours chill time	2 hours, 10 minutes	$\frac{1}{16}$ of cake

1¼ cups sugar-free graham cracker crumbs

¼ cup plus 1⅔ cups granulated sugar substitute

¼ cup unsalted butter, melted

5 (8-oz.) pkg. cream cheese, softened

3 TB. all-purpose flour

6 large eggs, beaten

1 tsp. vanilla extract

1 tsp. lemon juice

⅓ cup heavy cream

1. Preheat the oven to 475°F. Lightly coat a 10-inch springform pan with cooking spray, and wrap the outside with aluminum foil to seal. Place on a baking sheet.

2. In a small bowl, stir together sugar-free graham cracker crumbs, ¼ cup granulated sugar substitute, and unsalted butter until combined. Press into the bottom of the springform pan to create a crust.

3. In a large bowl, and using an electric mixer on medium-high, beat together cream cheese, remaining 1⅔ cups granulated sugar substitute, and all-purpose flour until smooth and creamy.

4. Beat in eggs 1 at a time. Add vanilla extract, lemon juice, and heavy cream, and beat for about 2 minutes or until mixture is well combined.

5. Pour batter over crust, and bake for 10 minutes. Immediately reduce heat to 200°F, and bake for about 1 hour or until somewhat firm.

6. Turn off the oven, and leave cheesecake inside with the door closed for 1 hour.

7. Cool for 20 minutes before refrigerating for at least 4 hours or overnight.

8. Slice, and serve well chilled.

SWEET SECRET

New York–style cheesecake, which often includes heavy cream and sometimes sour cream, is typically lightened in texture from the addition of eggs and usually has a hallmark graham cracker crust.

Crustless Pumpkin Cheesecake

A popular flavor for holiday entertaining, this pumpkin cheesecake is full of wonderfully fragrant spices and gets a nice flavor tang from low-fat yogurt.

Yield:	Prep time:	Cook time:	Serving size:
1 (9-inch) cheesecake	15 minutes, plus 4 hours chill time	1 hour, 10 minutes	1/16 of cake

3 (8-oz.) pkg. cream cheese, softened

1/3 cup granulated brown sugar substitute

3 large eggs

1 (15-oz.) can unsweetened pumpkin purée

1/2 cup low-fat plain yogurt

2 TB. all-purpose flour

1 1/2 tsp. ground cinnamon

1 tsp. ground ginger

1 tsp. vanilla extract

1. Preheat the oven to 350°F. Lightly coat a 9-inch springform pan with cooking spray, and wrap the outside with aluminum foil to seal. Place on a baking sheet.

2. In a large bowl, and using an electric mixer on medium-high speed, beat cream cheese and granulated brown sugar substitute until well combined.

3. Beat in eggs 1 at a time. Add pumpkin purée, low-fat yogurt, all-purpose flour, cinnamon, ginger, and vanilla extract, and beat for 2 minutes or until smooth and creamy.

4. Pour into the prepared pan, and bake for about 1 hour, 10 minutes or until outer rim is puffy and a bit golden but center is still a little jiggly.

5. Cool on a wire rack for 30 minutes. Carefully run a sharp paring knife around the upper edge of the pan, but do not remove cheesecake.

6. Refrigerate for at least 4 hours or up to 2 days.

7. Cut into slices using a large sharp knife dipped in hot water, and serve. Keep refrigerated or freeze.

TASTY TIP

Baked cheesecakes freeze extremely well and can be made at least a month before the holidays to save time later. You can even preslice the cake before freezing.

Chocolate Grasshopper Cheesecake

This tasty and refreshing dessert is easy to make and will delight everyone with its subtle minty flavor and not-too-sweet chocolate cookie crust and drizzle.

Yield:	Prep time:	Cook time:	Serving size:
1 (8-inch) cheesecake	15 minutes, plus 2 hours chill time	30 minutes	$\frac{1}{8}$ of cake

4 (3-oz.) pkg. cream cheese, softened

$\frac{1}{3}$ cup granulated sugar substitute

2 large eggs

1 tsp. vanilla extract

$\frac{1}{4}$ tsp. mint extract

2 drops green food coloring

1 (8-in.) sugar-free chocolate cookie crumb piecrust

$\frac{1}{2}$ cup sugar-free hot fudge sauce, warmed

1. Preheat the oven to 350°F.

2. In a large bowl, and using an electric mixer on medium speed, beat together cream cheese and granulated sugar substitute until smooth.

3. Beat in eggs 1 at a time. Add vanilla extract, mint extract, and green food coloring, and beat on medium-high speed for 1 minute.

4. Pour mixture into sugar-free chocolate cookie crumb piecrust, and bake for about 30 minutes or until filling is firm to the touch.

5. Refrigerate for at least 2 hours before slicing and serving with sugar-free hot fudge drizzled on top.

SWEET SECRET

The grasshopper pie gets its name from the cocktail of the same name, a bright green drink thanks to the addition of crème de menthe. Chocolate was never an original ingredient, but its natural pairing didn't take long to become embraced.

Amazing No-Bake Lemon Cheesecake

For a fast and refreshing dessert, nothing beats this impressive creamy and slightly tart lemon cheesecake that can be made with just about any gelatin flavor you choose.

Yield:	Prep time:	Serving size:
1 (8-inch) cheesecake	15 minutes, plus 4 hours chill time	$\frac{1}{8}$ of cake

1 (6-oz.) pkg. sugar-free lemon gelatin

1 cup boiling water

1 (8-oz.) pkg. cream cheese, softened

1 tsp. vanilla extract

1 cup frozen sugar-free nondairy whipped topping, thawed

1 (8-in.) sugar-free graham cracker or cookie crumb piecrust

1. In a small saucepan, dissolve sugar-free lemon gelatin in boiling water, stirring occasionally. Set aside to cool and thicken, but not to set.

2. In a large bowl, and using an electric mixer on medium speed, beat cream cheese and vanilla extract until smooth. Add thickened lemon gelatin, and beat until well combined.

3. Fold in sugar-free whipped topping, maintaining as much volume as possible.

4. Pour into sugar-free graham cracker piecrust, and smooth over top.

5. Refrigerate for at least 4 hours or overnight before slicing and serving.

TASTY TIP

Keep sugar-free packages of gelatin and pudding in your pantry for making quick desserts. Pie fillings, quick cheesecakes, and gelatin fruit molds all use these handy ingredients.

Pies, Tarts, and Cobblers

Chapter 18

In This Chapter

- Rolling out classic American pies
- Taste bud–tempting tarts
- Baking the best of old-fashioned crisps and cobblers
- Reducing added sugar while increasing flavor

Pies are just about as American as dessert can get. Who could imagine a Thanksgiving dinner without pumpkin pie to finish, or a fabulous apple pie, warm and fragrant straight from the oven when apples are plentiful? Unfortunately, many of our classic favorites contain a lot of added and unwanted sugar.

In this chapter, I show you how easy it is to adapt old-fashioned favorites to sugar-free versions, often with a little added twist to enhance the outcome. The results are perfect, and you'll wonder why you needed all that sugar in the first place.

Flavor Combos Rule

With selections like Creamy Chocolate Peanut Butter Pie or Cherry and Peach Cobbler, you'll love the way the flavor combos in these recipes complement each other and add excitement—not sugar—for your awaiting taste buds.

If pie-baking is your thing, you've definitely come to the right place. So let's get baking some of America's time-honored and super-delicious desserts.

Basic Sugar-Free Piecrust

With its wonderfully flaky texture and buttery flavor, this will become your go-to piecrust recipe for everything from apple to lemon meringue pies. Feel free to double for two-crusted pie recipes.

Yield:	Prep time:	Cook time:	Serving size:
1 (9-inch) crust	10 minutes, plus 15 minutes chill time	6 to 8 minutes	$\frac{1}{8}$ of crust

1 cup all-purpose flour, plus more for rolling

1 TB. granulated sugar substitute

$\frac{1}{2}$ tsp. salt

$\frac{1}{3}$ cup unsalted butter, diced

2 TB. cold water

1. In a medium bowl, whisk together all-purpose flour, granulated sugar substitute, and salt.

2. Add unsalted butter, and using a fork or pastry blender, mix into flour to create a sandy consistency.

3. Add cold water, 1 tablespoon at a time, gathering dough into a ball. Flatten slightly, wrap in plastic wrap, and refrigerate for 15 minutes.

4. Preheat the oven to 350°F.

5. Turn out dough onto a floured surface, and roll to fit a 9-inch pie pan, using extra flour as necessary to keep dough from sticking.

6. Transfer crust to the pie pan, crimp edges, and bake for 6 to 8 minutes or to desired doneness. Alternatively, chill rolled-out dough in the pie pan to fill and bake later.

TASTY TIP

Commercial frozen unbaked pie shells as well as refrigerated piecrusts generally don't contain sugar so they're fine to use. However, if you prefer a slightly sweet taste to your piecrust, making your own with a sugar substitute is recommended.

Healthy Holiday Pumpkin Pie

Deliciously low in fat as well as sugar, this must-have holiday pie, flavorful and fragrant with the aroma of autumn spice, will become your go-to recipe.

Yield:	Prep time:	Cook time:	Serving size:
1 (9-inch) pie	10 minutes	35 to 40 minutes	⅛ of pie

1 (15-oz.) can unsweetened pumpkin purée

½ cup granulated sugar substitute

¼ cup granulated brown sugar substitute

½ tsp. ground cinnamon

1½ tsp. pumpkin pie spice

Pinch salt

1 large egg

⅔ cup regular or fat-free half-and-half

1 TB. vanilla extract

2 TB. cornstarch

1 Basic Sugar-Free Piecrust (recipe in earlier in this chapter), unbaked

1. Preheat the oven to 400°F.

2. In a large bowl, and using an electric mixer on medium speed, beat together pumpkin purée, granulated sugar substitute, granulated brown sugar substitute, cinnamon, pumpkin pie spice, and salt until well combined.

3. Beat in egg.

4. In a small bowl, stir together half-and-half, vanilla extract, and cornstarch until smooth. Pour into pumpkin mixture, and beat on medium-low speed for 1 minute or until well combined.

5. Roll out Basic Sugar-Free Piecrust, place in a pie pan, and crimp edges. Pour filling into crust, and bake for 35 to 40 minutes or until crust is golden and a sharp knife tip inserted in the center comes out clean.

6. Cool on a wire rack before slicing and serving.

SWEET SECRET

The world's largest pumpkin pie on record was created on September 25, 2010, at the New Bremen, Ohio, Pumpkinfest. It had a diameter of 20 feet and weighed in at a little under 2 tons.

Lemon-Lime Meringue Pie

Doubly sweet and tart at the same time, you'll relish the tang of fresh lemon and lime in a smooth-as-silk filling topped with a light airy meringue.

Yield:	Prep time:	Cook time:	Serving size:
1 (9-inch) pie	15 minutes	18 minutes	⅛ of pie

1½ cups plus 5 TB. granulated
    sugar substitute
⅓ cup cornstarch
1½ cups water
3 large egg yolks, beaten
2 TB. unsalted butter
¼ cup fresh lemon juice

Juice of ½ lime
½ tsp. lemon zest
½ tsp. lime zest
3 large egg whites
¼ tsp. cream of tartar
1 Basic Sugar-Free Piecrust (recipe
    earlier in this chapter), baked

1. In a medium saucepan over medium heat, whisk together 1½ cups granulated sugar substitute, cornstarch, and water. Bring to a boil, and cook, stirring constantly, for about 5 minutes or until thickened. Cook 1 more minute as mixture bubbles.

2. Add a small amount of cornstarch mixture to beaten egg yolks, and stir well to combine. Pour back into the saucepan, and stir together with remaining cornstarch mixture, continuing to cook over low heat for 1 more minute.

3. Remove from heat, and stir in unsalted butter, lemon juice, lime juice, lemon zest, and lime zest. Set aside.

4. Preheat the oven to 425°F.

5. In a medium bowl, and using an electric mixer on high speed, beat egg whites with cream of tartar until soft peaks form.

6. Gradually add remaining 5 tablespoons granulated sugar substitute, and continue beating for 2 minutes or until firm, glossy peaks form.

7. Pour lemon-lime filling into baked Basic Sugar-Free Piecrust, and smooth over top. Dollop meringue over filling, and spread evenly to cover all the way to the rim of piecrust to prevent *weeping*. Make decorative peaks with the back of a spoon.

8. Bake for 6 to 8 minutes or until meringue peaks turn golden brown.

9. Cool completely before slicing and serving.

DEFINITION

Weeping refers to the oozing of liquid filling that may result after baking if a pie isn't well sealed by its top crust, meringue, or crumb topping.

Easy-as-Pie Apple Pie

A variety of apples add layers of fruity flavor to this not-too-sweet version of America's all-time favorite pie.

Yield:	Prep time:	Cook time:	Serving size:
1 (9-inch) pie	35 minutes	40 to 50 minutes	$\frac{1}{8}$ of pie

3 medium Granny Smith apples, peeled, cored, and sliced

2 medium Golden Delicious apples, peeled, cored, and sliced

2 medium Gala or *Honeycrisp* apples, peeled, cored, and sliced

1 cup granulated sugar substitute

2 TB. cornstarch

1 tsp. ground cinnamon

$\frac{1}{4}$ tsp. ground ginger

$\frac{1}{8}$ tsp. ground nutmeg

Pinch salt

2 Basic Sugar-Free Piecrusts (recipe earlier in this chapter), rolled out and unbaked

1. Preheat the oven to 425°F.

2. In a large bowl, toss together Granny Smith apples, Golden Delicious apples, and Gala apples.

3. In a small bowl, whisk together granulated sugar substitute, cornstarch, cinnamon, ginger, nutmeg, and salt. Sprinkle over apples, and using a rubber spatula, gently toss to evenly distribute and coat.

4. Transfer 1 Basic Sugar-Free Piecrust to a pie pan. Add apple mixture, and, using your fingers, arrange apples to create even layers.

5. Top with remaining piecrust, pinch edges to seal well, and cut a few small openings in the center with a sharp paring knife.

6. Place pie on a baking sheet lined with aluminum foil, and bake for 40 to 50 minutes or until apples are fork-tender and crust is golden brown. Serve warm or chilled.

Creamy Chocolate Peanut Butter Pie

A favorite summer picnic dessert, this sugar-free version lacks none of the peanut or dark chocolate flavor it's known for, while the soft and creamy texture will delight every pie grazer around.

Yield:	Prep time:	Serving size:
1 (9-inch) pie	20 minutes, plus overnight chill time	$\frac{1}{8}$ of pie

1 cup no-sugar-added creamy peanut butter

1 (8-oz.) pkg. cream cheese, softened

1 cup granulated sugar substitute

2 TB. unsalted butter, melted

1 cup heavy cream

1 tsp. vanilla extract

1 (9-in.) sugar-free chocolate cookie crumb piecrust

1 (12-oz.) jar sugar-free hot fudge sauce

1. In a large bowl, and using an electric mixer on medium speed, beat together no-sugar-added peanut butter, cream cheese, granulated sugar substitute, and unsalted butter for 2 or 3 minutes or until smooth and creamy.

2. In another large bowl, and using an electric mixer on high speed, beat together heavy cream and vanilla extract until stiff peaks form.

3. Spoon $\frac{1}{3}$ of whipped cream into peanut butter mixture, and stir well to combine. Add remaining whipped cream, and fold gently into peanut butter mixture, trying not to lose volume. Pour into sugar-free chocolate cookie crumb piecrust, and smooth over top. Refrigerate overnight.

4. Just before serving, heat sugar-free hot fudge sauce according to manufacturer's directions, and drizzle over top of pie. Slice and serve immediately.

TASTY TIP

Always save broken pieces and crumbs from your sugar-free cookies to make quick cookie-crumb piecrusts or to sprinkle over ice cream or puddings.

Southern Buttermilk Chess Tart

This sugar-free version of an old classic will surprise chess tart aficionados with its depth of rich, buttery flavor and authentic-tasting sweet filling.

Yield:	Prep time:	Cook time:	Serving size:
1 (9-inch) tart	10 minutes	40 to 45 minutes	⅛ of tart

1 Basic Sugar-Free Piecrust (recipe earlier in this chapter)

1¾ cups granulated sugar substitute

2 TB. all-purpose flour

4 large eggs, beaten

½ cup buttermilk

6 TB. unsalted butter, melted

1 tsp. vanilla extract

1. Roll out Basic Sugar-Free Piecrust to fit a 9-inch tart pan with a removable bottom, and carefully fit into the pan, pressing against the edges and bottom to create a seal. Refrigerate until ready to use.

2. Preheat the oven to 350°F.

3. In a large bowl, using an electric mixer on medium speed, beat together granulated sugar substitute, all-purpose flour, eggs, and buttermilk for 1 or 2 minutes or until well combined.

4. Add melted unsalted butter and vanilla extract, and beat for 1 more minute.

5. Pour mixture into the prepared tart pan, place on a rimmed baking sheet, and bake for 40 to 45 minutes or until crust is golden and the tip of a sharp paring knife inserted in the center comes out clean.

6. Cool completely before slicing and serving.

TASTY TIP

If you ever find yourself out of buttermilk and need just a small amount, add 1 teaspoon white vinegar to regular milk and allow it to curdle slightly for 10 to 15 minutes. It will fill in perfectly as a substitute!

Crispy Toasty Apple Crisp

With its sweet and crunchy oat topping and flavorful spices, this crisp will become a great dessert selection when apples are plentiful.

Yield:	Prep time:	Cook time:	Serving size:
4 cups	20 minutes	30 minutes	½ cup

4 large Golden Delicious or Granny Smith apples

½ cup granulated sugar substitute

¼ cup granulated brown sugar substitute

½ cup all-purpose flour

½ cup old-fashioned rolled oats

5 TB. unsalted butter, softened

1 tsp. ground cinnamon

¼ tsp. ground nutmeg

1. Preheat the oven to 375°F. Lightly coat an 8-inch-square baking pan with cooking spray.

2. Peel and core Golden Delicious apples, and cut into ½-inch-thick pieces. Spread evenly in the prepared baking pan.

3. In a medium bowl, stir together granulated sugar substitute, granulated brown sugar substitute, all-purpose flour, old-fashioned rolled oats, unsalted butter, cinnamon, and nutmeg. Sprinkle evenly over apples.

4. Bake for about 30 minutes or until topping is golden and apples are fork-tender. Serve warm or chilled.

TASTY TIP

To prevent sliced apples from browning before you're ready to bake or cook with them, submerge the slices in a bowl of cold water with a squeeze of lemon juice added.

Mixed Berry Crumble

Delectable berries highlight this easy-to-make version of a true favorite that's bursting with sweet natural fruit flavor and a tasty cinnamon-kissed crumb topping.

Yield:	Prep time:	Cook time:	Serving size:
3 or 4 cups	20 minutes	30 to 40 minutes	about $\frac{1}{2}$ cup

$\frac{1}{2}$ cup sugar-free strawberry jam

$\frac{1}{2}$ cup water

1 tsp. lemon juice

1 (16-oz.) bag frozen no-sugar-added mixed berries, thawed

$\frac{1}{4}$ cup ($\frac{1}{2}$ stick) unsalted butter, diced

$\frac{1}{2}$ cup granulated sugar substitute

$\frac{1}{3}$ cup all-purpose flour

$\frac{1}{2}$ tsp. ground cinnamon

1. Preheat the oven to 350°F. Lightly coat a 9-inch-square baking pan with cooking spray.

2. In a medium saucepan over medium heat, combine sugar-free strawberry jam, water, and lemon juice. Bring to a simmer, stirring until smooth. Remove from heat, and gently stir in no-sugar-added mixed berries.

3. Pour berry mixture into the prepared baking dish, and set aside.

4. In a medium bowl, combine unsalted butter, granulated sugar substitute, all-purpose flour, and cinnamon. Using a fork or your fingers, mix to create a crumblike consistency. Sprinkle evenly over berries.

5. Bake for 30 to 40 minutes or until topping is browned and edges of crumble are bubbly.

6. Cool slightly before serving warm.

TASTY TIP

Fruit pectin offers great thickening power when jams and jellies that contain it are used in fruit desserts and sauces. Adding a dollop to pie and tart fillings can prevent runny results.

Cherry and Peach Cobbler

This extraordinarily flavorful cobbler gets a nice tang from tart cherries while canned no-sugar-added peaches contribute to a tasty sauce, all topped with a buttermilk biscuit crust.

Yield:	Prep time:	Cook time:	Serving size:
3 or 4 cups	20 minutes	20 to 25 minutes	about $\frac{1}{2}$ cup

2 (15-oz.) cans no-sugar-added sliced peaches, with juice

1 (15-oz.) can tart cherries, drained

$\frac{1}{2}$ cup plus 1 TB. granulated sugar substitute

1 TB. cornstarch

$\frac{1}{2}$ tsp. vanilla extract

$1\frac{1}{4}$ cups sugar-free buttermilk biscuit baking mix

$\frac{1}{4}$ cup milk

$\frac{1}{4}$ cup sour cream

1. Preheat the oven to 375°F. Lightly coat a 9-inch-square baking pan with cooking spray.

2. In a medium saucepan over medium heat, combine no-sugar-added peaches with juice, tart cherries, $\frac{1}{2}$ cup granulated sugar substitute, cornstarch, and vanilla extract. Bring to a simmer, and cook for 5 minutes or until hot and somewhat thickened. Transfer to the prepared baking pan, and set aside.

3. In a small bowl, stir together remaining 1 tablespoon granulated sugar substitute, sugar-free buttermilk biscuit baking mix, milk, and sour cream until just combined. Drop by spoonfuls on top of peach mixture.

4. Bake for 20 to 25 minutes or until biscuits are lightly golden and fruit is bubbly.

5. Cool slightly before serving warm.

TASTY TIP

Cobblers can easily be made in individual baking dishes or ramekins for holiday presentations or entertaining. Serve with sugar-free whipped cream or ice cream on top!

Single-Serve Strawberry Shortcakes

More like a cobbler than a cake, this classic favorite consists of a not-too-sweet biscuit topped with sweet, succulent strawberries and oozing delicious juice and cream.

Yield:	Prep time:	Cook time:	Serving size:
6 shortcakes	35 minutes, plus 1 hour chill time	15 to 20 minutes	1 shortcake

3¾ cups fresh strawberries (2 lb.), stemmed, hulled, and sliced

4 TB. granulated sugar substitute

½ cup light agave nectar

1½ cups all-purpose flour

½ cup cake flour (not self-rising)

1 TB. baking powder

½ tsp. baking soda

¼ tsp. salt

6 TB. unsalted butter, diced and slightly softened

1 cup buttermilk

1 tsp. vanilla extract

1 cup light cream (optional)

1. In a medium bowl, toss strawberries, 2 tablespoons granulated sugar substitute, and light agave nectar. Refrigerate for 1 hour, occasionally tossing.

2. Preheat the oven to 375°F. Lightly coat a baking sheet with cooking spray, and dust with all-purpose flour.

3. In a large bowl, whisk together all-purpose flour, cake flour, baking powder, baking soda, and salt.

4. Add unsalted butter, and, using a pastry blender or your fingertips, gently work butter into dry ingredients until mixture resembles sand.

5. Add buttermilk and vanilla extract, and quickly stir in just to combine. Form mixture into a ball, adding a bit of flour if necessary to prevent sticking, and transfer to a floured work surface.

6. Pat dough into a 1-inch-thick circle. Using a 2-inch biscuit cutter, cut out 6 shortcakes and transfer to the prepared baking sheet.

7. Bake for 15 to 20 minutes or until a toothpick inserted in center comes out clean and bottoms are golden. Transfer to a wire rack to cool.

8. When ready to serve, use a serrated knife to cut shortcakes in half horizontally and place in a serving dish cut side up. Spoon strawberry mixture over top, and drizzle a little cream (if using) on top.

TASTY TIP

If you don't have (or can't find) round biscuit or cookie cutters, use the open end of a drinking glass or tumbler to form your shortcakes. Dip the glass in flour each time to prevent sticking.

Old-Fashioned Desserts and Treats

Part 6

Is it possible to re-create all your favorite desserts and treats to satisfy a discriminating sweet tooth? I'll let you be the judge after you taste-test a few recipes in Part 6. From rice pudding to peanut butter fudge, chocolate pudding to raspberry dessert sauce, the recipes in the following chapters feature one delicious treat after another—all sugar free.

And let's not forget the candy store confections that never seem to hold their own in the sugar-free department. That's not the case here! From divinity to chocolate bark, you'll have so many sugar-free sweets options, trying to decide which to make first could be a challenge.

Puddings, Custards, and Mousses

Chapter 19

In This Chapter

- Rich and creamy desserts without excess sugar
- Cooking classic comfort desserts
- Spoonfuls of delicious flavor
- Sweet puddings, mousses, and more

If the proof is in the pudding, this chapter leaves no doubt that your favorite creamy desserts don't need sugar to taste fantastic. From old classics like rice pudding and tapioca, to decadent chocolate pudding or coconut crème brûlée, you'll find every bowl of sweet goodness you can think of in this chapter, just waiting for your sweet tooth to dive in for a taste test.

With every little (or big!) spoonful you take, you'll be amazed at the intense flavors and rich creaminess that sugar-free puddings, custards, and mousses can contain. If chocolate is your passion, chocolate mousse may be your first choice. If light and not-too-sweet is more your style, you might favor the airy-textured lemon mousse that's sure to become a standard in your kitchen.

Homemade Wins Hands Down

Some of the pudding recipes you'll find in this chapter certainly can be found commercially produced for convenience's sake, so it's true—you could just purchase a sugar-free gelatin or pudding at your grocer and call it a day.

But guaranteed, your taste buds will know the difference once you try the homemade version, so why even bother to disappoint? You'll be whipping up these easy recipes on a regular basis anyway when you discover how quick and delicious they can be.

Are you ready? It's dessert time.

Easy Creamy Rice Pudding

One taste of this quick stovetop version of the comfort food classic, full of aromatic cinnamon, plump raisins, and a hint of vanilla, will have you whipping it up on a regular basis!

Yield:	Prep time:	Cook time:	Serving size:
4 cups	10 minutes	30 to 40 minutes	½ cup

2 cups water

¼ tsp. salt

1 cup long-grain rice

2 cups milk

1 cup light cream

½ cup granulated sugar substitute

¼ tsp. ground cinnamon

⅓ cup golden raisins

1 tsp. vanilla extract

1. In a heavy-bottomed saucepan over high heat, bring water to a boil. Stir in salt and long-grain rice, cover, reduce heat to low, and simmer for 12 to 15 minutes or until water is absorbed but rice is still somewhat firm.

2. Add milk, light cream, granulated sugar substitute, cinnamon, and golden raisins, and return to a simmer. Cook, stirring often, for 10 to 12 minutes or until creamy and rice is tender.

3. Stir in vanilla extract, divide among 4 dessert cups, and serve warm.

TASTY TIP

To reheat cold rice pudding, stir together with a splash of milk in a saucepan over low heat for 1 or 2 minutes or until creamy and warmed.

Simple Sugar-Free Tapioca

Five simple ingredients and just a few minutes will have you enjoying rich and wonderful homemade tapioca flavored with the delightful taste of vanilla.

Yield:	Prep time:	Cook time:	Serving size:
3 cups	2 minutes	12 to 15 minutes	½ cup

2½ cups milk

1 large egg, beaten

⅓ cup granulated sugar substitute

3 TB. *instant tapioca*

1 tsp. vanilla extract

1. In a medium saucepan, whisk together milk, egg, granulated sugar substitute, and instant tapioca. Set aside for 5 minutes.

2. Set the saucepan over medium heat, and cook, stirring constantly, for 12 to 15 minutes or until just boiling and thickened.

3. Remove from heat, stir in vanilla extract, and transfer to dessert cups to cool before serving.

DEFINITION

Instant tapioca is made of tapioca pearls that have been cracked, partially cooked, and dried to speed up the cooking process. It can be used for thickening sauces and gravies as well as in pudding.

Dark Chocolate Pudding

You might find it hard to believe that this amazingly rich pudding, with its intense chocolate flavor and creamy consistency, is sugar free.

Yield:	Prep time:	Cook time:	Serving size:
2 cups	20 minutes, plus 45 minutes chill time	10 minutes	$\frac{1}{2}$ cup

$1\frac{1}{2}$ cups milk

1 large egg, beaten

1 tsp. vanilla extract

2 TB. cornstarch

$\frac{1}{4}$ cup unsweetened cocoa powder

6 (1-g) pkt. concentrated sugar substitute

2 TB. chopped sugar-free dark chocolate

1. In a medium saucepan, combine milk, egg, and vanilla extract.

2. In a small bowl, whisk together cornstarch, unsweetened cocoa powder, and concentrated sugar substitute.

3. Add cornstarch mixture to milk mixture in the saucepan, set over medium heat, and bring to a simmer, whisking often. Cook, lightly bubbling, for 2 or 3 minutes or until thickened. Switch to a wooden spoon for stirring as mixture becomes thicker.

4. Remove from heat, and stir in sugar-free dark chocolate.

5. Transfer to dessert cups, and refrigerate for 45 minutes before serving.

TASTY TIP

When using cornstarch to thicken, remember that it must boil for 2 or 3 minutes in order for it to come to its full thickening power.

Spiced Pear Bread Pudding

Delicious and comforting straight from the oven, the aroma of exotic spices and sweet pear highlight this flavorful autumn dessert that's just as tasty any time of year.

Yield:	Prep time:	Cook time:	Serving size:
15 squares	30 minutes	30 to 40 minutes	1 square

1 (1 lb.) loaf country-style sliced white bread

4 large eggs

2 cups milk

1 cup heavy cream

1 cup granulated sugar substitute

1 tsp. vanilla extract

¼ tsp. ground allspice

¼ tsp. ground cinnamon

⅛ tsp. ground nutmeg

1 cup drained canned no-sugar-added diced pears

Sugar-free ice cream (optional)

1. Preheat the oven to 350°F. Lightly coat a 13×9-inch glass baking dish with cooking spray.

2. Using a serrated knife, cut bread slices in ½-inch cubes. Transfer to a large bowl, and set aside.

3. In another bowl, whisk together eggs, milk, heavy cream, granulated sugar substitute, vanilla extract, allspice, cinnamon, and nutmeg until well combined.

4. Pour wet mixture over bread cubes, and gently stir to moisten. Set aside for 10 minutes to absorb most of liquid.

5. Gently fold in no-sugar-added diced pears, and transfer mixture to the prepared baking dish. Smooth out evenly.

6. Bake for 30 to 40 minutes or until top is golden brown and a toothpick inserted in the center comes out clean. Allow to rest for 10 to 15 minutes before cutting. Serve warm or cold, with sugar-free ice cream (if using).

HONEY DON'T!

Watch when ordering bread pudding at restaurants because the accompanying sauce can often have more sugar than the actual pudding! Opt for a splash of light cream instead, or ask for the sauce on the side.

Incredible Caramel Custard

Traditionally made with caramelized sugar, this rich and flavorful dessert gets a sugar-free makeover with the help of sweetener, agave, and the intoxicating aroma of vanilla bean.

Yield:	Prep time:	Cook time:	Serving size:
2 cups	15 minutes, plus 2 hours chill time	30 to 40 minutes	½ cup

1 cup milk

1 (2-in.) piece vanilla bean, unopened and unscraped

2 (1-g) pkt. concentrated sugar substitute

2 tsp. sugar-free caramel syrup

5 large egg yolks, beaten

Boiling water

Amber agave nectar

1. In a small saucepan over medium heat, heat milk with vanilla bean for 2 or 3 minutes or until just warmed. Set aside for 10 minutes.

2. Preheat the oven to 325°F. Line a small, 3-inch-tall roasting pan with parchment paper. Lightly coat 4 (½-cup) ramekins or ovenproof dessert cups with cooking spray.

3. In a medium bowl, whisk together concentrated sugar substitute, sugar-free caramel syrup, and egg yolks until well combined.

4. Remove vanilla bean from milk, and slowly pour milk into egg mixture, whisking well. Divide mixture among the prepared ramekins, and place in the roasting pan.

5. Pour boiling water into the roasting pan to come halfway up the sides of the ramekins. Bake for 30 to 40 minutes or until custard is set and a toothpick comes out clean.

6. Remove from the oven, carefully lift the ramekins off the pan, and place them on a flat plate or tray. Refrigerate for at least 2 hours or until completely cooled.

7. To serve, run a sharp paring knife around the edge of the ramekin, and turn out custard onto a dessert plate. Drizzle with amber agave nectar, and serve.

TASTY TIP

Reserve and dry the unscraped vanilla bean for another purpose. You can also save scraped pods for flavoring other liquids for sauces and puddings.

Coconut Crème Brûlée

You'll delight in this heavenly dessert, thick and creamy with the tropical flavor of coconut, sure to satisfy every sweet tooth.

Yield:	Prep time:	Cook time:	Serving size:
2 cups	20 minutes, plus 2 hours chill time	35 to 40 minutes	½ cup

⅔ cup heavy cream

½ cup unsweetened coconut milk

5 large egg yolks

½ tsp. vanilla extract

½ cup plus 1 TB. granulated sugar substitute

Boiling water

1. In a small saucepan over medium heat, combine heavy cream and coconut milk for about 2 minutes or just until *scalding*.

2. Preheat the oven to 350°F. Line a small, 3-inch-tall roasting pan with parchment paper.

3. In a medium bowl, whisk together egg yolks, vanilla extract, and ½ cup granulated sugar substitute until pale yellow and thick. Slowly add warm milk mixture, whisking well to combine.

4. Divide mixture among 4 (½-cup) ramekins, and place the ramekins in the roasting pan. Pour boiling water into the roasting pan to come halfway up the sides of the ramekins. Bake for 30 to 40 minutes or until custard is almost set but still a little jiggly in the center.

5. Remove from the oven, carefully lift the ramekins off the pan, and place them on a flat plate or tray. Refrigerate for at least 2 hours or until completely cooled.

6. Just before serving, sprinkle remaining 1 tablespoon granulated sugar substitute over tops of custards, and using a kitchen torch or oven broiler, quickly brown tops. Serve immediately.

DEFINITION

A liquid, usually dairy, reaches **scalding** when it's just about to come to a boil and small bubbles appear around the edge of the pot.

Raspberry *Panna Cotta*

Deliciously sweet, but with a hint of fruity tartness, this impressive dessert will wow everyone at the table at the first taste.

Yield:	Prep time:	Cook time:	Serving size:
2 cups	15 minutes, plus 3 hours chill time	5 minutes	½ cup

1½ tsp. unflavored gelatin

1½ cups whole or reduced-fat milk

1 tsp. vanilla extract

1 cup frozen, no-sugar-added raspberries, thawed

2 TB. granulated sugar substitute

¼ cup fresh raspberries (optional)

1. In a small saucepan, combine unflavored gelatin and whole milk. Set aside for 2 minutes.

2. Add vanilla extract, set over medium-low heat, and cook, stirring often, for 2 or 3 minutes or until gelatin has dissolved. Do not boil. Set aside until cool.

3. Meanwhile, lightly coat 4 (½-cup) ramekins or dessert cups with cooking spray.

4. In a food processor fitted with a steel blade, pulse thawed no-sugar-added raspberries until completely smooth. Strain purée through a fine mesh sieve into a bowl to remove seeds.

5. When milk mixture is cool, stir into puréed raspberries. Add granulated sugar substitute, and mix well until dissolved. Divide mixture among the prepared ramekins, cover with plastic wrap, and refrigerate for at least 3 hours or preferably overnight until set and firm.

6. To serve, run a sharp paring knife around the edges of the ramekins, and unmold *panna cotta* onto dessert plates. Garnish with fresh raspberries (if using), and serve.

DEFINITION

Panna cotta means "cooked cream" in Italian and is usually made from cream, milk, sugar, and gelatin. It has a resulting custard consistency and is often served with fruit.

The Best-Ever Chocolate Mousse

This glamorous dessert—that's amazingly sugar-free and delectably rich—boasts tons of deep chocolate flavor.

Yield:	Prep time:	Cook time:	Serving size:
3 cups	35 minutes, plus 2 hours chill time	10 minutes	½ cup

1 cup whole or reduced-fat milk

3 (1-oz.) squares unsweetened chocolate

1 large egg

½ tsp. vanilla extract

½ cup granulated sugar substitute

1 tsp. cornstarch

½ cup heavy cream, whipped to soft peaks

1. In a small saucepan over medium heat, combine whole milk and unsweetened chocolate. Simmer, stirring often, for 2 or 3 minutes or until chocolate has melted. Set aside to cool slightly.

2. In a medium bowl, whisk together egg, vanilla extract, granulated sugar substitute, and cornstarch.

3. Add egg mixture to chocolate mixture, and return to medium heat. Cook, stirring constantly, for 3 to 5 minutes or until mixture is bubbly and thick. Whisk well to a creamy texture, transfer to a clean bowl, and refrigerate at least 2 hours until cool.

4. When chocolate mixture is cooled, fold whipped heavy cream into mousse mixture, trying to maintain as much volume as possible.

5. Spoon into serving dishes, or keep refrigerated until ready to serve.

TASTY TIP

Chocolate mousse can make a great filling for your sugar-free cakes and cupcakes! Be sure it's well chilled before spreading.

Light and Lovely Lemon Mousse

Nothing beats this light and airy dessert when you're craving a bit of refreshing lemony flavor with just a hint of sweetness.

Yield:	Prep time:	Cook time:	Serving size:
4 cups	15 minutes	5 minutes	½ cup

1 cup boiling water

1 (3-oz.) pkg. sugar-free lemon gelatin

½ cup cold water

¾ cup sugar-free frozen lemonade concentrate, thawed

1 cup sugar-free frozen whipped topping, thawed

1. In a medium bowl, combine boiling water and sugar-free lemon gelatin, and stir until dissolved.

2. Add cold water and sugar-free lemonade concentrate, and stir well.

3. Chill for at least 30 minutes until mixture becomes somewhat thickened but not completely set.

4. Using an electric mixer on low speed, beat in sugar-free whipped topping until well combined, thick, smooth, and creamy.

5. Spoon into dessert cups, and keep refrigerated until ready to serve.

TASTY TIP

Mousses of all kinds freeze well and are great treats in hot weather. Try freezing your fruit-flavored mousses in layers to make a rainbow effect.

Banana Strawberry Mousse

You'll love the fruity flavor and creamy texture of this light, no-cooking-required dessert, complete with a hint of delicious white chocolate peeking through.

Yield:	Prep time:	Serving size:
4 cups	20 minutes, plus 1 hour chill time	½ cup

1 (3-oz.) pkg. cream cheese, softened

1 TB. sour cream

3 TB. granulated sugar substitute

1 medium banana, peeled and mashed

½ cup chopped fresh or no-sugar-added frozen strawberries

1 TB. sugar-free strawberry jelly

½ tsp. vanilla extract

2 oz. sugar-free white chocolate, chopped and melted

½ cup heavy cream, whipped to soft peaks

White chocolate curls

1. In a medium bowl, and using an electric mixer on medium-high speed, combine cream cheese, sour cream, granulated sugar substitute, and banana until smooth.

2. Add strawberries, sugar-free strawberry jelly, and vanilla extract, and beat for 1 more minute or until well combined. Add sugar-free white chocolate, and beat in.

3. Fold whipped heavy cream into banana-strawberry mixture, trying to maintain as much volume as possible.

4. Transfer mixture to individual dessert cups, and chill for at least 1 hour before serving topped with white chocolate curls.

TASTY TIP

Use your vegetable peeler to make chocolate curls by running it along the side of a chocolate bar. Keep curls chilled or away from heat before sprinkling on top of mousse.

Dessert Toppings, Fillings, and Sauces

In This Chapter

- The perfect whipped toppings
- Opting for sugar-free alternatives
- Flavorful guilt-free fillings
- Sweet, sweet sauces

Finding tasty sugar-free desserts can be hard enough for a sugar-free eater, but discovering delicious extras like sweet whipped creams, fudgy fillings, and fruity sauces must make you feel as if you're dreaming.

Hold on to your taste buds! You're about to be whisked into a whole other realm of amazing sugar-free delights you thought were off the table!

Sweet Dreams Come Alive

It's true—you can have your cake, and cream, too! Whipping up delicious toppings for everything from ice cream to pie to pastries was never so easy and guiltless. Imagine classic French whipped cream with a hint of brandy or oozing with chocolate flavor. Or how about rich and smooth fillings like you find in the bakery? Or decadent chocolate or raspberry sauce? Ooh! Pinch me!

Complementary Sugar Free

Many of the recipes you'll find in this chapter complement the desserts also in this book. Try the Chantilly Cream on Holiday Pumpkin Pie (recipe in Chapter 18), or drizzle a bit of Homemade Chocolate Sauce on that Strawberry Mousse (recipe in Chapter 19).

With so much flavor going on, you'll wonder why sugar-free eaters complained so much in the past. Just give them a bite of your latest dessert creation, topped with one of your marvelous sugar-free sauces, and see how quickly they change their tune—and grab a spoon!

Chantilly Cream

Classic French whipped cream usually flavored with confectioners' sugar and a splash of brandy gets a sugar-free makeover in this tasty topping for desserts and coffee.

Yield:	Prep time:	Serving size:
2 cups	5 minutes	2 tablespoons

1 cup heavy cream, well chilled	½ tsp. vanilla extract
2 TB. granulated sugar substitute	½ tsp. brandy extract

1. In a medium bowl, and using an electric mixer on low speed, beat heavy cream, granulated sugar substitute, vanilla extract, and brandy extract for 1 minute or until slightly thickened.

2. Increase mixer speed to medium-high, and beat for 1 or 2 more minutes or until soft peaks form.

3. Transfer to a chilled serving bowl, and keep refrigerated until ready to use.

SWEET SECRET

Chantilly cream got its name in the late seventeenth century from the Chateau de Chantilly, outside Paris, where it was served. The chateau was particularly known for its refined gourmet food and elegant service.

Luscious Chocolate Whipped Cream

When it comes to feeding a chocolate craving, you can't do much better than this sugar-free delight that's great on ice cream, in hot chocolate, or even on its own!

Yield:	Prep time:	Serving size:
2 cups	5 minutes, plus 1 hour chill time	2 tablespoons

4 oz. unsweetened chocolate, broken into pieces
1 TB. unsweetened cocoa powder

1 cup heavy cream, well chilled
¼ cup granulated sugar substitute
½ tsp. vanilla extract

1. In the top of a double boiler over medium heat, melt unsweetened chocolate, stirring occasionally. Whisk in unsweetened cocoa powder, transfer to a medium bowl, and set aside to cool slightly.

2. In a medium bowl, beat heavy cream, granulated sugar substitute, and vanilla extract for 2 or 3 minutes or until stiff peaks form.

3. In one quick gesture, transfer whipped cream to the bowl with chocolate. Whisk vigorously for 1 minute or until completely combined. Chill for 1 hour before serving.

TASTY TIP

If you don't have a double boiler, you can create a makeshift version by placing a heatproof bowl over a saucepan of simmering water. Do not allow the bottom of the bowl to touch the water.

Mock Confectioners' Sugar Glaze

Here's a perfectly sweet, sugar-free rendition of a popular glaze that's perfect for topping cakes and cookies.

Yield:	Prep time:	Serving size:
¾ cup	5 minutes	1 tablespoon

1½ cups granulated sugar substitute

¼ cup cornstarch

4 or 5 tsp. water

1. In a blender, pulse granulated sugar substitute to a fine powder.

2. In a small bowl, combine powdered sugar substitute and cornstarch.

3. Whisk in water 1 teaspoon at a time until desired consistency is reached. Use immediately to spread or drizzle over baked goods.

Variation: Add flavor to your glaze with ½ teaspoon of any one of the following: vanilla extract, lemon zest, almond extract, or rum extract.

TASTY TIP

Pulse granulated sugar substitute to a fine powder and use in cold drinks for quick dissolving.

Sugar-Free Royal Icing

For perfect cookie icing that dries hard, this recipe can't be beat for flavor and ease of preparation.

Yield:	Prep time:	Serving size:
1 cup	5 minutes	1 tablespoon

2 cups granulated sugar substitute

1 large egg white

½ tsp. lemon juice

1. In a blender, pulse granulated sugar substitute to a fine powder.

2. In a medium bowl, whisk together powdered granulated sugar substitute, egg white, and lemon juice until smooth.

3. Use immediately to spread on cookies, or color with food coloring and place into piping bags for decorating. If icing gets too thick, thin with small amounts of warm water. Will keep for 2 days in the refrigerator before hardening completely.

Variation: Instead of using 1 large egg white, you could substitute 1 tablespoon *meringue powder* prepared according to the package directions.

DEFINITION

Meringue powder is a fine white substance made from dried egg whites that, when reconstituted with water, can be used as a substitute for fresh egg whites.

Quick Chocolate Frosting

You'll use this frosting, deliciously creamy with plenty of sweet chocolate flavor, again and again for cakes, brownies, or cupcakes.

Yield:	Prep time:	Serving size:
1½ cups	5 minutes, plus 20 minutes chill time	2 tablespoons

2 (1-oz.) squares unsweetened chocolate, melted and slightly cooled	½ cup (1 stick) unsalted butter, softened
⅓ cup heavy cream	¼ cup granulated sugar substitute
	1 tsp. vanilla extract

1. In a medium bowl, and using an electric mixer on medium speed, beat together melted chocolate and heavy cream.

2. Beat in unsalted butter, add granulated sugar substitute and vanilla extract, and continue beating until smooth and fluffy.

3. Refrigerate for 20 minutes to thicken, and spread or pipe on cake as desired.

TASTY TIP

You can intensify the flavor of your chocolate baked goods and frostings—and save calories at the same time—by adding a small amount of chocolate extract. This is available in the supermarket baking aisle alongside the vanilla and other extracts.

Vanilla Pastry and Cake Filling

This will become your go-to recipe for perfect vanilla filling that's sugar free but still full of rich, sweet flavor with the wonderful aroma of exotic vanilla and a creamy mouthwatering texture.

Yield:	Prep time:	Cook time:	Serving size:
about 2 cups	5 minutes	10 minutes	¼ cup

1 TB. cornstarch	2 large egg yolks, slightly beaten
2 TB. granulated sugar substitute	1 tsp. vanilla extract
1¾ cups milk	

1. In a medium saucepan over medium heat, whisk together cornstarch, granulated sugar substitute, and milk. Bring to a simmer, and cook, whisking constantly, for 4 to 6 minutes as mixture thickens. When it comes to a boil, switch to a wooden spoon and, stirring constantly, cook for 1 more minute. Remove from heat.

2. Pour about ⅓ of milk mixture into beaten egg yolks, and stir well to combine. Pour this mixture into remaining milk mixture in the saucepan, reduce heat to low, and cook, stirring constantly, for 3 minutes or until very thick.

3. Remove from heat, and stir in vanilla extract.

4. Press through a fine mesh sieve into a clean bowl, cover the surface with plastic wrap, and allow to cool somewhat before placing in the refrigerator to cool completely. Use within 3 days.

TASTY TIP

Vanilla filling can be used for all kinds of pastries—including éclairs, Napoleons, and tarts—or even as a topping for fresh fruit.

Rich Fudge Filling

Use this dark and full-flavored chocolate filling for cakes, cupcakes, and even as a thick icing for cookies and bars. You'll love the sweet, creamy taste of butter and cream that pops through.

Yield:	Prep time:	Serving size:
about 1 cup	10 minutes	1 tablespoon

$\frac{1}{3}$ cup light cream

$\frac{2}{3}$ cup unsweetened cocoa powder

$\frac{1}{2}$ cup (1 stick) unsalted butter, softened

$\frac{2}{3}$ cup light agave nectar

$\frac{1}{4}$ tsp. vanilla extract

1. In a medium bowl, and using an electric mixer on medium speed, beat light cream and unsweetened cocoa powder for 1 or 2 minutes or until smooth and creamy.

2. Add unsalted butter, light agave nectar, and vanilla extract, and beat for 1 or 2 more minutes or until well combined and creamy.

3. Refrigerate for at least 1 hour before using.

SWEET SECRET

Don't feel guilty about enjoying chocolate! Its antioxidant content and overall health benefits have been proven over and over. Just watch for the sugar.

Homemade Chocolate Sauce

You'll be glad to have this delicious and super-chocolaty sauce on hand for adding to milk, drizzling on top of ice cream or yogurt, or as a treat on fresh strawberries or other fruit.

Yield:	Prep time:	Cook time:	Serving size:
about 1 cup	2 minutes	8 to 10 minutes	1 tablespoon

¾ cup water

¼ cup granulated sugar substitute

⅓ cup unsweetened cocoa powder

½ tsp. vanilla extract

Dash ground cinnamon

1. In a medium saucepan over medium heat, whisk together water, granulated sugar substitute, unsweetened cocoa powder, vanilla extract, and cinnamon. Bring to a boil, reduce heat to low, and simmer, stirring often, for 6 to 8 minutes or until somewhat thickened and syrupy.

2. Remove from heat, transfer to an airtight container, and cool slightly before storing in the refrigerator.

HONEY DON'T!

Commercial chocolate sauce often contains high-fructose syrup as its main ingredient. Sometimes it even uses a chocolate "flavoring" rather than real cocoa. Steer clear!

Raspberry Dessert Sauce

Enjoy this super-flavored version of raspberry *coulis*, popular in restaurants alongside desserts because of its tangy taste and complementary pairings with many sweets, any time you like—guilt free!

Yield:	Prep time:	Cook time:	Serving size:
1¼ cups	5 minutes	8 to 10 minutes	2 tablespoons

3 cups fresh or frozen no-sugar-added raspberries

½ cup water

½ cup granulated sugar substitute

½ tsp. lemon juice

1. In a medium saucepan over medium heat, bring no-sugar-added raspberries, water, granulated sugar substitute, and lemon juice to a boil. Reduce heat to low, and simmer, stirring occasionally, for 5 minutes or until raspberries have broken down. Remove from heat, and set aside to cool slightly.

2. Transfer mixture to a blender, and purée for 1 minute or until smooth.

3. Pour through a fine-mesh strainer to discard seeds, and refrigerate raspberry sauce in an airtight container until ready to use.

DEFINITION

Coulis is the French culinary term used for a liquid purée derived from fruits or vegetables.

Sweet Yogurt Sauce

Delicious on fresh fruit as well as fruit pies, this healthy alternative to sugar and cream has a delightful tang from the yogurt and a sweet spiciness from agave and cinnamon.

Yield:	Prep time:	Serving size:
2 cups	5 minutes	¼ cup

2 cups nonfat or low-fat Greek yogurt

½ cup amber agave nectar

½ tsp. ground cinnamon

Dash nutmeg

1. In a medium bowl, combine Greek yogurt, amber agave nectar, cinnamon, and nutmeg.

2. Keep refrigerated in an airtight container for up to 2 weeks.

TASTY TIP

Greek yogurt's thick and creamy consistency makes it an excellent substitute for sour cream in many baking and cooking recipes.

Candies and Confections

Chapter

21

In This Chapter

- Smart candy options
- Sensational sugar-free treats
- Sweet confection perfection
- Easy candy-making methods

You've probably already written off candy since you decided to go sugar free, but wait just a minute. You don't have to completely eliminate candy from your diet, but you do have to be smart about your choices. With the sugar-free recipes in this chapter, you'll find yourself in candy heaven—without an ounce of guilt!

Creative Creations

How can this be so? Surely good-tasting candy can't be made without sugar. The answer lies in the creative approach you take. When you eliminate an excess of unwanted sugar, you replace it with something amazingly delicious and subtly sweet. How about the ever-popular maple walnut fudge made with agave instead? Or think about truffles without all that usual added sugar. You'll be surprised how easily you can do without all the excess and still enjoy the confections you crave.

Easy Candy-Making

If the idea of candy-making gives you a tad of trepidation, don't be concerned. Every recipe in this chapter is easy to make with all the vital instructions you need to get the results you're after. Don't shy away from your candy thermometer; it will become your best friend when you're whipping up these dynamite confections.

Best-Ever Chocolate Fudge

This dark chocolate fudge is low in sugar and high in rich chocolate flavor—and studded with your choice of toasted crunchy nuts.

Yield:	Prep time:	Cook time:	Serving size:
81 squares	10 minutes, plus 2 hours chill time	5 minutes	2 or 3 squares

1 (7-oz.) jar sugar-free marshmallow crème

½ cup unsalted butter, diced

⅔ cup unsweetened evaporated milk

3 cups sugar-free dark chocolate chips

1 TB. granulated sugar substitute

2 tsp. vanilla extract

1½ cups chopped toasted pecans, almonds, or walnuts

1. Line a 9-inch-square baking pan with aluminum foil, and lightly coat foil with cooking spray.

2. In a large saucepan over medium heat, combine sugar-free marshmallow crème, unsalted butter, and evaporated milk, stirring until smooth. Bring to a boil, and cook, stirring constantly, for about 5 minutes.

3. Remove from heat, and stir in sugar-free dark chocolate chips, granulated sugar substitute, and vanilla extract until chocolate is melted and consistency is smooth.

4. Stir in toasted pecans, and pour into the prepared pan, smoothing out the surface. Chill for at least 2 hours or overnight.

5. Carefully remove foil with fudge from the pan, and peel away foil from the surface. Using a large, sharp knife, cut into 1-inch squares.

6. Store in an airtight container in the refrigerator.

TASTY TIP

Look for sugar-free versions of marshmallow crème in your supermarket and health food store or online.

Peanutty Peanut Butter Fudge

A favorite combination of flavors comes together in this easy-to-make fudge that's smooth and creamy with the bite of crunchy, lightly salted peanuts.

Yield:	Prep time:	Cook time:	Serving size:
36 squares	5 minutes, plus 2 hours chill time	5 minutes	1 or 2 squares

2 (1-oz.) squares unsweetened chocolate, chopped

$^2\!/_3$ cup half-and-half

$^1\!/_2$ cup no-sugar-added creamy peanut butter

$^1\!/_2$ cup granulated sugar substitute

1 tsp. vanilla extract

1 cup lightly salted peanuts

1. Lightly coat an 8- or 9-inch-square baking pan with cooking spray.

2. In a medium saucepan over medium heat, melt together chocolate, half-and-half, and no-sugar-added peanut butter, stirring well until smooth and creamy.

3. Stir in granulated sugar substitute and vanilla extract, and remove from heat. Continue stirring until sugar substitute has dissolved.

4. Add peanuts, and stir to combine. Pour into the prepared baking pan, smoothing out the surface. Chill for at least 2 hours or overnight.

5. Cut into 36 squares. Store in an airtight container in the refrigerator.

TASTY TIP

Adding a pinch of sea salt or another coarse salt to chocolate and caramel confections helps bring out the sweet essence of the chocolate without any added sugar. Try sprinkling a bit on top of your homemade chocolate candies.

Agave Maple Walnut Fudge

Agave's delicious maple flavor fills in for half the maple syrup in this creamy and satisfying confection that's full of tender sweet walnuts and a hint of vanilla.

Yield:	Prep time:	Cook time:	Serving size:
36 squares	10 minutes, plus 2 hours chill time	10 minutes	1 or 2 squares

1 cup amber agave nectar

1 cup pure maple syrup

¾ cup light cream

1 tsp. vanilla extract

½ cup chopped walnuts

1. Lightly coat an 8-inch-square baking pan with cooking spray.

2. In a medium saucepan over medium heat, combine amber agave nectar, maple syrup, and light cream. Without stirring, bring mixture to a boil until bubbly and somewhat thickened or a candy thermometer reaches between 234°F and 240°F and a drop of syrup forms a soft ball in a cup of cold water. Remove from heat.

3. Stir in vanilla extract and walnuts, and pour into the prepared pan, smoothing the top. Cool for at least 2 hours.

4. Cut into 36 squares. Store in an airtight container in the refrigerator.

SWEET SECRET

In candy-making, when a sugar liquid reaches a temperature of about 234°F to 240°F, it's called the "soft ball stage" because it's still malleable at this temperature, unlike at the "hard ball stage," when the sugar becomes solid and is appropriate for hard candy-making.

Chocolate Peppermint Mints

If you've given up your favorite sugar-laden mint patties, you can start enjoying them once again with this delectable version flavored with deep dark cocoa and a hint of refreshing peppermint extract.

Yield:	Prep time:	Cook time:	Serving size:
24 candies	10 minutes, plus 2 or 3 hours chill time	5 minutes	1 or 2 candies

½ cup (1 stick) unsalted butter, softened

1 (8-oz.) pkg. cream cheese, softened

¼ cup unsweetened cocoa powder

¼ cup heavy cream

1 tsp. peppermint extract

⅔ cup granulated sugar substitute

4 oz. sugar-free dark chocolate, chopped and melted

1. Line 2 (12-cup) mini muffin tins with paper liners.

2. In a medium bowl, and using an electric mixer on medium speed, beat together unsalted butter and cream cheese for 2 minutes or until well combined.

3. Add unsweetened cocoa powder and beat for 1 more minute.

4. Beat in heavy cream and peppermint extract, and add granulated sugar substitute, continuing to beat for at least 1 minute or until well combined.

5. Divide mixture by spoonfuls among paper liners, and flatten mound with the back of a spoon dipped in hot water. Refrigerate for 1 hour.

6. Pour a little melted sugar-free dark chocolate over each patty, and chill for 1 or 2 more hours before serving.

7. Store in an airtight container in the refrigerator.

SWEET SECRET

Peppermint drinks and candies are often served after dinner because the essence of peppermint helps calm indigestion and counterbalance an overindulgent meal.

Dusted Chocolate Truffles

Not even rich and festive truffles are off the menu with this fabulous version that highlights the unique depth of dark chocolate flavor combined with a little sweetener and a fragrant hint of vanilla.

Yield:	Prep time:	Cook time:	Serving size:
36 truffles	15 minutes, plus 4 hours chill time	5 minutes	1 or 2 truffles

6 oz. sugar-free bittersweet chocolate (about 70 percent cocoa), chopped

1 cup heavy cream

1 tsp. vanilla extract

2 TB. granulated sugar substitute

1/4 cup unsweetened cocoa powder

1. Place chopped sugar-free bittersweet chocolate in a large mixing bowl.

2. In a small saucepan over medium heat, bring heavy cream just to a simmer. Pour over chocolate. Stir with a wooden spoon until all chocolate pieces have melted.

3. Stir in vanilla extract and granulated sugar substitute. Chill for about 4 hours or until quite firm.

4. Line a rimmed baking sheet with parchment paper.

5. Using a melon baller dipped in hot water, scoop out truffles and place on the prepared baking sheet. (If mixture becomes too soft while working, chill briefly to firm.) Chill truffles for several hours or overnight until very firm.

6. Place cocoa powder in a small bowl, and quickly drop in truffles, one at a time, tossing to coat. Transfer dusted truffles to a clean serving plate or individual paper cupcake liners.

7. Store in an airtight container in the refrigerator for up to 4 days.

Variation: For **Chocolate Rum Truffles,** replace the vanilla extract with rum extract or dark rum. Refrain from adding too much, however, as the alcohol can prevent the chocolate from firming and may result in flattened truffles.

Chocolate Peanutty Pretzels

The combination of sweet and salty never tasted as good as in these easy-to-make crunchy treats featuring the flavor of dark chocolate.

Yield:	Prep time:	Cook time:	Serving size:
3 cups	10 minutes, plus 30 minutes chill time	15 minutes	¼ cup

1 large egg white

¼ cup amber agave nectar

1 cup chopped peanuts

2 cups mini salted pretzels

1 cup sugar-free dark chocolate, melted

1. Preheat the oven to 350°F. Line a rimmed baking sheet with parchment paper.

2. In a large bowl, and using an electric mixer on high speed, beat egg white until frothy. Beat in amber agave nectar until well combined.

3. Add peanuts and mini pretzels, and stir to coat. Transfer to the prepared baking sheet, and spread into an even layer. Bake for about 15 minutes or until pretzels and nuts appear dry.

4. Remove from the oven. When cool enough to handle, break into bite-size pieces, and transfer to a clean piece of parchment paper to cool completely.

5. Drop cooled pretzel pieces in melted sugar-free dark chocolate, and stir to coat. Using a slotted spoon, remove pieces from chocolate, and set in a single layer on a baking sheet. Refrigerate for 30 minutes or until hardened.

6. Store in an airtight container for up to 3 weeks.

HONEY DON'T!

Most commercial chocolate-dipped pretzels contain an artificial flavoring and much added sugar. No worries about either with this delicious homemade version!

Chocolate Coconut Haystacks

One of the old-time favorites in homemade candy shops, these delightful treats get a sugar-free makeover by using dark chocolate and a barely sweetened flaky coconut that together taste like they're straight out of the gourmet candy box.

Yield:	Prep time:	Cook time:	Serving size:
36 candies	35 minutes, plus 1 hour chill time	2 minutes	1 or 2 candies

1½ cups unsweetened flaked coconut	½ tsp. vanilla extract
¼ cup light agave nectar	6 oz. sugar-free dark chocolate, chopped and melted

1. In a medium bowl, combine coconut, light agave nectar, and vanilla extract, and stir well to combine. Set aside for 20 minutes.

2. Line a rimmed baking sheet with parchment paper.

3. Pour melted sugar-free dark chocolate into coconut mixture, and stir well to coat.

4. Drop batter by heaping teaspoons on the prepared baking sheet. Chill for at least 1 hour before serving.

5. Store in an airtight container.

HONEY DON'T!

When melting chocolate, never allow it to bubble because it might seize up and ruin its consistency. Always melt over low heat, in a double boiler, or in the microwave at 5-second intervals, and stir well before deciding to add more heat.

Candied Brittle Peanuts

This treat will satisfy any peanut brittle lover, with its roasted peanut flavor and a hint of buttery agave.

Yield:	Prep time:	Cook time:	Serving size:
2 cups	5 minutes	20 to 25 minutes	¼ cup

2 cups dry-roasted peanuts, lightly salted

1 large egg white, beaten

⅓ cup light agave nectar

2 TB. unsalted butter, melted

1. Preheat the oven to 325°F. Line a rimmed baking sheet with parchment paper.

2. Place peanuts in a medium bowl. Stir in egg white to coat.

3. Add light agave nectar and unsalted butter, and stir well to combine.

4. Spread onto the prepared baking sheet, and bake for 20 to 25 minutes or until mixture is dry and slightly golden.

5. Remove from the oven and allow to cool on the baking sheet before breaking into desired sizes.

6. Store in an airtight container.

HONEY DON'T!

Between 1 and 2 percent of the American population is allergic to peanuts. Reactions can be mild or severe and are not always limited to ingesting peanuts. Be sure to make guests aware that you're serving peanuts in case this is an issue for them.

Marvelous Marshmallows

You can whip up these sweet nothings without a bit of sugar and savor them as they melt in your mouth—or in your sugar-free hot chocolate.

Yield:	Prep time:	Cook time:	Serving size:
78 marshmallows	15 minutes, plus 4 hours chill time	15 minutes	1 or 2 marshmallows

1½ (.25-oz.) pkg. unflavored gelatin

¼ cup cold water

⅓ cup confectioners' sugar

1½ cups light agave nectar

Pinch salt

1 tsp. vanilla extract

1. In a medium bowl, stir together unflavored gelatin and cold water. Set aside.

2. Lightly coat a 13×9-inch baking dish with cooking spray. Cut parchment paper to fit and place on the bottom. Lightly coat parchment paper with cooking spray, and dust with 2 tablespoons confectioners' sugar.

3. In a medium saucepan over medium-high heat, combine light agave nectar and salt, and cook for about 6 minutes or until a candy thermometer reaches about 240°F (or soft ball stage).

4. Using an electric mixer on medium speed, add agave in a slow stream to gelatin mixture, and beat for 2 minutes. Increase speed to high, and continue beating for about 10 minutes or until mixture is very thick and still slightly warm. Stir in vanilla extract.

5. Pour mixture into the prepared pan, and sprinkle with 2 tablespoons confectioners' sugar. Place another fitted sheet of parchment on top, and chill for at least 4 hours.

6. Slide entire sheet of marshmallow onto a cutting board. Carefully remove parchment paper, and using a sharp knife or pizza cutter, cut into 78 squares.

7. Dredge cut marshmallows in remaining confectioners' sugar. Store in an airtight container for up to 1 week.

TASTY TIP

You can add flavoring or color to your homemade marshmallows by adding a small amount of extract or food coloring before pouring into the pan.

Buttery Vanilla Caramels with Sea Salt

This easy recipe features the delicious, smooth, and buttery taste of traditional caramels plus the subtle sweetness of agave and the alluring flavor of vanilla and sea salt.

Yield:	Prep time:	Cook time:	Serving size:
64 caramels	1 minutes	15 minutes	2 or 3 caramels

2 cups heavy cream

½ cup (1 stick) unsalted butter

1⅓ cups light agave nectar

2 TB. vanilla extract

½ tsp. coarse sea salt

1. Lightly coat an 8-inch-square glass baking dish with butter.

2. In a medium saucepan over medium heat, combine 1 cup heavy cream, unsalted butter, and light agave nectar. Cook, stirring often, for 3 to 5 minutes or until mixture comes to a rolling boil.

3. Continue cooking and stirring for 5 to 10 more minutes as mixture turns darker and thickens.

4. In a small bowl, combine remaining 1 cup heavy cream and vanilla extract. Stir into thickened agave mixture, return to a rolling boil, and cook, stirring often, for about 5 minutes or until a candy thermometer reaches about 245°F.

5. Pour mixture into the prepared baking dish, and set aside to cool at room temperature. After 5 minutes, sprinkle with sea salt.

6. When completely cooled, cut into 64 (1-inch) squares and wrap in candy wrappers if desired.

HONEY DON'T!

Whenever boiling cream, be very mindful of your heat setting and never leave unattended as it can quickly boil over and ruin your hard work.

Frozen Desserts

No sugar-free cookbook would be complete without a section on ice creams and other frozen desserts. So last but not least, I introduce Part 7, full of those cool and creamy desserts you crave. Delicious versions of all your favorites are here, from simple French vanilla ice cream to rich chocolate-chocolate chip, and even a green tea gelato for you frozen dessert aficionados.

Let's not forget the fruity and flavorful array of sorbets and ices that await as well. You'll be amazed at how easy it is to prepare mango sorbet and love the delightfully delicious chocolate sorbet. Popsicles have a place, too, with a treat for kids of all ages and an especially healthy version for the discriminating adult. Enjoy every refreshing bit of these final chapters as you think to yourself, *Sugar free never tasted so good!*

Ice Cream, Gelato, and Frozen Yogurt

In This Chapter

- Cool and creamy frozen treats
- Sweet sugar-free favorites
- Easy recipes for great taste
- Flavorful frozen ice creams, gelatos, and yogurts

If you're an ice-cream fan, you might be less than thrilled with the commercial sugar-free offerings in your local supermarket freezer case. If they've left you out in the cold, this chapter is for you.

In the following pages, I share recipes for all your favorite ice-cream flavors, from French vanilla to chocolate to green tea. They're all here, just waiting to be whipped up in delicious sugar-free versions that will make your taste buds smile.

Flavor, Not Filler

Too often sugar-free frozen desserts contain numerous unpronounceable ingredients that will make you wonder what the real scoop is. Unfortunately, many of these mystery ingredients are added to improve consistency and taste, but with very little success.

That's not the case with the recipes in this chapter. Every natural ingredient is included to enhance the final outcome, whether it be for creaminess, sweetness, or just plain great flavor.

Churned-Up Taste

If you have an ice-cream maker, you'll be able to whip up these selections in no time. The machine does all the work for you while you just wait for the amazing result.

If you don't have an ice-cream maker, you can always churn the old-fashioned way by freezing the ice-cream mixture in a bowl and giving it an occasional stirring to increase texture and volume. Happy churning!

French Vanilla Ice Cream

Ooh la la! You'll love the fabulous flavor of this deliciously creamy sugar-free version of classic vanilla ice cream, perfect for topping pies and tarts, or terrifically tasty on its own.

Yield:	Prep time:	Cook time:	Serving size:
3 cups	20 minutes, plus overnight chill time and freeze time	10 minutes	$\frac{1}{2}$ cup

1 cup light cream

$1\frac{1}{2}$ cups half-and-half

4 large egg yolks

$\frac{1}{2}$ cup granulated sugar substitute

1 TB. vanilla extract

Pinch salt

1. In a medium saucepan over medium heat, combine light cream and half-and-half. Heat just to scalding. Remove from heat.

2. In a medium bowl, and using an electric mixer on medium speed, beat together egg yolks and granulated sugar substitute until pale yellow and somewhat thickened.

3. While still beating, slowly pour in half of warm milk mixture, and beat for 30 seconds. Pour this mixture into remaining milk mixture in the saucepan. Add vanilla extract and salt, and using a wooden spoon, stir constantly over medium-low heat for about 5 minutes or until mixture is very thick and coats the back of the spoon.

4. Remove from heat and transfer to a clean bowl. Cover and chill overnight.

5. Freeze in an ice-cream maker according to the manufacturer's directions. Transfer to an airtight container, and keep frozen.

SWEET SECRET

Vanilla ice cream that is made with an egg custard base and cream and has a strong vanilla aroma is called French vanilla, after the French style of making ice cream, as opposed to eggless versions.

Agave Butter Pecan Ice Cream

Amber agave nectar adds a delightful maple flavor to this creamy and rich-tasting ice cream that's loaded with the buttery, toasted taste of crunchy pecans.

Yield:	Prep time:	Cook time:	Serving size:
3 cups	10 minutes, plus freeze time	5 minutes	$\frac{1}{2}$ cup

2 TB. unsalted butter

$\frac{2}{3}$ cup roughly chopped pecans

Pinch salt

$1\frac{1}{2}$ cups whole or reduced-fat milk

$1\frac{1}{2}$ cups heavy cream

2 TB. granulated brown sugar substitute

2 TB. amber agave nectar

1. In a medium nonstick skillet over medium heat, melt unsalted butter. Add pecans and salt, and cook, stirring often, for about 3 minutes or until lightly toasted, reducing heat if necessary to avoid butter burning. Set aside.

2. In a medium bowl, whisk together whole milk, heavy cream, granulated brown sugar substitute, and amber agave nectar until well combined. Stir in toasted pecans.

3. Freeze in an ice-cream maker according to the manufacturer's directions. Transfer to an airtight container, and keep frozen.

TASTY TIP

To prevent ice crystals from forming on the surface of your ice cream in the freezer, place plastic wrap directly on the surface before closing the container lid.

Chocolate-Chocolate-Chip Ice Cream

Lovers of deep, rich chocolate flavor will adore this ice cream sweetened with agave nectar and studded with dark chocolate bits to enhance every flavorful bite.

Yield:	Prep time:	Cook time:	Serving size:
4 cups	10 minutes, plus overnight chill time and freeze time	15 minutes	½ cup

½ cup light agave nectar

2 (1-oz.) squares unsweetened chocolate, chopped

1 TB. granulated sugar substitute

3 cups half-and-half

⅓ cup unsweetened cocoa powder

Pinch salt

4 large egg yolks, beaten

¾ cup chopped sugar-free dark chocolate

1. In a small saucepan over medium heat, combine light agave nectar, chopped unsweetened chocolate, and granulated sugar substitute, stirring constantly until chocolate is melted. Pour into a large bowl, and set aside.

2. Pour 1½ cups half-and-half into the clean saucepan, and whisk in unsweetened cocoa powder and salt. Bring to a simmer over medium heat, whisking often to break up any clumps, and allow to bubble for 30 seconds. Pour into the bowl with chocolate-agave mixture, and stir well to combine.

3. Place egg yolks in a medium bowl.

4. In the saucepan over medium heat, heat remaining 1½ cups half-and-half just to scalding. Slowly whisk hot half-and-half into egg yolks to *temper*. Return mixture to the saucepan, and cook over medium heat, stirring constantly, for about 5 minutes or until mixture thickens and coats the back of a spoon.

5. Pour cooked egg mixture through a fine-mesh strainer into chocolate mixture, and stir well to combine. Chill overnight.

6. Freeze in an ice-cream maker according to the manufacturer's directions, adding chopped sugar-free dark chocolate during the final 5 minutes of churning. Transfer to an airtight container, and keep frozen.

DEFINITION

To **temper** ingredients such as eggs means to slowly raise their temperature to prevent cooking and curdling when a hot liquid is added.

Great Spiced Pumpkin Ice Cream

The earthy flavors of autumn come together in this amazing ice cream, fragrant with cinnamon, ginger, and nutmeg and delectably rich in texture and taste with a hint of maple.

Yield:	Prep time:	Cook time:	Serving size:
4 cups	10 minutes, plus 2 hours chill time and freeze time	15 minutes	½ cup

3 cups half-and-half

½ tsp. ground cinnamon

¼ tsp. ground ginger

¼ tsp. ground nutmeg

4 large egg yolks, beaten

¼ cup granulated brown sugar substitute

½ cup amber agave nectar

1 cup canned unsweetened pumpkin purée

1 tsp. vanilla extract

½ tsp. maple extract

1. In a medium saucepan over medium heat, combine half-and-half, cinnamon, ginger, and nutmeg. Bring to a simmer, whisking often, just to scalding. Set aside.

2. In a medium bowl, whisk together egg yolks and granulated brown sugar substitute until well combined. Slowly pour warm half-and-half mixture into egg mixture, whisking constantly. Pour back into the saucepan, stir in amber agave nectar, and cook, stirring constantly, over medium-low heat for about 5 minutes or until mixture is slightly thickened and coats the back of a spoon.

3. Remove from heat and stir in pumpkin purée, vanilla extract, and maple extract.

4. Strain through a fine-mesh sieve into a clean bowl, cover, and chill for at least 2 hours or overnight.

5. Freeze in an ice-cream maker according to the manufacturer's directions. Transfer to an airtight container, and keep frozen.

TASTY TIP

Adding a lot of alcohol-based extracts at the end of cooking can often leave a "boozy" aftertaste. Look for alcohol-free, glycerin-based extracts in health food stores and online if you prefer to cook without alcohol.

Chocolate-Covered Almond Gelato

Sugar-free chocolate-coated nuts highlight this easy Italian version of ice cream with the enticing aroma of almond and just a hint of vanilla.

Yield:	Prep time:	Cook time:	Serving size:
4 cups	5 minutes, plus 2 hours chill time and freeze time	5 minutes	½ cup

1½ cups whole or reduced-fat milk

1½ cups heavy cream

1 cup granulated sugar substitute

1 TB. cornstarch

1 tsp. vanilla extract

1 tsp. almond extract

¾ cup sugar-free chocolate-coated almonds, roughly chopped

1. In a medium saucepan over medium heat, combine whole milk, heavy cream, granulated sugar substitute, and cornstarch. Bring to a simmer, whisking often. Reduce heat to low, and allow to bubble lightly, still whisking, for 2 minutes. Set aside to cool slightly.

2. Whisk in vanilla extract and almond extract, and pour into a medium bowl. Cover and chill for at least 2 hours or until very cold.

3. Freeze in an ice-cream maker according to the manufacturer's directions, adding sugar-free chocolate-covered almonds during the final 5 minutes of churning. Transfer to an airtight container, and keep frozen.

TASTY TIP

Local candy and confection shops that make their own chocolates often carry sugar-free coated nuts and other similar treats. Look for sugar-free chocolate-coated peanuts, walnuts, or even bridge mix to add to your ice creams.

Japanese Green Tea Gelato

You'll be surprised how easy this gelato is to make and delighted at the result when you savor the uniquely wonderful taste of green tea combined with the zip of ginger and a subtle hint of vanilla.

Yield:	Prep time:	Cook time:	Serving size:
3 cups	15 minutes, plus overnight chill time and freeze time	15 minutes	½ cup

2½ cups half-and-half

1 (½-in.) slice fresh peeled ginger

⅔ cup granulated sugar substitute

1 TB. *matcha*

½ tsp. vanilla extract

4 large egg yolks, beaten

1. In a medium saucepan over medium heat, combine half-and-half and ginger. Bring to a simmer, and set aside for 15 minutes to steep and cool slightly.

2. Meanwhile, in a medium bowl, whisk together granulated sugar substitute, matcha, vanilla extract, and egg yolks until well combined.

3. Remove ginger slice from half-and-half mixture, and slowly pour into egg mixture to temper, whisking constantly. Pour back into the saucepan, reduce heat to medium-low, and cook, stirring with a wooden spoon, for about 5 minutes or until mixture is thickened and coats the back of a spoon.

4. Pour through a fine-mesh strainer into a clean bowl, cover, and chill overnight.

5. Freeze in an ice-cream maker according to the manufacturer's directions. Transfer to an airtight container, and keep frozen.

DEFINITION

Matcha is powdered green tea used in Japanese ceremonial tea services as well as cooking. It has a strong, pungent flavor and a bright green color and can be found in most tea shops or online.

Greek-Style Frozen Yogurt

Very little sweetness is required in this refreshing frozen treat that boasts the delicious tartness of yogurt and the rich, creamy consistency Greek yogurt is known for. Top with fresh fruit or your choice of sugar-free dessert sauces.

Yield:	Prep time:	Serving size:
3 cups	10 minutes, plus freeze time	½ cup

2 cups nonfat or reduced-fat plain Greek yogurt

1 cup whole milk plain traditional yogurt

¼ cup granulated sugar substitute

2 TB. light agave nectar

1. In a medium bowl, whisk together Greek yogurt, traditional yogurt, granulated sugar substitute, and light agave nectar until well combined and sugar substitute has dissolved.

2. Freeze in an ice-cream maker according to the manufacturer's directions. Transfer to an airtight container, and keep frozen.

SWEET SECRET

Greek yogurt gets its incredibly creamy consistency by being strained of all whey. As an added bonus, strained yogurt contains more protein and less carbohydrates and sugar than unstrained varieties.

Peachy Keen Frozen Yogurt

Sweet, juicy peaches and slightly tart yogurt are natural flavor partners, particularly in this custard-based frozen yogurt that's perfect for end-of-summer fresh peaches.

Yield:	Prep time:	Cook time:	Serving size:
6 cups	25 minutes, plus 2 hours chill time and freeze time	10 minutes	1 cup

¾ cup low-fat evaporated milk

1 large egg yolk

⅓ cup granulated sugar substitute

1 tsp. vanilla extract

3 medium ripe peaches, peeled and diced

2 cups plain low-fat yogurt

1. In a medium saucepan over medium heat, whisk together evaporated milk, egg yolk, and granulated sugar substitute. Cook, whisking constantly, for about 5 minutes or until mixture is slightly thickened. Do not boil. Remove from heat.

2. Stir in vanilla extract, pour into a bowl, and chill for at least 2 hours or until very cold.

3. Meanwhile, in a medium bowl, combine peaches and yogurt. Chill while waiting for milk mixture to cool.

4. Stir chilled peaches and yogurt into chilled milk mixture, being sure to combine well without separation.

5. Freeze in an ice-cream maker according to the manufacturer's directions. Transfer to an airtight container, and keep frozen.

TASTY TIP

To easily peel peaches, drop the peaches briefly—not more than 30 seconds—into a pot of boiling water and then submerge in ice water. The skin will peel right off!

Key Lime Pie Frozen Yogurt

You'll love the tart yet sweet flavor of this creamy frozen treat that's two desserts in one, complete with the unique taste of *Key limes* and the added crunch of graham crackers.

Yield:	Prep time:	Serving size:
3 cups	15 minutes, plus freeze time	$\frac{1}{2}$ cup

2 cups nonfat or reduced-fat plain Greek yogurt

1 cup whole milk plain traditional yogurt

$\frac{3}{4}$ cup granulated sugar substitute

2 TB. Key lime juice

3 TB. light agave nectar

$\frac{1}{2}$ cup crumbled sugar-free graham crackers

1. In a medium bowl, whisk together Greek yogurt, traditional yogurt, granulated sugar substitute, Key lime juice, and light agave nectar until well combined and sugar substitute has dissolved.

2. Freeze in an ice-cream maker according to the manufacturer's directions, adding crumbled sugar-free graham crackers during the last 5 minutes of churning. Transfer to an airtight container, and keep frozen.

DEFINITION

Key limes are indigenous to the Florida Keys. Smaller than common limes, they have a uniquely pleasant tart and bitter flavor and are commonly used in Key lime pie and other Southern desserts. Find Key lime juice bottled in your supermarket's baking aisle.

Chocolate Yogurt Fudgsicles

Healthy and delicious, these frozen yogurt pops will delight chocolate fans of all ages.

Yield:	Prep time:	Freeze time:	Serving size:
8 pops	10 minutes	3 hours	1 pop

2 cups plain nonfat or low-fat
   yogurt

½ cup granulated sugar substitute

½ cup sugar-free cocoa mix

1 TB. unsweetened cocoa powder

1. In a large bowl, whisk together yogurt, granulated sugar substitute, sugar-free cocoa mix, and cocoa powder until well combined.

2. Spoon into 8 long, thin Popsicle molds, and insert sticks.

3. Freeze for at least 3 hours or overnight until solid.

SWEET SECRET

Popsicles were first created in 1905 when soda pop was left outside overnight to freeze by accident. Today, Popsicle, Fudgsicle, and Creamsicle are all registered trademarks of Unilever.

Sweet Sorbets and Ices

Chapter 23

In This Chapter

- Cooling down with frozen treats
- Freezing the essence of fruit flavor
- Creating sugar-free (and low-fat!) iced refreshers
- Relishing old favorites with a new twist

Unlike ice creams, gelatos, and frozen yogurt, sorbets and ices have no dairy content, so most of their makeup is sugar, water, and some type of flavoring. This means that regular versions normally have quite a bit of added sugar, depending on the natural sweetness of the fruit or other flavoring used. Enjoying them has always been easy, but avoiding the sugar has not—until now.

Sugar-Free Sorbets

With the recipes in this chapter, you can now enjoy sugar-free sorbets any time you like. From popular flavors like mango and chocolate, to dynamic combos like pineapple and coconut, you'll no longer worry about dipping into the sorbet bowl after dinner or even at snack time with these sugar-free friendly versions.

Pops Are Tops

Popsicles are back in fashion, now made with pure, authentic flavors and a touch of sugar substitute to bring out the sweetness. You'll feel like a kid again when you experience the flavor of the terrific grape popsicles you're about to create. You'll also get a dose of some healthy nutrition when you enjoy the blueberry acai versions as well. Either way you look at it, frozen pops (and sorbets) are definitely the tops!

Easy Mango Sorbet

With only three ingredients, you're on your way to delicious sugar-free sorbet. This flavorful frozen treat features the sweet and unique flavor of ripe mangos.

Yield:	Prep time:	Serving size:
1 pint	20 minutes, plus freeze time	½ cup

½ cup light agave nectar

½ cup water

4 large mangoes, peeled, seeded, and chopped

1. In a small bowl, whisk together light agave nectar and water until combined.

2. In a food processor fitted with a steel blade, purée mangoes. While puréeing, slowly add agave mixture, and continue processing until smooth and pourable.

3. Freeze in an ice-cream maker according to the manufacturer's instructions. Transfer to an airtight container, and keep frozen.

TASTY TIP

Combining equal parts agave nectar and water makes the equivalent of simple syrup, a sugar-and-water mixture often called for in fruit desserts and cocktails. You could use agave simple syrup for the same recipes.

Piña Colada Sorbet

The tropics beckon with this tantalizing flavorful sorbet made from fresh, sweet pineapple and the rich and fragrant taste of coconut milk.

Yield:	Prep time:	Serving size:
1 pint	15 minutes, plus freeze time	½ cup

2 cups fresh pineapple chunks

¼ cup unsweetened flaked coconut

1 cup unsweetened coconut milk

½ cup light agave nectar

1 TB. lemon juice

1. In a food processor fitted with a steel blade, process pineapple and flaked coconut until as smooth as possible.

2. Pour ¹/₂ of mixture into a medium bowl and the other ¹/₂ in a blender. Add coconut milk, light agave nectar, and lemon juice to the blender, and purée until smooth. Pour into the bowl with unblended mixture, and stir well to combine.

3. Freeze in an ice-cream maker according to the manufacturer's instructions. Transfer to an airtight container, and keep frozen.

TASTY TIP

Use sugar-free sorbets to make sugar-free frozen cocktails by blending with your choice of alcohol and a splash of club soda.

Dark Chocolate Sorbet

Naturally low-fat chocolate sorbet gets a sugar-free makeover in this richly flavored version made with intense-tasting unsweetened cocoa and a bit of dark chocolate for another level of distinct, decadent flavor.

Yield:	Prep time:	Serving size:
1 pint	15 minutes, plus 3 hours chill time and freeze time	¹/₂ cup

1 cup unsweetened cocoa powder

1 cup granulated sugar substitute

2 cups boiling water

1 oz. unsweetened chocolate, chopped

Dash salt

¹/₂ tsp. vanilla extract

1. In a medium bowl, whisk together cocoa powder and granulated sugar substitute. Slowly pour in boiling water, whisking constantly until smooth.

2. Whisk in unsweetened chocolate until melted, and add salt and vanilla extract. Set aside to cool slightly, and refrigerate for at least 3 hours or until cold.

3. Freeze in an ice-cream maker according to the manufacturer's instructions. Transfer to an airtight container, and keep frozen.

HONEY DON'T!

Never allow chocolate mixtures to boil as it can ruin the flavor of the final product.

Lemon Cup Italian Ice

Refreshing and light, traditional Italian ice can unfortunately be laden with sugar, but this version, in addition to being fun to eat, is actually full of tangy lemon flavor and plenty of sugar-free sweetness to delight the senses.

Yield:	Prep time:	Cook time:	Freeze time:	Serving size:
1 pint	15 minutes	5 minutes	4 hours	$\frac{1}{2}$ cup

3 medium lemons, cut in $\frac{1}{2}$

2 cups water

6 (1-g) pkt. concentrated sugar substitute

Mint sprigs

1. Line a baking sheet with parchment or waxed paper.

2. Juice lemons, remove seeds, and measure out $\frac{1}{2}$ cup juice. (Set aside rest of juice for another use.)

3. Using a grapefruit spoon or a teaspoon, carefully scrape out and discard remaining pulp from lemons. Place lemon halves cut side down on the prepared baking sheet, and freeze for at least 2 hours.

4. In a medium saucepan over high heat, bring water to a boil. Remove from heat, and stir in concentrated sugar substitute and reserved $\frac{1}{2}$ cup lemon juice. Set aside to cool.

5. Pour lemon mixture into a 9-inch baking pan, and freeze for at least 2 hours or until solid.

6. When ready to serve, remove lemon halves and lemon ice from the freezer, and allow to stand for 10 minutes. Scrape surface of lemon ice with a serving spoon to create a snow-cone texture. Spoon ice into lemon halves, garnish with mint sprigs, and serve immediately.

Raspberry Passion Fruit Granita

Uniquely flavored and wonderfully refreshing, this granita is like a snow cone for adults, although kids will flip for it, too, after the first fruity taste.

Yield:	Prep time:	Cook time:	Freeze time:	Serving size:
2 cups	10 minutes	5 minutes	2 hours	$\frac{1}{2}$ cup

1 cup water

1 tsp. lemon juice

$\frac{2}{3}$ cup granulated sugar substitute

$\frac{1}{2}$ cup *passion fruit* juice

2 cups fresh or frozen raspberries, puréed

1. In a medium saucepan over high heat, bring water to a boil. Stir in lemon juice and granulated sugar substitute, and stir until dissolved. Remove from heat, and allow to cool completely.

2. In a medium bowl, whisk together passion fruit juice and puréed raspberries. Add cooled sugar mixture, and continue whisking until well combined. Pour into an 8-inch-square stainless-steel baking pan, and place in the freezer.

3. Every 20 minutes, stir mixture with a fork until it reaches a grainy frozen consistency, about 2 hours total.

4. Spoon into dessert cups, and serve.

DEFINITION

The **passion fruit** is a sweet and slightly acidic fruit, either large and yellow or purple and small, prized for its unique exotic flavor.

Classic Grape Popsicles

Kids love 'em, and now you can, too! Intense grape flavor highlights these refreshing, easy-to-make treats the whole family will enjoy.

Yield:	Prep time:	Freeze time:	Serving size:
12 popsicles	10 minutes	3 hours	1 popsicle

½ (.14-oz.) pkg. unsweetened powdered grape drink mix

2 cups water

2 cups no-sugar-added grape juice

¼ cup granulated sugar substitute

1. In a large measuring cup or pitcher, combine powdered grape drink mix, water, no-sugar-added grape juice, and granulated sugar substitute. Stir until drink mix and sugar substitute are dissolved.

2. Pour into popsicle molds, and freeze for 1 hour.

3. Insert popsicle sticks into pops, and freeze for 2 more hours or until solid. Unmold and serve. Keep extras frozen.

TASTY TIP

You can make popsicles using almost any type or shape of mold or even a small plastic or paper cup. Try other fruit flavors as well.

Blueberry Acai Super Pops

Not only do these popsicles taste great, they're also full of super-nutritious antioxidants, thanks to the blueberries as well as acai, a slightly tart but fruity-flavored berry that will surprise you with its delicious and exotic taste.

Yield:	Prep time:	Cook time:	Freeze time:	Serving size:
6 popsicles	20 minutes	10 minutes	3 hours	1 popsicle

4 cups fresh or frozen no-sugar-added blueberries

½ cup water

1 tsp. lemon juice

¼ cup light agave nectar

1 cup no-sugar-added *acai berry juice*

1. In a medium saucepan over medium heat, bring no-sugar-added blueberries, water, and lemon juice to a boil. Reduce heat to low, and cook, stirring often, for 6 to 8 minutes or until berries have broken down and liquefied. Remove from heat, and allow to cool slightly.

2. Transfer mixture to a blender or a food processor fitted with a steel blade, and purée until smooth. Pour through a fine-mesh strainer, and collect juice in a clean bowl. Press on berries to extract as much juice as possible, and discard pulp.

3. Whisk in light agave nectar and no-sugar-added acai berry juice, and set aside to cool.

4. Pour into popsicle molds, and freeze for 1 hour.

5. Insert popsicle sticks into pops, and freeze for 2 more hours or until solid. Unmold before serving. Keep extras frozen.

DEFINITION

The **acai berry,** native to Central and South America, is a tiny, deep-purple-colored fruit gaining in worldwide popularity due to its high levels of antioxidants. You can drink the juice; it's available in the refrigerated section of most supermarkets.

Watermelon Kiwi Pops

The delicious flavors of summer are featured in these guilt-free pops that will cool you off on a hot afternoon.

Yield:	Prep time:	Freeze time:	Serving size:
8 pops	20 minutes	6 hours	1 pop

2 cups seeded and diced watermelon

4 medium kiwis, peeled and diced

$\frac{1}{3}$ cup granulated sugar substitute

1 tsp. lemon juice

1. In a food processor fitted with a steel blade or a blender, purée watermelon, kiwis, granulated sugar substitute, and lemon juice until smooth.

2. Force through a fine sieve into a medium bowl, pressing on solids firmly, to extract juice. Discard pulp.

3. Pour remaining liquid into 8 popsicle molds, and add sticks. Freeze for at least 6 hours or overnight before serving.

TASTY TIP

When selecting kiwis for juice, be sure they're very soft. Soft kiwis will extract the most liquid and have the most sweetness.

Glossary

acai berry A tiny, deep-purple fruit native to Central and South America gaining in worldwide popularity due to its high antioxidant levels.

agave nectar A substitute sweetener for sugar, honey, and maple syrup. Made from the agave plant, it's also called agave syrup and has a lower impact on glucose levels in the body than sugar.

all-purpose flour Flour that contains only the inner part of the wheat grain. It's suitable for everything from cakes to gravies.

allspice A spice named for its flavor echoes of several spices (cinnamon, cloves, nutmeg). It's used in many desserts and in rich marinades and stews.

apple pie spice A blend of ground cinnamon, nutmeg, and allspice.

arugula A spicy-peppery green with leaves that resemble a dandelion and have a distinctive and very sharp flavor.

aspartame An artificial sweetener about 200 times sweeter than sucrose used as a low-calorie sugar substitute.

baguette A long, thin loaf of French bread, characterized by a crispy crust and a chewy interior.

bake To cook in a dry oven. Dry-heat cooking often results in a crisping of the exterior of the food being cooked. Moist-heat cooking, through methods such as steaming, poaching, etc., brings a much different, moist quality to the food.

baking powder A dry ingredient used to increase volume and lighten or leaven baked goods.

balsamic vinegar Vinegar produced primarily in Italy from a specific type of grape and aged in wood barrels. It's heavier, darker, and sweeter than most vinegars.

basil A flavorful, almost sweet, resinous herb delicious with tomatoes and used in all kinds of Italian- and Mediterranean-style dishes.

baste   To keep foods moist during cooking by spooning, brushing, or drizzling with a liquid.

beat   To quickly mix substances.

blanch   To place a food in boiling water for about 1 minute or less to partially cook the exterior and then submerge in or rinse with cool water to halt the cooking.

blend   To completely mix something, usually with a blender or food processor, more slowly than beating.

boil   To heat a liquid to the point where water is forced to turn into steam, causing the liquid to bubble. To boil something is to insert it into boiling water. A rapid boil is when a lot of bubbles form on the surface of the liquid.

braise   To cook with the introduction of some liquid, usually over an extended period of time.

brine   A highly salted, often seasoned liquid used to flavor and preserve foods. To brine a food is to soak, or preserve, it by submerging it in brine. The salt in brine penetrates the fibers of meat and makes it moist and tender.

broil   To cook in a dry oven under the overhead high-heat element.

broth   *See* stock.

brown   To cook in a skillet, turning, until the food's surface is seared and brown in color, to lock in the juices.

brown rice   A whole-grain rice, including the germ, with a characteristic pale brown or tan color. It's more nutritious and flavorful than white rice.

buckwheat groats   The hulled grains of buckwheat cereal, a popular grain in Eastern European cooking, often made as a porridge. Also called kasha.

cake flour   A high-starch, soft, and fine flour used primarily for cakes.

caper   The flavorful buds of a Mediterranean plant, ranging in size from *nonpareil* (about the size of a small pea) to larger, grape-size caper berries produced in Spain.

caramelize   To cook vegetables, especially onions, or meat in butter or oil over low heat until they soften, sweeten, and develop a caramel color.

caraway   A distinctive spicy seed used for bread, pork, cheese, and cabbage dishes. It's known to reduce stomach upset, which is why it's often paired with foods like sauerkraut.

cardamom   An intense, sweet-smelling spice used in baking and coffee and common in Indian cooking.

carob   A tropical tree that produces long pods from which the dried, baked, and powdered flesh—carob powder—is used in baking. The flavor is sweet and reminiscent of chocolate.

cayenne   A fiery spice made from hot chile peppers, especially the cayenne chile, a slender, red, and very hot pepper.

chickpea (or **garbanzo bean**)   A roundish yellow-gold bean used as the base ingredient in hummus. Chickpeas are high in fiber and low in fat.

chile (or **chili**)   Any one of many different "hot" peppers, ranging in intensity from the relatively mild ancho pepper to the blisteringly hot habanero.

chili powder   A warm, rich seasoning blend that includes chile pepper, cumin, garlic, and oregano.

chipotle   Red jalapeño peppers that have been dried and smoked. They can be purchased as a powder, whole, or canned in a marinade.

chive   A member of the onion family, chives grow in bunches of long leaves that resemble tall grass or the green tops of onions and offer a light onion flavor.

chop   To cut into pieces, usually qualified by an adverb such as "*coarsely* chopped" or by a size measurement such as "chopped into $\frac{1}{2}$-inch pieces." "Finely chopped" is much closer to mince.

cider vinegar   A vinegar produced from apple cider, popular in North America.

cilantro   A member of the parsley family used in Mexican dishes (especially salsa) and some Asian dishes. Use in moderation because the flavor can overwhelm. The seed of the cilantro plant is the spice coriander.

cinnamon   A rich, aromatic spice commonly used in baking or desserts. Cinnamon can also be used for delicious and interesting entrées.

clementine   A type of mandarin orange. They're small, easy to peel, usually seedless, and generally very sweet.

clove   A sweet, strong, almost wintergreen-flavor spice used in baking.

Colman's dry mustard   The gold standard of mustards in England and most chef kitchens because of its fine, pure, and zesty flavor.

compote   A chilled dish of fresh or dried fruit that's slowly cooked in a sweet syrup made of liquid and spices.

coriander   A rich, warm, spicy seed used in all types of recipes, from African to South American, from entrées to desserts.

cornstarch   A thickener used in baking and food processing. It's the refined starch of the endosperm of the corn kernel. To avoid clumps, it's often mixed with cold liquid to make into a paste before adding to a recipe.

coulis   A French term used to describe a liquid purée derived from fruits or vegetables.

count   In terms of seafood or other foods that come in small sizes, the number of that item that compose 1 pound. For example, 31- to 40-count shrimp are large appetizer shrimp often served with cocktail sauce; 51- to 60-count are much smaller.

couscous   Granular semolina (durum wheat) that's cooked and used in many Mediterranean and North African dishes.

cream   To beat a fat such as butter, often with another ingredient, to soften and aerate a batter.

cream of tartar   An acidic powder used in cooking to activate baking soda, stabilize egg whites, and prevent crystallization of sugar syrups.

Creole seasoning   A blend of herbs and spices that generally contains paprika, a variety of peppers, and onion and garlic powder.

crudité   Fresh vegetables served as an appetizer, often all together on one tray.

cumin   A fiery, smoky-tasting spice popular in Middle Eastern and Indian dishes. Cumin is a seed; ground cumin seed is the most common form used in cooking.

curry   Rich, spicy, Indian-style sauces and the dishes prepared with them. A curry uses curry powder as its base seasoning.

curry powder   A ground blend of rich and flavorful spices used as a basis for curry and many other Indian-influenced dishes. Common ingredients include hot pepper, nutmeg, cumin, cinnamon, pepper, and turmeric. Some curry can also be found in paste form.

custard   A cooked mixture of eggs and milk popular as a base for desserts.

dash   A few drops, usually of a liquid, released by a quick shake.

deglaze To scrape up bits of meat and seasoning left in a pan or skillet after cooking. Usually this is done by adding a liquid such as wine or broth and creating a flavorful stock that can be used to create sauces.

devein To remove the dark vein from the back of a large shrimp with a sharp knife.

diabetes A disease in which blood glucose (blood sugar) levels are above normal. Type 2 diabetes, also known as adult-onset or non-insulin-dependent diabetes mellitus, is the most common form of diabetes.

dice To cut into small cubes about ¼ inch square.

dietary fiber The indigestible part of plant foods that moves through the digestive system. It can be soluble (dissolves in water) or insoluble (stays intact). Both types of fiber are essential for moving waste through the digestive tract and maintaining overall good health.

Dijon mustard A hearty, spicy mustard made in the style of the Dijon region of France.

dill An herb perfect for eggs, salmon, cheese dishes, and, of course, vegetables (pickles!).

dollop A spoonful of something creamy and thick, like sour cream or whipped cream.

double boiler A set of two pots designed to nest together, one inside the other, and provide consistent, moist heat for foods that need delicate treatment. The bottom pot holds water (not quite touching the bottom of the top pot); the top pot holds the food you want to heat.

dredge To coat a piece of food on all sides with a dry substance such as flour or cornmeal.

drizzle To lightly sprinkle drops of a liquid over food, often as the finishing touch to a dish.

emulsion A combination of liquid ingredients that do not normally mix well that are beaten together to create a thick liquid, such as a fat or oil with water. Creating emulsions must be done carefully and rapidly to ensure the particles of one ingredient are suspended in the other.

endive A green that resembles a small, elongated, tightly packed head of romaine lettuce. The thick, crunchy leaves can be broken off and used with dips and spreads.

entrée The main dish in a meal.

extra-virgin olive oil   *See* olive oil.

extract   A concentrated flavoring derived from foods or plants through evaporation or distillation that imparts a powerful flavor without altering the volume or texture of a dish.

fennel   In seed form, a fragrant, licorice-tasting herb. The bulbs have a mild flavor and a celery-like crunch and are used as a vegetable in salads or cooked recipes.

fiber   The indigestible part of plant foods that moves through the digestive system. It can be soluble (dissolves in water) or insoluble (stays intact). Both types of fiber are essential for moving waste through the digestive tract and maintaining overall good health.

flour   Grains ground into a meal. Wheat is perhaps the most common flour, but oats, rye, buckwheat, soybeans, chickpeas, etc., can also be used. *See also* all-purpose flour; cake flour; self-rising flour; whole-wheat flour; whole-wheat pastry flour.

fold   To combine a dense, light mixture with a circular action from the middle of the bowl.

frittata   A skillet-cooked mixture of eggs and other ingredients that's not stirred but is cooked slowly and then either flipped or finished under the broiler.

fructose   A sugar compound digested by the body that provides energy for it to function properly and found primarily in fruit.

fry   *See* sauté.

garlic   A member of the onion family, a pungent and flavorful vegetable used in many savory dishes. A garlic bulb contains multiple cloves. Each clove, when chopped, provides about 1 teaspoon garlic.

ginger   A flavorful root available fresh or dried and ground that adds a pungent, sweet, and spicy quality to a dish.

glucose   A sugar compound digested by the body that provides energy for it to function properly. Blood glucose levels are an important factor in evaluating diabetes.

Greek yogurt   A strained yogurt that's a good natural source of protein, calcium, and probiotics. Greek yogurt averages 40 percent more protein per ounce than traditional yogurt.

handful   An unscientific measurement, it's the amount of an ingredient you can hold in your hand.

herbes de Provence A seasoning mix of basil, fennel, marjoram, rosemary, sage, and thyme, common in the south of France.

high-fructose corn syrup A common sweetener made by processing corn syrup to increase its fructose content.

Honeycrisp A type of apple developed in the 1970s for its sweet yet pleasantly tart flavor.

hors d'oeuvre French for "outside of work" (the "work" being the main meal), an hors d'oeuvre can be any dish served as a starter before a meal.

horseradish A sharp, spicy root that forms the flavor base in condiments such as cocktail sauce and sharp mustards. Prepared horseradish contains vinegar and oil, among other ingredients. Use pure horseradish much more sparingly than the prepared version, or try cutting it with sour cream.

hummus A thick, Middle Eastern spread made of puréed chickpeas, lemon juice, olive oil, garlic, and often tahini.

infusion A liquid in which flavorful ingredients such as herbs have been soaked or steeped to extract their flavor into the liquid.

instant tapioca Tapioca pearls that have been cracked, partially cooked, and dried to speed up the cooking process. Instant tapioca can be used for thickening sauces and gravies as well as in puddings.

Italian seasoning A blend of dried herbs, including basil, oregano, rosemary, and thyme.

julienne A French word meaning "to slice into very thin pieces."

kalamata olive Traditionally from Greece, a medium-small, long, black olive with a rich, smoky flavor.

Key lime A very small lime grown primarily in Florida known for its tart taste.

knead To work dough to make it pliable so it holds gas bubbles as it bakes. Kneading is fundamental in the process of making yeast breads.

kosher salt A coarse-grained salt made without any additives or iodine.

lentil A tiny lens-shaped pulse used in European, Middle Eastern, and Indian cuisines.

liquid smoke A seasoning that consists of flavored wood-chip smoke that's been dissolved in water and made through a distillation process.

mace   A seasoning derived from the red covering of the nutmeg fruit seed. It's similar in taste to nutmeg, with a bit more pungency.

marinate   To soak meat, seafood, or another food in a seasoned sauce, a marinade, that's high in acid content. The acids break down the muscle of the meat, making it tender and adding flavor.

marjoram   A sweet herb, cousin of and similar to oregano popular in Greek, Spanish, and Italian dishes.

matcha   A powdered green tea used in Japanese ceremonial tea services as well as cooking.

meatloaf mix   A combination of equal parts ground beef, veal, and pork found in the meat section of the supermarket. Also sometimes referred to as meatball mix.

meld   To allow flavors to blend and spread over time. Melding is often why recipes call for overnight refrigeration and is also why some dishes taste better as leftovers.

meringue powder   A fine white substance made from dried egg whites that, when reconstituted with water, can be used as a substitute for fresh egg whites.

mesclun   Mixed salad greens, usually containing lettuce and other assorted greens such as arugula, cress, and endive.

mince   To cut into very small pieces, smaller than diced, about $\frac{1}{8}$ inch or smaller.

miso   A fermented, flavorful soybean paste, key in many Japanese dishes.

mouthfeel   The overall sensation in the mouth resulting from a combination of the temperature, taste, smell, and texture of a food.

muddler   A bartender's tool shaped like a pestle used to crush ingredients like fruit, spices, and herbs to release their essential flavors.

no-sugar-needed pectin   Commercial pectin specifically designed for using in sugar-free jams and jellies. Regular pectin, which contains sugar, normally requires the addition of granulated sugar in order to thicken. Find both in your supermarket fruit or baking aisle.

nutmeg   A sweet, fragrant, musky spice used primarily in baking.

Old Bay Seasoning   A classic blend of herbs and spices created in the 1940s for flavoring crab, shrimp, and other shellfish.

olive   The fruit of the olive tree commonly grown on all sides of the Mediterranean. Black olives are also called ripe olives. Green olives are immature, although they're also widely eaten. *See also* kalamata olive.

olive oil   A fragrant liquid produced by crushing or pressing olives. Extra-virgin olive oil—the most flavorful and highest quality—is produced from the first pressing of a batch of olives; oil is also produced from later pressings.

oregano   A fragrant, slightly astringent herb used in Greek, Spanish, and Italian dishes.

orzo   A rice-shaped pasta used in Greek cooking.

oxidation   The browning of fruit flesh that happens over time and with exposure to air. Minimize oxidation by rubbing the cut surfaces with lemon juice.

panko breadcrumbs   A Japanese variety of breadcrumbs that result in a light crispy crust when used for frying.

panna cotta   Italian for "cooked cream," it's usually made from cream, milk, sugar, and gelatin. It has a resulting custard consistency and is often served with fruit.

paprika   A rich, red, warm, earthy spice that lends a rich red color to many dishes.

parboil   To partially cook in boiling water or broth.

parsley   A fresh-tasting green leafy herb, often used as a garnish.

passion fruit   A sweet and slightly acidic fruit, either large and yellow or purple and small, prized for its unique exotic flavor.

pectin   Commercial pectin is a substance used in jam- and jelly-making as a thickener. It comes regular, which contains sugar, and sugar free.

pesto   A thick spread or sauce made with fresh basil leaves, garlic, olive oil, pine nuts, and Parmesan cheese.

phenylketonuria   An inherited disorder that increases the levels of a substance called phenylalanine (found in aspartame) in the blood, a building block of proteins. If not treated, phenylalanine can build to harmful levels in the body, causing intellectual disability and other serious health problems.

pickling spice   A combination of herbs and spices, including bay leaf, coriander, peppercorns, and dill. You can find it in the spice section of most supermarkets.

pilaf   A rice dish in which the rice is browned in butter or oil and then cooked in a flavorful liquid such as a broth, often with the addition of meats or vegetables. The rice absorbs the broth, resulting in a savory dish.

pinch   An unscientific measurement for the amount of an ingredient—typically a dry, granular substance such as an herb or seasoning—you can hold between your finger and thumb.

pine nut   A nut that's rich (high in fat), flavorful, and a bit pine-y. Pine nuts are a traditional ingredient in pesto and add a hearty crunch to many other recipes.

pita bread   A flat, hollow wheat bread often used for sandwiches or sliced pizza style. They're terrific soft with dips or baked or broiled as a vehicle for other ingredients.

poach   To cook a food in simmering liquid such as water, wine, or broth.

preheat   To turn on an oven, broiler, or other cooking appliance in advance of cooking so the temperature will be at the desired level when the assembled dish is ready for cooking.

purée   To reduce a food to a thick, creamy texture, typically using a blender or food processor.

reduce   To boil or simmer a broth or sauce to remove some of the water content, resulting in more concentrated flavor and color.

render   To cook a meat to the point where its fat melts and can be removed.

reserve   To hold a specified ingredient for another use later in the recipe.

rice noodles   A popular alternative to flour-based noodles in Eastern and Southeast Asian cuisine. Usually made from rice flour and water, they become chewy and transparent when cooked.

rice vinegar   Vinegar produced from fermented rice or rice wine, popular in Asian-style dishes. (It's not the same thing as rice wine vinegar.)

roast   To cook something uncovered in an oven, usually without additional liquid.

rosemary   A pungent, sweet herb used with chicken, pork, fish, and especially lamb. A little goes a long way.

roux   A mixture of butter or another fat and flour used to thicken sauces and soups.

saccharin   An artificial sweetener about 500 times sweeter than sucrose used as a calorie-free sugar substitute.

sage   An herb with a musty yet fruity lemon-rind scent and "sunny" flavor.

San Marzano tomatoes   A variety of plum tomatoes grown near Naples, Italy, and considered the most flavorful of all tomatoes used in Italian cooking.

sauté   To pan-cook over lower heat than what's used for frying.

savory   A popular herb with a fresh, woody taste. Can also describe the flavor of food.

scald   To heat milk just until it's about to boil and then remove it from heat. Scalding milk helps prevent it from souring.

scallops   Also called scallopini, these are thin, boneless cuts of meat—usually veal, pork, or beef—that are tender and quick-cooking.

scant   An ingredient measurement directive not to add any extra, perhaps even leaving the measurement a tad short.

sear   To quickly brown the exterior of a food, especially meat, over high heat.

self-rising flour   Flour that already has the addition of a leavener such as baking powder. It's available as all-purpose flour for general baking as well as in cake flour and pastry flour versions.

sesame oil   An oil made from pressing sesame seeds. It's tasteless if clear, and is aromatic and flavorful if brown.

shallot   A member of the onion family that grows in a bulb somewhat like garlic but has a milder onion flavor. When a recipe calls for shallot, use the entire bulb.

shellfish   A broad range of seafood, including clams, mussels, oysters, crabs, shrimp, and lobster.

shiitake mushroom   A large, dark brown mushroom with a hearty, meaty flavor. It can be used fresh or dried, grilled, as a component in other recipes, and as a flavoring source for broth.

short-grain rice   A starchy rice popular in Asian-style dishes because it readily clumps, making it perfect for eating with chopsticks.

simmer   To boil gently so the liquid barely bubbles.

skillet (also **frying pan**)   A generally heavy, flat-bottomed, metal pan with a handle designed to cook food over heat on a stovetop or campfire.

skim   To remove fat or other material from the top of liquid.

spaetzle   A small, soft-textured type of egg noodle popular in German and Austrian cuisine, traditionally made by forcing dough through a fine sieve.

steam   To suspend a food over boiling water and allow the heat of the steam (water vapor) to cook the food. This quick-cooking method preserves a food's flavor and texture.

steep   To let sit in hot water, as in steeping tea in hot water for 10 minutes.

stevia   A naturally sweet noncaloric herb used as a sugar substitute.

stew   To slowly cook pieces of food submerged in a liquid. Also, a dish prepared by this method.

stir-fry   To cook small pieces of food in a wok or skillet over high heat, moving and turning the food quickly to cook all sides.

stock   A flavorful broth made by cooking meats and/or vegetables with seasonings until the liquid absorbs these flavors. The liquid is strained, and the solids are discarded. Stock can be eaten alone or used as a base for soups, stews, etc.

sucralose   A sugar substitute derived from sucrose that is 600 times sweeter and is both water soluble and heat resistant.

sucrose   A sugar compound digested by the body that provides energy for it to function properly. Overeating of sucrose-containing products can release too much glucose into the bloodstream at one time, making the body stressed and forcing the pancreas to work harder and release more insulin to lower blood glucose levels.

sweetener   A natural or artificial substance used in cooking and baking to add a sweet taste in place of sugar.

tahini   A paste made from sesame seeds used to flavor many Middle Eastern recipes.

tarragon   A sweet, rich-smelling herb, perfect with seafood, vegetables (especially asparagus), chicken, and pork.

temper   To slowly raise the temperature of ingredients such as eggs to prevent cooking and curdling when a hot liquid is added.

Thai basil   An Asian type of basil with purple stems and licorice-flavored leaves.

thyme   A minty, zesty herb.

tofu   A cheeselike substance made from soybeans and soy milk.

turmeric A spicy, pungent yellow root used in many dishes, especially Indian cuisine, for color and flavor. Turmeric is the source of the yellow color in many prepared mustards.

tzatziki A Greek dip traditionally made with Greek yogurt, cucumbers, garlic, and mint.

veal Meat from a calf, generally characterized by its mild flavor and tenderness.

vegetable steamer An insert with tiny holes in the bottom designed to fit on or in another pot to hold food to be steamed above boiling water. *See also* steam.

Vidalia A type of sweet onion grown in Georgia. It's prized for its crisp and flavorful, sweet taste.

vinegar An acidic liquid widely used as a dressing and seasoning, often made from fermented grapes, apples, or rice. *See also* balsamic vinegar; cider vinegar; rice vinegar; white vinegar; wine vinegar.

wasabi Japanese horseradish, a fiery, pungent condiment used with many Japanese-style dishes. It's most often sold as a powder to which you add water to create a paste.

water chestnut A white, crunchy, and juicy tuber popular in many Asian dishes. It holds its texture whether cool or hot.

weeping The oozing of liquid filling that may result after baking if any type of pie is not well sealed by its top crust, meringue, or crumb topping.

whisk To rapidly mix, introducing air to the mixture.

white mushroom A button mushroom. When fresh, white mushrooms have an earthy smell and an appealing soft crunch.

white vinegar The most common type of vinegar, produced from grain.

whole grain A grain derived from the seeds of grasses, including rice, oats, rye, wheat, wild rice, quinoa, barley, buckwheat, bulgur, corn, millet, amaranth, and sorghum.

whole-wheat flour Wheat flour that contains the entire grain.

whole-wheat pastry flour Wheat flour that contains the whole grain but has less gluten and also has been ground finer and softer to lessen its weight. It's good for pastry and delicate baking.

wild rice   Not a rice at all, this grass has a rich, nutty flavor and serves as a nutritious side dish.

wine vinegar   Vinegar produced from red or white wine.

zest   Small slivers of peel, usually from a citrus fruit such as a lemon, lime, or orange.

Resources

Now that you're a sugar-free cooking and baking expert, you'll probably want to keep informed on all matters sugar free. The following books and websites will assist you in your journey.

Books

Here are some books you might like to check out to help you learn more about your health and sugar-free cooking and baking:

American Diabetes Association. *American Diabetes Association Complete Guide to Diabetes, Fourth Edition.* New York, NY: Bantam, 2006.

American Heart Association. *The New American Heart Association Cookbook, Seventh Edition.* New York, NY: Clarkson Potter, 2007.

Catalano, Ania. *Baking with Agave Nectar.* Berkeley, CA: Celestial Arts, 2008.

Gittleman, Anne Louise. *Get the Sugar Out!* Boston, MA: Three Rivers Press, 2008.

Holzmeister, Lea Ann. *Diabetes, Carbohydrates and Fat Gram Guide.* New York, NY: American Diabetes Association, 2000.

Koch, Marlene. *Unbelievable Desserts with Splenda Sweetener.* Lanham, MD: M. Evans, 2009.

Niall, Mani. *Sweet!* Boston, MA: Da Capo, 2008.

Teitelbaum, Jacob, MD. *Beat Sugar Addiction Now.* New York, NY: Fair Winds Press, 2010.

Websites

A quick web search turns up dozens of sites supporting sugar-free eating, but check out the following for important verified information about how sugar can be detrimental to your health with links on the latest research about sugar substitutes:

American Diabetes Association
diabetes.org

American Heart Association
americanheart.org

American Stroke Association
strokeassociation.org

Mayo Clinic Nutrition and Healthy Eating
mayoclinic.com/health/nutrition-and-healthy-eating/MY00431

U.S. Department of Agriculture, Food and Nutrition Information Center
fnic.nal.usda.gov

U.S. Food and Drug Administration
www.fda.gov

Weight Watchers
weightwatchers.com

Easy Substitutions

Working with concentrated and granulated sugar substitutes can get confusing when it comes to translating how much sweetener you need to replace sugar in a recipe. The following table should help.

Sugar	Concentrated Sugar Substitute*	Granulated Sugar Substitute**
1 teaspoon	½ packet	1 teaspoon
2 teaspoons	1 packet	2 teaspoons
1 tablespoon	1½ packets	1 tablespoon
¼ cup	6 packets	¼ cup
⅓ cup	8 packets	⅓ cup
½ cup	12 packets	½ cup
⅔ cup	16 packets	⅔ cup
¾ cup	18 packets	¾ cup
1 cup	24 packets	1 cup

*Includes sucralose, stevia, aspartame, and saccharin.

**Includes sucralose and stevia.

Index

D

E

X–Y–Z